The Pilgrims had their blind spots but there is much in their example we can learn from. They were men and women of deep conviction, uneasily daunted, willing to suffer for principle's sake. They loved their children, they loved the body of Christ, and they abandoned everything that was familiar to them in order to serve both. They exhibited enormous courage: can you imagine cramming 102 passengers into a ship's hold the size of a school bus and making a sixty-five-day voyage to a strange world? Having taken that initial step of faith, they then persevered in the face of unspeakable hardship and loss, half of the colony dying from exposure that first winter. Because the Mayflower stayed at Plymouth until the spring of 1621, the survivors could have returned to England, but none did. Finally, they exhibited a faith in God's sovereignty that humbles me. What we remember as the "first Thanksgiving" was a celebration primarily of widowers and orphans. (Fourteen of the eighteen wives who made the voyage had died by spring.) That the Pilgrims could celebrate at all in this setting was a testimony both to human resilience and to heavenly hope.

Robert Tracy McKenzie
Holmes Professor of Faith and Learning
Wheaton College

For many Americans, the word "Pilgrims" brings to mind little more than the Mayflower, Plymouth Rock, and eating turkey. However, the history of the Pilgrims is actually a story of Reformed Christians who embraced convictions that led them to separate from the Church of England, fleeing persecution, to establish a colony on the wild shores of the New World. This well-written and helpful collection of biographical and historical essays highlights both the foibles and courage of these Christians who played a major role in the foundation of a new nation. Implicit practical lessons relevant to the calling of contemporary Christians who strive to live biblically and faithfully abound in this enlightening book.

Dr. Joel R. Beeke
President of Puritan Reformed Theological Seminary,
Grand Rapids, Michigan

Strangers and Pilgrims on the Earth: Remembering the Mayflower Pilgrims 1620–2020 dissects providential myths of the religious group in a previously untapped way—centring their faith and theology. Through this transnational collection of views, bridging various traditions, this book gives the *Mayflower* Pilgrims great body and presence for the reader. The importance of Congregationalism in the story is not forgotten and its role in the construction of Christianity in America; a tradition founded on gathering perspectives and collective decision making, this book exhibits a similar sense of coming together. In particular, Piesse's and Gray's contributions on John Robinson will surely act as an essential reference for any future resource on the pastor of the Pilgrims. *Strangers and Pilgrims on the Earth* reminds us to be journeymen in the world we inhabit; to truly be pilgrims in our hearts, minds and spirits and to ask: "What am I doing about what I believe?"

Joseph Nockels
Congregational Federation's National Council,
Nottingham, UK

The story of the United States does not begin with the arrival of the Mayflower in 1620, but that event is certainly an important part of the national story. To understand the significance of 1620, however, mandates a broader look. This book, *Strangers and Pilgrims on the Earth: Remembering the Mayflower Pilgrims, 1620–2020*, helps to provide a broader context to the story of the landing at Plymouth Rock.

The volume includes chapters on John Robinson, William Bridge, Francis Johnson, and Robert Browne, each of whom is a significant person among the early dissenting churches. Additionally, there are considerations of topics like: "The Ecclesiological Legacy of the Pilgrim Fathers," "The Mayflower Compact and Its Long Impact on American Values," "Encounter with the Indians," and "The Pilgrim Mothers." *Strangers and Pilgrims on the Earth* is a significant addition to the collection of books on the Mayflower Pilgrims. It will prove valuable for personal study as well as for use in a group setting.

Michael Chittum
Executive Director of the National Association of
Congregational Christian Churches,
Oak Creek, Wisconsin

The 400th Anniversary of the Mayflower Pilgrims leaving Plymouth to find freedom in the new world is being marked in lots of different ways and this book is just one of them. It is a collection of different chapters covering different angles of this epic adventure, and you will be spoiled for choice as to which to read first. It was especially interesting to think about the events through the eyes of the women who are to be remembered for their strong faith and perseverance.

Yvonne Campbell
General Secretary of the Congregational
Federation in Great Britain.
Liverpool, UK

Generations of American schoolchildren have learned the story of the Mayflower. Or at least parts of it. While many people have a vague understanding that the Pilgrims were seeking religious freedom, few are familiar with the religious beliefs of these Separatist sojourners, how their faith was nurtured in places like England and Holland, and how that faith was lived out in the New World. The four-hundredth anniversary of the Mayflower voyage is the perfect occasion to revisit the Pilgrims and their legacy. *Strangers and Pilgrims on the Earth* is a timely resource that will inform historians, equip pastors, and edify the saints.

Nathan A. Finn
Provost / Dean of the University Faculty
North Greenville University

Strangers and Pilgrims on the Earth: Remembering the Mayflower Pilgrims, 1620–2020
Edited by Michael A.G. Haykin, Roy M. Paul, with John Clements

Copyright © H&E Publishing 2020

Cover and layout design: Dustin Benge

Front cover image:
Pilgrims Going To Church (1867)
Oil on Canvas by George Henry Boughton (1833–1905),
The Robert L. Stuart Collection, New York Historical Society

Paperback ISBN: 978-1-989174-63-0
Hardcover ISBN: 978-1-989174-65-4
eBook ISBN: 978-1-989174-64-7

Strangers and Pilgrims on the Earth

REMEMBERING THE MAYFLOWER PILGRIMS, 1620–2020

EDITED BY
Michael A.G. Haykin,
Roy M. Paul, with John Clements

To
Dustin Benge,
a dear friend and colleague,
and a lover of the Puritans and their piety—
may the faith of these Pilgrims inspire all of
us on our journey today.

Contents

Contributors		11
Introduction JOHN CLEMENTS		17
Editorial Note		21
1	The Mayflower Pilgrims D. MARTYN LLOYD-JONES	23
2	John Robinson: His Life and Teaching JONATHAN PIESSE	39
3	John Robinson's Country ADRIAN GRAY	61
4	William Bridge, A Norfolk Puritan MICHAEL A.G. HAYKIN	75
5	Francis Johnson: Life, Controversies, and Freedom TOM NETTLES	91
6	The Voyages of the Pilgrims FRANCIS J. BREMER	113
7	Robert "Troublechurch" Browne and the "Brownist Emigration" GARY BRADY	121

8	Stepping-Stones on the Congregational Way: The Ecclesiological Legacy of the Pilgrim Fathers NATHAN TARR	137
9	"Such Like Weighty Employments": A Vindication of Elder William Brewster's Quest for Religious Liberty ANDREW S. BALLITCH	157
10	The Pilgrim Fathers: The First Critical Years ROLAND BURROWS	171
11	The Mayflower Compact and its Long Impact on American Values JASON DEES	187
12	Spiritual Lessons from the First Thanksgiving DAVID ROACH	197
13	Encounter with the Indians ROY M. PAUL	211
14	The Pilgrim Mothers PRISCILLA WONG	225
15	The Pilgrims and Religious Liberty RYAN RINDELS	241
16	The Spirituality of the Pilgrim Fathers NATE PICKOWICZ	255
Afterword MICHAEL A.G. HAYKIN		265
Bibliography		267

Contributors

Andrew S. Ballitch (PhD, Southern Baptist Theological Seminary) is Associate Pastor of Preaching and Ministries at Westwood Alliance Church in Mansfield, Ohio. His research interests center around the sixteenth- and seventeenth-century Puritans as part of the larger Reformed tradition. He is the author of *The Gloss and the Text: William Perkins on Interpreting Scripture with Scripture*.

Gary Brady, originally from Cwmbran, South Wales, has studied at Aberystwyth, Cardiff and London Seminary. In 1983 he became pastor of the London church where he still ministers. In 2012 he gained a Westminster Seminary ThM in historical theology and has written a number of popular books, including one on *The Great Ejection of 1662* and a history of the church he has pastored all these years, *Childs Hill Baptist Church, A Unique opportunity*. He recently contributed to *Glory to the Three Eternal: Tercentennial Essays on the Life and Writings of Benjamin Beddome*. He is currently chairman of The Evangelical Library in London and serves on the committee that arranges The Westminster Conference, an annual church history conference begun by Dr Lloyd-Jones. He runs a number of Internet blogs, the main one being about Heavenly Worldliness. He also helped edit a book about the Dutch rock band Focus. He and his wife, Eleri, have five Welsh-speaking sons, two of whom are also ministers, and four grandchildren. Most of the family now live in Wales, to where Gary and Eleri hope to return one day.

Francis J. Bremer Coordinator of New England Beginnings, a partnership of institutions and individuals organized to educationally promote the commemoration of the cultures that shaped New England four hundred years ago. He is Professor Emeritus of History at Millersville University of Pennsylvania and has held visiting at Oxford and Cambridge universities in England, and Trinity College in Dublin, Ireland. He has published over a dozen books on Puritanism in the Atlantic world, including the prize-winning *John Winthrop, America's Forgotten Founding Father*. He is one of the co-editors of the recently released Four Hundredth Anniversary Edition of William Bradford's *Of Plimoth Plantation*. His study of the religion of the Pilgrims, *One Small Candle: The Story of the Plymouth Puritans and the Beginnings of English New England* will be published this summer by Oxford University Press.

Roland Burrows was born in Grappenhall, Cheshire in 1949. After a short career in teaching, he studied at the LTS (London Theological Seminary) and the LRBS (London Reformed Baptist Seminary) before entering the ministry in 1985. He served two congregations, one in rural Suffolk, and the other in Old Hill, near Birmingham. He lectures at the London Reformed Baptist Seminary and the newly formed Salisbury Reformed Seminary. He has served on several Committees and is currently an honourary vice-chairman of the Trinitarian Bible Society and Chairman of The Cherith Trust. He has written several titles including *John Wesley in the Reformed Tradition*; *How the Eighteenth Century Revival saved Britain*; *A Miscellany of British Church History* and *Our Priceless Christian Heritage*. He is married to Anne, and together they are the Coordinators of the "Christian Heritage Centre" in the West Midlands. They have two grown-up children and three grandchildren.

John Clements was born in 1948, the son of an Anglican clergyman. In 1975 he completed a 3-year teacher training course validated by Durham University at Neville's Cross College, Durham, qualifying him to be a teacher of religious and moral education. There are two great passions in John's life, his deep love of God out of which come his love for serving others. His first book, *Make Your Walls Tumble: How to Change Your Impossible to Merely Difficult, Then Achieve Success*, was published by Lexington House Books, in 2001. Other books have followed, his latest being *How to Get What Money Can't Buy: Personal Peace and Happiness in a World of Unrest*. Following further training and gaining a ThD in theology, John currently serves as Pastor of the Old Meeting House Congregational Church in Colegate, Norwich, which was founded in 1643 by the Puritan William Bridge (see www.oldmeetinghousechurch.org.uk for further details). Parson Porch Books has recently published his *A Brief History of The Old Meeting House Congregational Church (founded in 1643): Our Story So Far*. John and his wife Sarah have an adult son and daughter, Timothy and Rose, and a boxer dog named Daisy.

Jason Dees is the pastor of Christ Covenant in Atlanta, GA. He and his wife Paige have 3 children Emery Anna, John Kellis, and Raynor. Jason grew up in Alabama and earned a degree from Auburn University. He went on to earn an MDiv in Christian Ministry and PhD in Historical and Biblical Spirituality from the Southern Baptist Theological Seminary. He has served as the Senior Pastor of New Washington Christian Church (IN), First Baptist Covington (GA), and Valleydale Church (AL). His work in these churches has included bringing new vision, revitalization, and a deeper commitment to the mission of Christ. In 2017 he led the effort to plant Christ Covenant in the heart of Atlanta seeking to reach one of the most secular areas of the Southeastern United States for Christ. Jason has served as an adjunct professor for Midwestern Seminary and Reformed Theological Seminary and teaches regularly for the Kanakuk Institute. His articles have been published in The Gospel Coalition, For the Church, among other newspapers and publications. He has also had multiple papers selected for presentation at Evangelical Theological Society's annual meeting. During his free time, Jason enjoys travel, the outdoors, keeping up with Auburn Athletics, and spending time with his family.

Adrian Gray has an MA in History from Cambridge University and is the author of more than twenty books on a wide range of historical issues including *From Here We Changed the World* and *Restless Souls, Pilgrim Roots* which explore the diverse and rich Christian heritage of Lincolnshire and Nottinghamshire. He is historical adviser to the community and church groups which are developing interest in this heritage—Pilgrims & Prophets Christian Heritage Tours and Bassetlaw Christian Heritage as well as a figure in the Christian Heritage Network UK.

Michael A.G. Haykin is Chair and professor of church history at The Southern Baptist Theological Seminary in Louisville, KY, and the Director of the Andrew Fuller Center for Baptist Studies at Southern. He is also on the core faculty of Heritage Seminary and Bible College in Cambridge, ON, where he teaches church history. His areas of research are the church in late Antiquity and British and Irish Dissent in the long eighteenth century.

D. Martyn Lloyd-Jones (1899–1981) was one of the finest expositors of the Scriptures in the twentieth century. Welsh by birth, his main ministry was at Westminster Chapel in London till his retirement in the late 1960s. Under God he was a key figure in the recovery of biblical Calvinism in the Evangelical world.

Tom Nettles is Senior Professor of Historical Theology at the Southern Baptist Theological Seminary in Louisville, Kentucky. He retired from full-time teaching in 2014. He has written books in Baptist studies: biographies, historical studies, and theological analysis. He and his wife Margaret live in Louisville, Kentucky. They are active together at Lagrange Baptist Church.

Roy M. Paul was born in Perth, Ontario. He completed a BA in Chemistry and Psychology from Queen's University, and an Honours BSc in Biomedical Science from the University of Guelph. After a successful 25-year career as a drug product development scientist for Johnson and Johnson, he took an early retirement. Dr. Paul subsequently attended Heritage Theological Seminary in Cambridge, Ontario, completing a Master of Theological Studies, magna cum laude. He went on to complete a ThD in Church History. Dr. Paul serves as the Executive Research Assistant at the Canadian office of The Andrew Fuller Centre for Baptist Studies. He is author of *Jonathan Edwards and the Stockbridge Mohican Indians: His Mission and Sermons*, and co-editor of *Glory to the Three Eternal: Tercentennial Essays on the Life and Writings of Benjamin Beddome*.

Nate Pickowicz (BA, Muhlenberg College; MA, Trinity Theological Seminary) is the pastor of Harvest Bible Church in Gilmanton Iron Works, New Hampshire. In addition to writing *Reviving New England*, *Why We're Protestant*, and co-authoring *The American Puritans* with Dustin Benge, he has also edited several books. He and his wife, Jessica, have three children.

Jonathan Piesse was born in London and brought up in Norwich. He attended the Norwich School, and went onto Durham University, where he obtained a BA (Hons.) Upper Second in Modern History, finding particular interest in possible links between Christian faith, philosophy and history. Employment after this degree and a diploma in Personnel Management included working in Personnel Management in the electronics industry and a number of forms of Christian ministry; visiting Christian Unions in polytechnics and colleges on behalf of the Universities and Colleges Christian Fellowship, a ministry to those on the margins of society and working as a Pastoral Assistant for Greyfriars Church in Reading. He then returned to study, obtaining another BA (Hons.) Upper Second in Theological and Pastoral Studies and a post-graduate diploma in Theology from Oak Hill College in London. The earlier interest in theology, philosophy and history was taken further with a dissertation on theological responses to the Fall of Rome in 410 AD, the Lisbon Earthquake of 1755 and the Holocaust. Today he combines work for the local council and letting out property with involvement in St Andrew's Church, Norwich.

Ryan Rindels is pastor of First Baptist Church in Sonoma, CA. He earned his PhD in historical theology from Gateway Seminary of the Southern Baptist Convention where he also teaches as adjunct professor. His doctoral thesis examined Andrew Fuller's theology of Revival. You can follow him on Twitter @RyanRindels.

David Roach is a church historian and journalist. He teaches across the theological disciplines at several Christians colleges and seminaries, including Midwestern Baptist Theological Seminary, New Orleans Baptist Theological Seminary, and Anderson University. His writing has appeared in *Christianity Today* and *Baptist Press*, among other outlets. He has pastored a Baptist church in Shelbyville, Kentucky, and served on staff at churches in Kentucky and New Mexico. He holds a Doctor of Philosophy in church history and a Master of Divinity from The Southern Baptist Theological Seminary as well as an undergraduate degree in philosophy from Vanderbilt University. He lives with his wife Erin and three children in Nashville, Tennessee.

Nathan Tarr (PhD, The Southern Baptist Theological Seminary) was most recently Pastor of Discipleship and Missions at Christ Baptist Church in Raleigh, North Carolina. He enjoys, with his wife Devon, a full house with five children. The Tarr family can usually be found playing board games, exploring the mountains, or at the pool.

Priscilla Wong has a degree in English and French from York University and a Master of Theological Studies degree from Toronto Baptist Seminary. She also received a diploma in Radio and Television Broadcasting from Seneca College and a certificate in Creative Writing from the University of Toronto. Professionally, she has worked as an English tutor, technical writer, copywriter, and intern news reporter. Priscilla is the author of *Anne Steele and her Spiritual Vision: Seeing God in the Peaks, Valleys and Plateaus of Life* (Reformation Heritage Books, 2012). Her articles have appeared on The Gospel Coalition Canada as well as in *Barnabas* and *The Gospel Witness*. Her book *The Bold Evangelist: The Life and Ministry of Selina Hastings, Countess of Huntingdon* will be published by H&E Publishing. Priscilla lives in Richmond Hill, Ontario, with her husband Lee, and her three children Nathaniel, Jenuine, and Josiah. They attend Sovereign Grace Church. At present she is balancing home-schooling with pursuing her passion for writing.

A sculpture depicting the embarkation of the Pilgrim Fathers
to the Mayflower at the base of the National Monument
to the Forefathers in Plymouth, MA.
It was dedicated in 1889.
(Photo: Michael A.G. Haykin)

Introduction

JOHN CLEMENTS

The pages of this book describe one of the most important events in the history of the American Church, and arguably of America itself: the story of how God chose and guided a handful of oppressed religious refugees from England to found one of the greatest nations on earth.

When I started looking into the story in depth, I came to realize that my earlier understanding had been informed by myths and legends, some of them popularized by writers wearing rose-tinted glasses. *Strangers and Pilgrims on the Earth: Remembering the Mayflower Pilgrims 1620–2020* helps to dispel some misconceptions by giving me—as I hope it will give you—fresh and exciting insights into the remarkable story of the Mayflower Pilgrims.

The God we worship is, of course, a God of history; thus, all accounts of the Pilgrims are based on facts which are, to a greater or lesser extent, historically verifiable. As a pastor, however, I feel moved to ask you to read these pages with your eyes of faith open, for the narratives within have God's handprints all over them. Indeed, I believe that he has seen fit to perform yet another miracle in bringing about the publication of this book!

Some years ago, I was rummaging through a pile of old papers in my Chapel—the Old Meeting House Congregational Church—when I came across the first three photocopied pages of a book that had been published in Norwich, England, to commemorate the Tercentenary of the Mayflower Pilgrims.[1] I instantly wanted

---

[1] For further information about this Chapel, see a little book I wrote in 2019, *A Brief History of The Old Meeting House Congregational Church (founded in 1643): Our Story So Far* (Cleveland, TN: Parson Porch Books, 2019); Walter Stephenson, *Norwich and the Pilgrim Fathers: The Mayflower Centenary* (Norwich, Norfolk: Jarrold and Sons, 1920).

to obtain a copy; but the book was a rarity and took much searching for. At length, I was able to purchase one from a second-hand bookshop in London. Perusing that slim volume again recently, I sensed that God was wanting such a book to be written for the 400th Anniversary. Oh, woe is me! I am only a lowly minister (albeit the Pastor of the oldest remaining Congregational Chapel in the UK). I don't have a degree in history. I could not be the one to write that book. How, then, could it be written? I started to pray, and miracles started to happen!

Dr. Michael Haykin, Professor of Church History at the Southern Baptist Theological Seminary in Louisville, KY, offered his help. To find one writer capable of completing this important task seemed unlikely; but perhaps God might bring together a team of men and women of sufficient professional expertise who could each contribute a chapter. Within, you'll find details of everyone who has contributed to this landmark publication. It has been my privilege to have worked alongside these eminent folks, who have freely given their time to this project because they believe that God wants the Church in America, as well as in the UK, to rediscover its spiritual foundations.

The times in which we live are far from normal. Since early 2020, the COVID-19 virus has devastated commercial organisations and the communities they are (or were) a part of. The epidemic has also disrupted church services and the congregations that attend them (or would if they could). And in the midst of such widespread upheaval, God has moved to enable this book to be published! Do I overstate the case in calling this miraculous? Let me give you one example of divine intervention. I made a phone call to a retired minister of my acquaintance, asking whether he might contribute. Prior commitments meant he couldn't; but he became instrumental in enabling permission to include an essay written by the late Dr. Martyn Lloyd-Jones that he delivered at a meeting of the British Evangelical Council held on October 1, 1970, in Westminster Chapel, to commemorate the 350th anniversary of the sailing of the Pilgrims to the New World.[2] That 50-year-old essay could so easily have been written today, because the questions currently facing the Church are so similar. Among the most significant is: Why study church history? You may find the answer to that question, and a host of others, in the following pages. For this is no ordinary book: its tone, structure, content, and authoritative drive may even be near-unique in the field. It is not the work of a single author; rather it is a collection of essays compiled by a diverse group of professionals from both sides of the Atlantic. I hope you'll enjoy this richness as you explore the book. You'll notice that the chapters cover a wide range of topics. Some go into detail about the theological teachings of the Puritan founders; others give

---

[2] Lloyd-Jones was a minister at Westminster Chapel in London for 40 years. For a brief biography, see Iain H. Murray, *The Life of Martyn Lloyd-Jones 1899–1981* (Edinburgh: The Banner of Truth, 2013); Jason Meyer, *Lloyd-Jones on the Christian Life: Doctrine and Life as Fuel and Fire* (Grand Rapids, MI: Crossway, 2018).

graphic details about the living conditions of the Pilgrims during their perilous sea-crossing and early days of settlement; still others will draw your attention to the invaluable lessons that we, four centuries later, can still learn from those exceptional pioneers.

On a personal note, I have to say that working on this book has been among the richest experiences of my life. It has opened my eyes to one of the greatest miracles ever seen in the world. I always knew about the Mayflower Pilgrims, of course; but I had not realised that around 38 million people in America today can trace their ancestry back to them. Nor had I been aware that 95% of the early churches in New England were founded on Congregational principles; nor that Christians from Norwich (where I have lived for the past 30 years) played significant roles in laying the spiritual foundations of America.

Can I now suggest that you pick up a Bible and read 2 Kings 22–23? They tell the story of the rediscovery of the Book of Law in the Temple during the reign of King Josiah, and how this led to a major legislative and spiritual revival. I, for my part, strongly feel that, if the churches in America could rediscover the spiritual foundations laid by the Pilgrims, nothing on earth would stop America from once again becoming "one nation under God"—and thereby restoring its true greatness.

In closing, dear reader, I hope, pray, and trust that you will become infused and enthused by the tone, texture, and structure of the informative, authoritative and sometimes provocative material that follows!

Dr. John Clements
Pastor of the Old Meeting House Congregational Church
(founded in 1643 by the Puritan William Bridge)
Norwich, England

Editorial Note

The essays in this book are designed to provide a comprehensive look at the historical context and ideas that led the Mayflower Pilgrims to sail across the Atlantic to America as well as to delineate their legacy for today. They are each self-contained essays and can be read individually or as a continuous narrative. If read in the latter way, the reader will encounter areas of overlap in the essays. In the view of the editors, this is intentional and actually provides the reader with a more variegated picture of this remarkable group of Christians. It should also be noted that the essays are not uniform in their style: some are scholarly, others are much less so—but all take this historical event as a key event in history.

The cover portrait is by the Anglo-American artist George Henry Boughton (1833–1905) and was entitled by him as "Early Puritans of New England going to worship armed, to protect themselves from Indians and Wild Beasts"! It was his only exhibit at the Royal Academy in London for the year 1867. It signalled a series of Boughton paintings that depicted New England history. Boughton was particularly taken with the Pilgrim Fathers, as a number of his pictures in this book reveal. This particular painting was inspired by his reading of William Henry Bartlett's best-selling *The Pilgrim Fathers*, and was painted in the depths of the English winter of 1866–1867.[1]

The editors wish to thank Dr. Christopher E. Osterbrock for his fabulous proof-reading, Dr. Dustin Benge for his tremendous design of the entire book, and Chance Faulker and Corey Hughes at H&E Publishing for another great project with these brothers.

---

[1] W.H. Bartlett, *The Pilgrim Fathers*, rev. ed. (London: Arthur Hall, Virtue & Co., 1854).

Photograph of the statue of Samuel Chapin, known as "The Puritan," in Springfield, Massachusetts, which was cast by Augustus St. Gaudens in 1887. Photographed in 1905 for the Detroit Publishing Company (Public Domain).

CHAPTER ONE

The Mayflower Pilgrims

D. MARTYN LLOYD-JONES

Now why did a number of us feel that this notable event in the history of the human race and of the church should be commemorated? If we had no other reason for doing so, it is because it is one of the great epic stories of all history and it is good to be reminded in these flabby, easy-going days of men of character and strength, conviction and stature. One of the American poets has put this strikingly in very well-known words:

> Lives of great men all remind us
> We can make our lives sublime,
> And, departing, leave behind us
> Footprints on the sands of time;
>
> Footprints, that perhaps another
> Sailing o'er life's solemn main,
> A forlorn and shipwrecked brother,
> Seeing, may take heart again.[1]

So I believe that as we continue to look together at the footprints of these Pilgrim Fathers and their sons in New England, we shall, under the blessing of Almighty God, take heart again and resolve to go forward in the fight.

---

[1] Henry Wadsworth Longfellow (1807–1882), "A Psalm of Life," *The Knickerbocker; Or, New-York Monthly Magazine* 12 no. 2 (September 1838): 189.

Why we should study church history

I am particularly interested in this commemoration because, in a most extraordinary manner, there is a very close parallel between what happened in those early days of the seventeenth century and what is happening today. This is why it seems to me that one of the most important things for all Christians to do at the present time is to study church history, and particularly this period. Why? Well because it was an age of transition and ours is as well. Everybody is agreed about this. The period of the Renaissance, the Reformation and a century or so afterwards was one of those great climactic points in the history of the whole human race.

You and I are in a similar situation and notwithstanding all its problems and difficulties, it is a privilege to be alive at this time. We are involved in one of those great turning-points of history and, as I see it, it is a most astonishing and remarkable thing that, as members of the Christian church, we are confronted by precisely the same question as confronted those men 350 years ago and more. Now, what is that? Well, the great question confronting them and us is the nature of the Christian church and the character of Christian worship. That is what the crisis then was all about and that, as we have been reminded, is the great question which faces us today.

The great value of church history is that it not only presents us with doctrine—and that is all-important and primary—but it also concentrates on its practical application. Many people fail at this point. They may be correct in their doctrines, but they never apply them. They are theorists. Their attitude is entirely objective. It seems to me, however, that the moment you read history and are confronted with what people actually did, you are compelled to ask yourself the question: "What am I doing about what I believe?"

Another particular gain from church history, as I see it, and of this history about which we are concerned, is that we are called upon to think. May I interject here that I am one of those who does not fear to say that in some respects I am grateful for the ecumenical movement. Let me explain what I mean by that lest I be excommunicated immediately. What I mean is that this movement has thrown all the major denominations into a melting-pot situation. They say so themselves. Very well, I think that is a good thing because it should compel all Christians to think these things through once more. Of course, we should think in a different way from the ecumenical people and arrive at a different conclusion. But I am grateful in days like these for anything that even helps us to think because the main trouble is that people will not do so. They are content to rest with what they were brought up in, and in their indolence and laziness they will not face the issues. In this age of transition, everything is undergoing reconsideration and we are therefore being required to face challenging questions.

A further benefit of studying history is that we can look at how issues were faced in the past and become aware, not only of some of the dangers godly men have faced, but also of some of the errors into which even they have fallen. This is what we are going to do with the Pilgrim Fathers and we will find that even they were not perfect.

Who were the Pilgrim Fathers?
It seems important to me that we spend at least a moment in an exact definition concerning these Pilgrim Fathers. People are no longer aware of church history and they do not understand these things. In the sixteenth century a Reformation of the church took place in this country but immediately there were some who were not satisfied with it. In effect they said, "We have reformed the doctrine but we have not carried the reformation right through in our church practice and government." And they began to agitate about this. These were the people who were called Puritans. They felt that the Reformation was incomplete and that in this country it had not been carried through with the same thoroughness as it had in most of the European countries and nations.

But unfortunately a division developed even amongst these Puritans—not immediately, but from about 1562 to the end of the century. Three main groups emerged. There were those who believed in staying in the Church of England with the aim of bringing pressure to bear, trusting that things would gradually be improved and they would obtain a complete reformation. But then others soon appeared who were not content with this. They said that a different form of church government must be immediately introduced. For instance, there was a man like Thomas Cartwright (c. 1535–1603), who was in many ways the first Presbyterian. He was ejected from his post as Professor of Divinity in the University of Cambridge in 1570 because he was teaching Presbyterian rather than Episcopalian principles. Well, there was that group. They did not believe in separating from the state, nor did they believe in separating from the church. But they wanted to turn the Church of England from an Episcopalian church into a Presbyterian church on the lines Calvin laid down for the church in Geneva. Another group arose. These were men who said, "We must leave the church immediately and not wait. This is all wrong." They were led by a man called Robert Browne (1550s–1633) and were known as the Brownists. In many ways, he was the originator of Congregationalism and Independency. Yet another group began to appear. These agreed substantially with Browne but thought that it was not necessary to leave the Church of England because Congregational churches could be formed within it.

It is indeed important that we should know something about this history. All the Puritans were agreed with what John Foxe (1516/7–1587), the great martyrologist, stated. He said that there were still remnants of popery left in the Church of England which he wished God would remove, for God knew that they were the cause of much blindness and strife. Foxe pleaded for more conformity to the law of Christ and to primitive Christianity. All to whom I have referred agreed about this but they differed about how further reformation should be pursued.

Their view of the church
Why have I said all this? Because we are confronted by exactly the same situation at the present time. There are people who are equally evangelical who disagree on this point in much the same way as in the sixteenth century. But the great and the basic question of this debate can, in the last analysis, it seems to me, be put like this: are all in every parish who are baptized automatically Christians and members of the Christian church? Was Richard Hooker (1553–1600), whose work on ecclesiastical polity has been the main governing book of the outlook of the Church of England, right when he said that the English state and the Church of England were coextensive? This meant that every baptized person—and by law all were to be baptized—was thereby a Christian. Now is that the right view of the church? Or is the church a body that consists only of gathered saints—not of those who have been baptized, but of those who can be regarded as saints because of the evidence which they give of that fact?

Now, that is still the great issue before us and there are still these two basic views of a Christian church. Are all baptized people Christians and members of the church, or is it only those who can testify to their belief and who give evidence of their regeneration? This was the basic issue then and it is still the great and the basic issue today.

It was, of course in the light of this that the church was formed in Gainsborough and in Scrooby which spread out to Leyden and further. These Pilgrim Fathers who left Holland were not revolutionaries. There are people who are interested in the Pilgrim Fathers purely in a political sense, regarding them as politicians, as rebels, as revolutionaries. They were nothing of the sort. They were anxious to go out to form this new land in America which would be a colony of England and they were very anxious to swear their allegiance to James I (1566–1625). There is no question whatsoever but that their main motive in crossing the Atlantic was a religious one and that was furthered and accentuated by the other reasons which have been given to us. The great Dr. John Owen (1616–1683), the Puritan, put it perfectly, I think, in these words: "Multitudes of pious, peaceable Protestants were driven, by the severities of church and state, to leave their native country and seek a refuge for their lives and liberty with freedom for the worship of God in a wilderness in the ends of the earth."[2] That, undoubtedly, is the reason why they went.

Now what did they establish there? It is important, I think, that we should know that they established Congregational churches. They neither established new branches of the Church of England nor Presbyterian churches. Their beliefs, as we have been reminded, were the beliefs of all Puritans at that time. These

---

[2] John Owen, *The Works of John Owen*, ed. William H. Goold (Edinburgh: T&T Clark, 1862), 15:209.

men were all Calvinists. Perhaps you did not know that John Robinson, the pastor of these people in Leyden, was a great protagonist of the truth of the Canons of Dort and was greatly respected and admired by the Dutch theologians. He was put up to defend those canons and did so in a very masterly manner. He was a very able and erudite man. His books prove that quite clearly. They all held what we would call the Reformed faith, and that is the truth about every single one of them. I know that there was a mixed multitude on board the *Mayflower*, but I am talking about the people who formed the core of the Pilgrim Fathers.

As a consequence, they had certain rules for the formation of their churches and they were very punctilious about these. You could not just join the church at will. You had to be examined. All members had to make a confession of their faith and to make it clear that they believed the great cardinal articles of this Reformed faith as it had been taught by Luther and Calvin and so on. But in addition to that, they had to subscribe to a particular covenant in order to belong to an individual church because, to them, a church was a gathering of people who, holding certain views, covenanted together to live together, to worship God together so as to make the gospel known. So they covenanted together to do this and no one would be received as a member of the church unless that person signed the covenant.

Another thing for us to note about them is that they had no bishops. They had ministers, elders and deacons, and what is really important is that each church chose and ordained its own minister and admitted and expelled members of the church. No outside body decreed this. You see, it was a real departure from Anglicanism, from Episcopacy, and indeed also from Presbyterianism. It was a Congregational church and the other churches were influenced by them. Now as you read the story of the various emigrations that went out during the following years you will find that many of them went with different and varying ideas, but what has been outlined became the common principle and practice. The New England churches, speaking generally, were Congregational churches.

At this point I would venture on a few criticisms. The Pilgrim Fathers, as I have said just now, were not perfect. They were men of their age and of their own generation, as we are, and this is where we can learn from them. We should note that they attempted to form a theocracy. There is no question about this. Only church members were allowed to vote, for instance, in appointing the officers of the state. There is no question but that they still carried with them certain tyrannical ideas and were not clear upon the relationship between the church and state at that point. It took a number of years for these settlers in America to get clear on this issue in all the various denominations and there is no connection between church and state in America at this present time.

It seems to me that they were also guilty of imagining that the conditions of church membership and church government could be so laid down that the church could continue like that in perpetuity. This, of course, is always the danger that confronts reformers, men who have to start afresh. They have left a particular body because they feel that they have clearly seen its errors. Their danger is to think that they can make it impossible for the church ever to go astray again. They recall that the church which went wrong was right at the beginning, and so a new church has to be safeguarded by definitions to prevent the same thing happening again. They believe they can do that. History, however, has proved that it cannot be done.

I have a particular reason for pointing this out. There are people in this country today who are disturbed about the general situation and about their own denomination. What many of these friends tell me is holding them in their denomination is that they have no guarantee, if they were to leave, that what they form or join will be all right in a hundred years' time. So they stay where they are. Well, both those attitudes are wrong. It is true that we cannot legislate for prosperity, as the Pilgrim Fathers thought. But we must also realize, as they did, that we are responsible to God for our own day and generation Let us learn both those lessons from the Pilgrim Fathers.

There is a very wonderful statement by John Robinson (1576–1625) himself about this, and I want to read it to you. It not only establishes the point which I have just made, but it helps me to deal with an error with regard to him. There is a statement of his which is most frequently quoted by theological liberals and which leads them to think that he is on their side. He made it at the end of his last sermon to the Pilgrim Fathers before they sailed from Holland. Incidentally, he preached on Ezra 8. That was an excellent choice of text for that event. And so let those of us who are preachers learn from it the lesson of preaching suitably to an occasion.

This is how he ended:

Brethren, we are now quickly to part from one another, and whether I may ever live to see your faces on earth any more, the God of heaven only knows. But whether the Lord have appointed that or no, I charge you before God and before his blessed angels that you follow me no further than you have seen me follow the Lord Jesus Christ. If God reveal anything to you by any other instrument of his, be as ready to receive it as ever you were to receive any truth by my ministry.

Then he said what is the material phrase: "For I am verily persuaded, I am very confident the Lord hath more truth yet to break forth out of his Holy Word."

Now it is crucial that we do not stop there for an understanding of his meaning. He continued: "For my part, I cannot sufficiently bewail the condition of the reformed churches who are come to a period in religion; and will go at present no further than the instruments of their first reformation. The Lutherans cannot be drawn to go beyond what Luther saw: whatever part of his will our good God has imparted and revealed unto Calvin, they will rather die than embrace it. And the Calvinists, you see, stick first where they were left by that great man of God who yet saw not all things."

What a balanced and sane man this great pastor of the Pilgrim Fathers was! He went on to say, "This is a misery much to be lamented, for they were 'burning and shining lights' in their times. Yet they penetrated not into 'the whole counsel of God' but were they now living, they would be as willing to embrace further light as that which they first received. I beseech you to remember it—it is an article of your church covenant, 'That you will be ready to receive whatever truth shall be made known unto you from the written Word of God.' Remember that and every other article of our most sacred covenant. But I must herewithall exhort you heed what you receive as truth, examine it, consider it, compare it with the other Scriptures of truth, before you do receive it. For it is not possible the Christian world should come so lately out of such thick anti-Christian darkness and that perfection of knowledge should break forth at once."[3]

What a great and glorious statement! We all need to pay heed to it.

The phrase that is so frequently quoted by liberals is, "I am verily persuaded, I am very confident the Lord hath more truth yet to break forth out of his Holy Word." This has become their great keyword. They interpret that statement to mean that it is very wrong of us, as Christians, still to adhere to the Thirty-Nine Articles, or the Westminster Confession of Faith, or the teaching of the Protestant Fathers. They claim that because science has developed the whole situation today is different. What those men of the seventeenth century believed was only for their own age. We have more light. That is the kind of thinking which governs their own theological understanding.

It is abundantly clear from the context that John Robinson at this point was talking about one thing only, and that was church government. He was an honest man, you see. There was a time when he had adopted and espoused the teachings of Robert Browne, but having been persuaded by a Congregationalist called Henry Jacob (1563–1624) that he was wrong, he modified his opinion. Great men are ready to change their opinions if they can be convinced that they have been wrong! These men were not rigid bigots. They were godly men and they were ready to consider points of view and to evaluate them carefully in the light of the teaching of the Scripture. They were open to conviction and, as John Robinson in effect says so clearly and so excellently, "Don't imagine that Luther or Calvin in a few years could put everything right. They dealt with these great

---

[3] It does not appear from the section of Robinson's sermon found in Cotton Mather's *Magnalia Christi Americana* (1:64) that he was thinking exclusively of church government in the words quoted. Whether this is so or not, the famous sentence cannot be made to include the notions of modernism. To construe them in that way would be to make Robinson endorse the possibility that the opposite of his own views could arise from the Word of God. His express stipulation to test everything new by the Word is enough to dispose of such a fiction.

central fundamental truths of the faith but they had not got the time, apart from anything else, to work out all these other matters." It is here that he suggests that further light may yet break out from the Scriptures. So if ever you hear anybody again justifying his heterodoxy or liberalism in theology in terms of the statement of John Robinson give him the lie direct and put him right on his facts.

What explains the Pilgrim Fathers?
What, then, is it that explains these Pilgrim Fathers? What is it that led to this epic story? There is no doubt about this answer. It was their *knowledge of God*. Above everything else, they were godly men, sober men. Nobody would ever mistake any one of these men for a film star. They were men who lived under the eye of God and they walked in the fear of the Lord. I told you about their theological views, but these were not held in a merely intellectual manner. They penetrated the very fibre of their being. Their lives were entirely submitted and subordinated to this. They believed also very deeply in God's guidance and in his providential care, even down to the minutest details of their lives. And that, of course, led to their very characteristic view of life. Life to these men was a pilgrimage. This, of course, was the great note of that century. John Bunyan (1628–1688), we know, wrote his *Pilgrim's Progress*, but there were many other men before Bunyan who had written along these same lines. The great secret of these men was that to them the whole of life in this world was nothing but a pilgrimage. They were journeymen in this world.

William Haller (1885–1974), who has written a most excellent book on the *Origins of Puritanism*, uses a very pregnant statement when he says, "Heaven was theirs already, and if presently they demanded possession of the earth as well, that was no more than human."[4] That is a profoundly acute and true remark. The men who were mainly concerned about heaven and were assured that they were going there have incidentally been the men who have done the greatest things in this world and have been the Pioneers in so many respects. These men, before ever they decided to go to America, were pilgrims towards eternity. They had already been pilgrims on earth for eleven years in Holland before they set sail for America, which was but a further step. If you decide to leave England and to go to Holland because of your principles, well, it is only a little bit further to cross the Atlantic and to go to America. It all depends upon your point of view, and the governing thought of these men was what we find so much emphasized in the epistle to the Hebrews: "Here have we no continuing city, but we seek one to come."[5]

They were not interested in affluent societies. They did not talk about settling

---

[4] William Haller, *The Rise of Puritanism: Or, The Way to the New Jerusalem as Set Forth in Pulpit and Press from Thomas Cartwright to John Lilburne and John Milton, 1570–1643* (New York: Columbia University Press, 1938), 90.

[5] Hebrews 13:14.

down in this world and having a good time. No, no! They were strangers and pilgrims; they were travellers and journeymen. They said with Paul, "Our citizenship is in heaven."[6] That was their whole view of life. Or as the author of the epistle to the Hebrews puts it, "These men were looking for a city which had foundations, whose builder and maker is God."[7] They knew that they would never have it in this world, so their eye was set on the ultimate. They believed in making the best they could of life in this world while they were left in it because it was God's will, but they never expected much from this life and from this world. They knew it was a world of sin, a Vanity Fair, and so they passed through it as quickly as they could, as it were, untouched and untarnished by its tinsel and by all its sham and pretence. They went as pilgrims to America because they were already pilgrims in their minds and hearts and spirits. That seems to me to be the real ultimate explanation of these men. It was not merely their theological orthodoxy. What turned them into men of God was that they knew they were strangers and pilgrims in this evil world, journeymen on the way to God and to glory.

One other thing I would like to emphasize is this. What explains what happened to them? Here it seems to me that there is only one answer possible. It was *the providence of God* and his blessing upon them. Their original idea was to go to Virginia, but they soon had to abandon that. Then they thought to settle along the Hudson River, but they were not allowed to do so. There is some dispute about the reason. Some say it was the treachery of the captain of the ship, although recently people have been trying to exonerate him. But whether it was that he was in league with the Dutch or not, and that they did not want them there, the fact is that they landed more in the neighbourhood of Cape Cod. The truth is that they never planned to go where they eventually landed.

I can draw no other conclusion from that amazing fact than that it was God who contrived this. Why? Well, for this reason: if they had landed near the Hudson River, as they intended, there is very little doubt but that every single one of them would have been killed. There were large numbers of vicious Indians there who killed many who landed in that particular area. God, I believe, did not allow them to land there. They had to go further north and eventually they landed in what we now know as Plymouth. And that was another most amazing providence. Did you know, I wonder, that only six months before they landed a pestilence had broken out amongst the Indians who lived in that area and, according to some authorities, nineteen-twentieths of the Indian population had been killed? So, six months before the pilgrims arrived, well ahead of time, nineteen-twentieths of the Indians who were to be their enemies had been removed out of the way. Is this accident? My dear friends, the story of the Pilgrim Fathers

---

[6] Philippians 3:20.

[7] Hebrews 11:10.

tells us not of the God of the Deists but of the living God, who knows us one by one, who has counted the very hairs of our head and who watches over us and takes care of us in his fatherly and providential care.

Then another thing, which seems almost accidental, if you do not view things from the biblical standpoint, is that they were able to capture corn from some of the surviving Indians. That corn proved to be their salvation. It not only gave them food immediately, but it gave them seed for sowing later on in the year. During that first terrible winter half these people died of various illnesses. Do you know that even there one can see the providence of God? Because if those had not died, it is more than likely that, with the limited supply of food that they had, they would all have died of starvation. So God, as it were, mercifully took half away and left this remnant to carry on with the work.

But I have yet to tell you the most extraordinary thing of all. Two Indians appeared amongst them, quite unexpectedly. The Indians that remained had done their best to get rid of them. They had employed sorcerers to curse them and had invoked their devils, but all to no avail. Then two of them suddenly appeared amongst these settlers, welcoming them in broken English. Now how did this remarkable and providential happening in the life of these pilgrims come about?

One of these two Indians was named Squanto (1585–1622). My dear friends, I am telling you this that we may know that we have a living God, who sees the end from the beginning. Nothing happens by accident. Do you know the story of Squanto? It is this. Certain English adventurers landed from time to time in this very area. They went there to fish and for various other reasons. Unfortunately, they were bad and evil men and they would occasionally capture some of these Indians, take them on board their ships and use them as slaves. That is what happened to poor Squanto. He had become a slave to the English. Eventually they had sold him to someone in Spain but he managed to escape from there and make his way to England, where he lived for some time. It was while he was here that he picked up his little knowledge of English. And then, through the kindness of some men in this country he was able to go home and, believe it or not, this man Squanto arrived back in this very area six months before the arrival of the Pilgrim Fathers. He and his companion, as I say, visited the little settlement and were able to tell them about the number of the Indians and their attitude towards them, and were able to instruct them how to use the Indian corn. Everything that they needed most urgently these two men were able to provide for them.

So it all happened in that way. As God allowed Joseph to be wrongly taken captive and to go down into Egypt to prepare the way for the children of Israel in the famine, I believe he did precisely the same thing with Squanto in order to make it possible for the Pilgrim Fathers to settle in their plain. Indeed, subsequently, he was able to bring amongst them one of the greatest Indian chiefs in that whole area, and he made a treaty of peace with the Pilgrims and indeed became an English subject himself. I give you but these brief details in order that you may see that what ultimately accounts for the Pilgrim Fathers and all that their settlement there has led to during the intervening 350 years was not only their own sterling quality, their orthodox faith, their godliness and everything that I have emphasized concerning them, but it was ultimately the guiding hand of God. That is what emerges most clearly as you go through the history.

How are we to react?
Very well then, I shall try to sum up what we have been trying to say. How are we to react to all this? This is the big question. Surely none of us would be content with reacting merely in an antiquarian or merely historical manner. There are people who do that you know—there are church historians and church historians. I have known church historians who could speak eloquently about the facts of the past but who in their own lives were utter contradictions of everything that they had been saying. Their interest was merely that of the historian or the antiquarian. I am sure that nobody here tonight is animated merely by such an antiquarian interest.

I also imagine that you will agree with me when I say that we must not react to this story in the way that Christopher Hill, the present Master of Balliol College, Oxford does.[8] I am going to quote you a sentence in his biography on Oliver Cromwell, entitled *God's Englishman*. From the purely historical standpoint this book has many things to commend it, until Mr. Hill begins to give us his own theological opinions. This is one of them: he says, "An approach to the world which in that period produced a Luther, a Milton and a Bunyan, will today produce nothing but psychiatric cases."[9] You see the idea, an approach to life which 350 and 400 years ago would produce a Luther or a Milton or a Bunyan will today produce nothing but a psychiatric case. In other words, his view is that if we are going to pay too much attention to the views of the Pilgrim Fathers on God, men and the purpose of existence, the result will be that we shall all become psychiatric cases. My only comment is this: would to God that England had more psychiatric cases! Is not this the very need? Look around at what happens when you reject these views! No, no, let us learn from the Pilgrim Fathers that this is the only true view of life. The opposite has been tried, and look at what it leads to! See the lawlessness among us—among students, in the homes, in industry, politically, everywhere. Lawlessness and confusion. This country may go down from industrial crises. Why? Because men no longer believe in God and are ready to bow before him. Every man is his own god; every man is as good as anybody else; every man's view is right. There was no king in Israel and every man did that which was right in his own sight. That is chaos, and we have it

---

[8] Christopher Hill (1912-2003) was an English Marxist historian who specialized in seventeenth-century English history.

[9] Christopher Hill, *God's Englishman: Oliver Cromwell and the English Revolution* (Reprint; London: Penguin Books, 1990), 234–235.

today. What is therefore needed is a return to the very views of life and this world which were held by these men.

So I say we do not react like Mr. Christopher Hill. It is equally important that we do not react as our Lord says that the Pharisees and scribes behaved in his time and in his day. Listen to him in Matthew 23:29–32: "Woe unto you, scribes and Pharisees, hypocrites! Because ye build the tombs of the prophets, and garnish the sepulchres of the righteous, and say, If we had been in the days of our fathers, we would not have been partakers with them in the blood of the prophets. Wherefore ye be witnesses unto yourselves, that ye are the children of them which killed the prophets. Fill ye up then the measure of your fathers."

Why do I say this? I say it because there are men, who have and are proposing to pay tribute to the Pilgrim Fathers, who deny their spirit and the practice. The ecumenical idea today is denying the spirit, the practice and the life of the Pilgrim Fathers and any tribute that they may attempt to pay to these men is hypocritical. These men stood for the great principles which we have been reminded of and if we do not stand for those principles we cannot honour them.

Very well, then, how do we honour them? I leave the answer in the form of a number of questions. Do we hold the same doctrines as they held? This is the first great question. Do we hold the same general doctrines about the Scriptures and their inerrancy? Do we hold the same view of the way of salvation as they held? But, more particularly, here is a question to evangelicals: are you subscribing to recent teaching, in the name of evangelicalism, which says that bishops are essential to the church, that they belong to the bone structure and skeleton of the Christian church? The Pilgrim Fathers did not and evangelicals, hitherto, have not done so either. Do we follow them in this that bishops are not essential to a new unified church? Do we agree with them in their view of sacramentalism and its practices? Are we equally clear in rejecting baptismal regeneration and various other sacramental errors? Do we agree with them in their view of the church of Rome, which to them was the great whore?

Now it is no use paying tribute to the Pilgrim Fathers unless you ask yourself these questions. Their views were quite unequivocal; they were perfectly clear. I therefore ask, do we take these things seriously? These men took these things so seriously that they did what they did. Are these matters vital to us? Evangelical people, I am addressing you in particular, are you content to go on just as you are? Do you not think it is about time you faced these issues? These are not issues merely for preachers. They are issues for every member of the church.

So I go on to my next question: *are we ready to act on our beliefs as they were?* These men left the churches in which they had been brought up and nurtured. They left their homes; they left their relatives; they left their friends; they left their occupations; they even left their country! Eleven years in Holland and the rest in that wilderness in America! They faced the Atlantic, they faced the wilderness and all its horrors and possibilities and the antagonism of the Indians.

They faced it all because of the principles which animated them.

But let me emphasize this as I close. History is vital, and exact history, precision, is important. 1620, remember, was in the age of James I. It was pre-Charles I. We know how things deteriorated sadly when Charles I (1600–1649) came to the throne. But let me remind you that these men acted before Charles ever became king. Indeed, they also acted as they did in pre-Laudian days. You know how things deteriorated under Archbishop Laud (1573–1645). But these men acted before Laud ever became archbishop. These men separated in the pre-Charles, pre-Laudian days.

And let me remind you again, they were in general theological agreement with the others I have referred to. That was not the difference. The difference was over these matters of rites and ceremonies and church government. It was on those issues, in spite of the general theological agreement, they settled the question and faced the rigours of a cruel, Atlantic and an unknown wilderness in the West. Now this is all I ask, if they were prepared to endure all that for those issues, if they were prepared to separate on those issues, are we not prepared to separate from those who are liberal in their doctrine, who deny the Christian faith, who preach actively against it and ridicule it Sunday by Sunday from supposedly Christian pulpits? That is the challenge of the Pilgrim Fathers to us.

If they acted on their own issues, how much more should we act on this issue of Liberalism, a denial of the very elements of the Christian faith, and a rejection of the inerrancy and total authority of the Scripture? Are we not also ready to divide on this issue of sacramentalism, this issue of fraternizing with Rome? Indeed, is not the call to us to separate from everything that is represented by the World Council of Churches and the ecumenical movement? Are you content to say, "I do not want any trouble, I have always been brought up in this chapel and I have always worshipped here"? There are many evangelicals who are saying that to their pastors and ministers today. They say, "We agree about your theology but we do not want to be disturbed. We have always done this."

My dear friends, if you think like that and can sleep tonight after hearing what you heard about the Pilgrim Fathers, I am in utter despair with respect to you. You have no right to mention the Pilgrim Fathers and pretend that you honour their memory. Face the issues; face the facts. Or are you one of those who say, "I am still hopeful that I can reform the church in which I have been brought up." The answer of history to that is that the Pilgrim Fathers anticipated by forty-two years the Great Ejection of 1662. It took the rest forty-two years to see what these men had previously seen. By 1662 it was seen to be impossible and they took a stand which led to their ejection from the Church of England. This is the testimony of history. No, no! When a church is apostate or refuses repeated attempts to discipline those in error on these matters, you cannot reform her. This is the testimony of history. You must try to do so; you must try to get discipline to be exercised. If they will not do so, separate yourself from them and "be not partaker of their evil deeds".[10]

Have you heard the challenge of the Pilgrim Fathers? This is how it comes to me:

> A noble army, men and boys,
> The matron and the maid
> Around the Savior's throne rejoice
> In robes of light arrayed.
> They climbed the steep ascent of heaven
> Through peril, toil and pain.
> O God, may grace to us be given
> To follow in their train.[11]

---

[10] 2 John 11.

[11] Reginald Heber (1783–1826), "St. Stephen's Day [The Son of God goes forth to war]," *Hymns, Written and Adapted to the Weekly Church Service of the Year* (London: John Murray, 1827), 18.

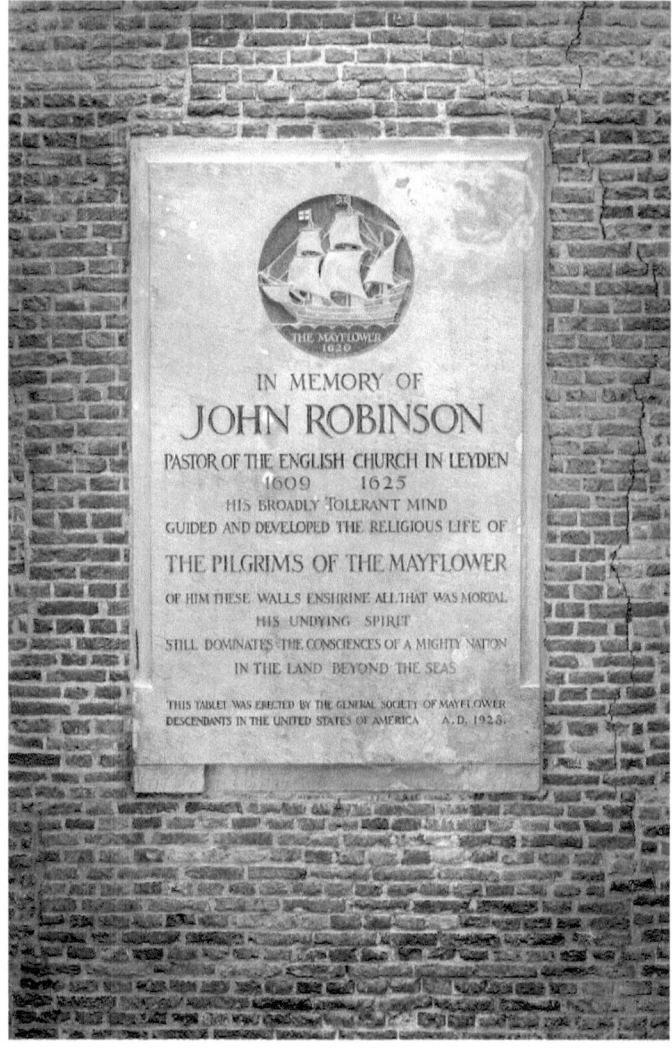

The memorial plaque to John Robinson at the
Pieterskerk, Netherlands
(Public Domain).

CHAPTER TWO

John Robinson: His Life and Teaching

JONATHAN PIESSE

John Robinson was a Christian leader who lived from about 1575 to 1625. He served briefly in 1604–1605 as a deputy to the minister of St. Andrew's Church, Norwich, but left the Church of England and later was involved in leading independent churches in Lincolnshire and Leiden in Holland. A large group from the Leiden Church formed the core of those known as the Pilgrim Fathers who sailed to the New England on the *Mayflower* in 1620 and had a lasting influence on the life of America.

Early Life
John Robinson was born about 1575 in Sturton, now known as Sturton-le-Steeple, in Nottinghamshire in England. The village had about 650 residents, and was quite prosperous, partly because of the quality of the soil. The Robinson family were farmers, and probably moved to Sturton in the 1540s. The first mention of a Robinson is Christopher in a list of taxpayers dated 1544, and the amount of tax he pays—five shillings and four pence—is paid by John Robinson's father John in 1585. John Robinson the elder is trusted to carry out the terms of his neighbours' wills, which suggests he was respected in the community. He and his wife Ann had a faith strongly influenced by the Reformation from the evidence of the way they commend their souls to God in their wills of 1614 and 1616. Traditional Catholic phrasing would be likely to commend a person's soul to Almighty God, the Virgin Mary and the whole company of heaven. John the elder's will bequeaths his "soul to Almighty God my Creator and to Jesus Christ my Redeemer

by whose precious blood shedding I have an assured hope of salvation;" his widow Ann's commends her soul to God "assuredly hoping and trusting in and by the merits, death and passion of his dear Son Jesus Christ my only Lord and Saviour to be one of his elect and blessed Company in the kingdom of heaven and by no other way or means whatsoever."[1]

It is therefore likely that as John grew up, he was taught the Christian faith in ways understood by the Reformers. He himself said his Christian conversion came about in the Church of England. Other features of life in Sturton, no doubt, also left their impression, including the rivalries between some families such as the Lassells and the Thornhaghs, and the local magnate the Earl of Shrewsbury and the Stanhopes. Lawsuits, even violence could occur, including an occasion in 1594, when a local vicar called John Quippe reported George Lassells, the local lord of the manor, for not attending church and received verbal and physical abuse from him. Perhaps the difference between the teaching of the Christian faith and the way it was lived out at times influenced the way John Robinson believed the church should be later on in his life.

In 1592 he went to Corpus Christi, Cambridge University, probably as a sizar. This term referred to the lowest tier of Cambridge students, and relates to an arrangement whereby intelligent youths with limited means could pay their way through university by doing chores for those who were better off. The lectures, given in Latin, involved the study of logic, making use of ideas by the French Protestant mathematician and philosopher, Peter Ramus, on the importance of method, which led to a strong emphasis on setting out in logical form laws of reasoning implicit in human speech. There were lectures too, on books of the Old and New Testament. Robinson made some effort to learn original Hebrew and gained a good knowledge of New Testament Greek. Students were also involved in disputations, initially listening to discussions by sophisters and taking part once they were approved as sophisters themselves, as Robinson was. In 1598, having completed his Bachelor of Arts degree, he became a Fellow of Corpus Christi, which meant he had board, lodging and a small amount of pay. The appointment gave him freedom to make contacts and look for opportunities elsewhere, but only while he remained unmarried. The appointment as Fellow was followed by the grant of a Master of Arts degree and election as Reader in Greek in 1599 and election as Dean, involving some responsibility for other students, in 1600.

Apart from the foundation provided through his studies, Robinson was influenced by a number of Christian leaders. John Jegon (1550–1618), Master of the College, was Calvinist in outlook, and his brother Thomas (1575–1626) was Robinson's tutor. Laurence Chaderton (c.1536–1640), Master of Emmanuel College from 1584–1622, was also a Calvinist and took part in a major disputation

---

[1] Walter H. Burgess, *John Robinson, Pastor of the Pilgrim Fathers: A Study of His Life and Times* (London: Williams and Norgate, 1920), 14–15.

on the soundness of the opinions of Dr. John Overall (1559–1619), Regius Professor of Theology, at which Robinson is likely to have been present. Chaderton's sermon on Romans 12:3–8 was published by members of the Pilgrim Church in Leiden, and Robinson refers to it more than once in his works. Most significant in influence was probably William Perkins (1558–1602), the lecturer at the Church of Great St. Andrew. He was well-balanced in thought, fervent in spirit and expounded Calvinism in a way which people could grasp and apply. Perkins was, however, opposed by Jacobus Arminius (1560–1609), whose views Robinson later argued against in disputes at the University of Leiden. Robinson's biographer, Walter H. Burgess observed, rightly it seems, that the way Robinson later contended for a Calvinist understanding of the Christian faith owed much to what he had known in Cambridge and concluded "Robinson was deeply indebted to Perkins for the general structure of his scheme of religious thought and his interpretation of Christianity."[2] The theological outlook to which Robinson held and which he defended came not only from what Calvin, Perkins and others taught, but from the Scriptures. Robinson's "general scheme of theology," wrote Burgess, "seemed to have ample scriptural warrant in the Pauline epistles, and that was enough for him."[3]

Scheme of Theology

Robinson's theological outlook is not one which is stated in the form of a catechism or a textbook, but it emerges in his writings about Christian teaching and life on a number of issues he encountered.

The nature of God and the nature of man

God is, he affirmed, the Creator and Ruler of all. "The sun and moon teaching God ... God the creator and governor of the world."[4] His ways are, furthermore, made known in "the law, which is natural and written by creation in the heart of every man."[5] Man, in response, should seek God, "as he, that lying in a dungeon, sees some little glimpse of light, and gropes after it, by the wall, hoping to come in time to some door or window,"[6] and his conscience lead him to seek for reconciliation with God. This is needed because of man's sinfulness: in reflecting on Romans 5:19 ("as by one man's disobedience many were made sinners") Robinson observes that Adam's sin has not only set a bad example, but brought actual corruption to human beings, a fact observable in the way children, "coming to

---

[2] Burgess, *John Robinson*, 48.

[3] Burgess, *John Robinson*, 55.

[4] John Robinson, *The Works of John Robinson*, ed. Robert Ashton (London: John Snow, 1851), 1:343.

[5] Robinson, *Works*, 1:343.

[6] Robinson, *Works*, 1:344.

some discerning, will lie, filch and revenge themselves, though they never heard a lie told etc."[7] Our sinfulness leads to an inability to keep the law God intended in creation, and this means we are in debt to God:

> The inability of the debtor, and his heirs, especially by their own default, is no sufficient discharge of the debt unto the creditor who lent it: so neither doth man's inability prejudice the Lord's right, but that he may in the course of justice, require that obedience to his holy law, unto which by creation he enabled mankind.[8]

Rather than having a right standing and relationship with God, Robinson observes, heathens remain in a state of ignorance (for which they are responsible) of the ways of reconciliation and salvation, satisfying themselves with their own inventions and being given up by God to the lusts of their hearts and to reprobate minds.[9]

God's love of himself and his own holiness means that he is opposed to man's sin, but this judgement is mitigated by God's love. As Robinson states,

> … even in the very execution of his most fearful vengeance upon the reprobate, men and angels, he retaineth the general love of a Creator; and out of it, preserveth the being of the creature, which in itself, and in respect of the universal is better than not to be, though not so in the case of the person: and also moderateth the extremity of that torment, which he both could and might in justice, inflict.[10]

The reconciliation of God and man—penal substitution

God's justice meant that he passed by the angels who sinned, as Hebrews 2:16 indicates, and could have meant he passed by the human race too, but his mercy led him to provide for our redemption in Christ.[11] To reconcile the world to himself through Christ, as described in 2 Corinthians 5:19, meant God dealt with his wrath against us, although the reconciliation leads to the taking away of our hatred and enmity towards God.[12]

Robinson's understanding of what the cross achieved is a statement of the doctrine of penal substitution, but much of his focus is on who benefits from Christ's

---

[7] Robinson, *Works*, 1:406

[8] Robinson, *Works*, 3:250–251.

[9] Robinson, *Works*, 1:344–345.

[10] Robinson, *Works*, 3:254.

[11] Robinson, *Works*, 3:260.

[12] Robinson, *Works*, 3:264–265.

death. He opposes strongly the view represented by Thomas Helwys (1575–1616), that Gentile sacrifices which are prompted by troubled consciences and involve a kind of acknowledgement of a false Christ are a means of salvation. "Is there any other name under heaven, by which men are saved," he asks, "than by the name of the true Christ, Jesus the Son of God, crucified by the Jews … and raised again by God from the dead?"[13] The apostle Paul taught, he observes, that the focus of Gentile sacrifices is with devils, and that they are incompatible with the "remembrances of Christ's body and blood."[14] Thus Robinson does not go into detail about how much truth about Jesus needs to be apprehended for someone to be saved, but he clearly sets his face against the idea that any kind of acknowledgment will do, and usefully raises the issue of who, or what, is being worshipped.

The reconciliation of God and man—limited atonement and election
Moreover, although Robinson acknowledged that Christ's death is in itself sufficient for all, he denied that God's purpose was to pay the price of the sins of the whole world and everyone in it.[15] This was given in reply to a treatise by John Murton (c.1583–c.1625/26) and his associates against the Articles of the Synod of Dort of 1618–1619, a treatise which asserted that "Christ died unfeignedly for all without exception; by whose death all might be saved, if they did not reject it."[16] Verses which could support Christ's death as potentially benefiting all are interpreted by Robinson in ways which limit its scope. Thus the statement Christ gave himself "a ransom for all" (1 Timothy 2:6) is understood to refer to "all sorts of people," and the statement that God "is the Saviour of all men, especially those who believe" (1 Timothy 4:10) to refer to his providence rather than the scope of his salvation.[17]

Robinson's belief in "limited atonement"—that God's purposes in Christ's death were intended to benefit a limited number of people—connects closely with the conviction that salvation is not something which we choose, but which God gives. He told Christians that when thinking of those who had not received God's grace they should, "give the glory to God's grace, and not to your own freewill, that you believe, repent and obey, rather than they."[18] In addressing the

---

[13] Robinson, *Works*, 1:341.

[14] Robinson, *Works*, 1:342.

[15] Robinson, *Works*, 1:329.

[16] Robinson, *Works*, 1:329. John Murton, *A Discription of What God hath Predestinated Concerning Man, in his Creation, Transgression, & Regeneration. As also an Answere to Iohn Robinson; touching Baptisme* (London, 1620), 44–46.

[17] Robinson, *Works*, 1:331–2.

[18] Robinson, *Works*, 1:316.

issue of how people come to faith in Christ, he affirmed,

> they err with great error, in holding this election [the choosing of people for salvation] is for the quality which God finds in persons, and upon the condition of faith and repentance going before, and that God only chooseth and electeth where he finds faith and obedience to his Son.[19]

Regeneration is not the same as faith and repentance, as some said: rather faith and repentance come about in those whom God has regenerated.[20]

Teaching on perfection and perseverance
How those whom God had brought to faith could be expected to continue was an issue of concern to Robinson and to others. Robinson argued cogently that a believer would neither become perfect in this life, nor finally fall away. Some thought that John Smyth (c.1554–c.1612), a Separatist who also made his way to the Netherlands, reached a state of perfection in holiness. In response Robinson observed that Christ's perfect righteousness was imputed to the believer to justify—to declare them righteous—before God, and that a perfection "of parts" could come about in the life of a believer, but stated the notion a person could reach a state of perfection, which removed the need to deal with sin, was "a most dangerous delusion of that prince of darkness transforming himself into an angel of light."[21]

Some also held the view that a person could be truly and effectually called, but wholly fall away from the grace of Christ. In response, Robinson agreed that the promise of salvation is to those who persevere to the end, but observed that this depends on election. He also notes that there are verses which exhort the godly to turn to the Lord, but that these should be taken as the means God uses to warn the faithful against apostasy rather than statements that people can fall away. On Jesus' statement "If the salt loses its savour" (Matthew 5:13), for example, he comments "It is sufficient for the truth of a conditional proposition, that the latter part follow infallibly upon the former; if it be; but requires not that it [the latter] should be."[22] Overall, he notes,

> where there is in the Scriptures, either mention, or insinuation of man's falling away from the grace of God, there is withal commonly an item given in

---

[19] Robinson, *Works*, 1:320.

[20] Robinson, *Works*, 1:400–401.

[21] Robinson, *Works*, 3:271–272.

[22] Robinson, *Works*, 1:372–373.

the same place, that such persons were never effectually sanctified.[23]

Double predestination
Belief that God chooses some who will come to faith in Christ connects with the view that others are destined not to do so—an outlook known as double predestination. The latter is not however, the logical corollary of the former. God does not condemn those in the latter group without any condition, but for their sins which he knows about in advance, to which he is opposed, and in which they are hardened. Esau, for example, is said to be destroyed because of his "obstinacy in sin."[24] Hardening takes place not because God wishes men to perish, but for the purpose of displaying his power and wrath.[25] Robinson also shows well that God's purposes are worked out using human sinfulness; likening this to the way a husbandman will set up ditches and trenches to guide the flow of water towards particular ends. His just judgement on David's sin against Uriah, for example, involved the use of the "horrible sin of Absalom."[26]

Robinson's theological outlook is formed in logical ways, but he does not take every point to its possible conclusion. God's choosing that some will believe, for example, does not mean we should neglect our part. Robinson states preachers are needed so that people may believe, citing Romans 10:14–15, and observes there are places where Christ has not been named, citing Romans 15:20–21.[27] Infants share in sin because of Adam and, he writes, are "under condemnation," but "that actual faith in Christ is required for their reconciliation to God, doth not follow hereupon … Actual sins indeed require actual faith; but for sin in disposition (called original) why not faith in disposition suffice, through the mercy of God, for the applying of it."[28]

The evidence of Robinson's writing largely supports the observation of Burgess that there was a strong vein of religious rationalism implicit in Robinson's system of thought, that if

> men and women would but apply their reason and common sense to the interpretation and understanding of the Divine message enshrined in the Scriptures, they would soon grasp the truths it conveyed.[29]

---

[23] Robinson, *Works*, 1:392.

[24] Robinson, *Works*, 1:355.

[25] Robinson, *Works*, 1:349.

[26] Robinson, *Works*, 1:278–279.

[27] Robinson, *Works*, 1:348.

[28] Robinson, *Works*, 1:412.

[29] Burgess, *John Robinson*, 363.

Robinson believed further that there was the need for God to reveal himself to man, but his grasp of what this meant was guided by careful reflection on the Scriptures.

Life after Cambridge

In February 1604, Robinson resigned his fellowship at Corpus Christi, and within a few days married Bridget White (c.1575–c.1643), from his home village of Sturton. Later in 1604, he came to Norwich as a deputy to the minister of St. Andrew's Church, Thomas Newhouse (d.1611), an arrangement which might have been expected to work well. Newhouse had been a student about five or six years ahead of Robinson at Cambridge, at Christ's College, and had been profoundly influenced by William Perkins. He had become the minister of St. Andrew's in 1602, and shared Robinson's theological outlook, shown by lectures he gave on some Thursday afternoons at the church defending double predestination. The bishop of Norwich was John Jegon, former master of Corpus Christi.

However, in 1604 there was pressure to impose conformity on the Church of England throughout the nation in ways which caused disquiet. This meant full acceptance of the rubrics in the Prayer Book and measures put forward by the Archbishop of Canterbury, Richard Bancroft (1544–1610), in a new Book of Canons. Some demands were worthwhile—clergy, for example, were forbidden to gamble and pulpits were to be installed in churches—but demands to, for example, use the sign of the cross in baptism and kneel at communion were regarded as "popish," and there was concern that the requirements came from the use of royal prerogative rather than act of Parliament.

Robinson came to question the scriptural authority for diocesan bishops and was suspended from his ministry. Since Bancroft's Canons required churchwardens to report offences such as private gatherings or unlicensed preaching, it is not surprising Robinson's attempt to exercise an unofficial ministry was opposed. Henry Ainsworth (1571–1622), a writer from the early seventeenth century dissatisfied with the Church of England, wrote to Mr. Crashaw of,

> the late practice in Norwich, where certain citizens were excommunicated for resorting unto and praying with Mr. Robinson, a man worthily reverenced of all the city for the grace of God in him, as yourself also, I suppose, will acknowledge, and to whom the cure and charge of their souls was erewhile committed.[30]

Robinson then seems to have returned to Sturton and reflected further on what the church should be. This involved a visit to Cambridge where he wrote,

---

[30] Robinson, *Works*, 1:xvii.

"I hoped most to find satisfaction to my troubled heart."[31] On this visit, he went to hear Laurence Chaderton, from whose sermon on Mary's message about the resurrection to the disciples he took the point that,

> the things which concerned the whole Church were to be declared publicly to the whole Church and not to some part only; bringing for instance and proof the words of Christ, Matt.18:17: "Tell it to the Church," confirming one main ground of our difference from the Church of England.

Issues could not be addressed by the "whole church" in local parish churches because of the way the Church of England was governed, and this was of great concern to him. Later in the day he heard Paul Baynes (c.1573–1617) on the need for God's people to be separate from the apparently wicked, as light is from darkness.[32] This visit appears to have confirmed him on the path of leaving the Church of England, and joining gathered, also known as Separatist, congregations. He was to write further on what the Church should, and should not, be.

Scrooby

In Robinson's home area there were two Separatist congregations, in Gainsborough and in Scrooby. Scrooby was a few miles from Sturton, and the congregation met in the Manor House, the home of William Brewster (1560–1644), a postmaster attracted to Separatism. The congregation had three leaders, Brewster being the elder, Richard Clyfton (d.1616)—the former rector of nearby Babworth church, who was ejected for failing to follow the Archbishop of York's attempts to impose conformity—being the pastor, and Robinson becoming the third, the teacher of the congregation. Another person in the congregation was William Bradford (1590–1657), a young man, who was to become a leader of the Pilgrim Fathers and a chronicler of their history. The pattern of Sunday worship involved meeting from 8 a.m. to 5 or 6 p.m. with a two-hour break at noon; singing psalms, reading, and discussing the biblical text. This points to a strong commitment of people to each other within the congregation, a commitment which lasted and was probably strengthened through adversity. Adversity was to come in the immediate and more distant future.

Scrooby was close to the main route to the north of England, and the visibility of the Manor House meant it was likely the activities of the congregation would be noticed. Brewster lost his job as the postmaster, probably due to his involvement with the Separatist congregation. The manor house belonged to the Archbishop of York, who exerted pressure on the congregation. Brewster and three others from the congregation were imprisoned in York, while there was a

---

[31] Burgess, *John Robinson*, 69.

[32] Burgess, *John Robinson*, 69.

danger, not only of falling foul of rules on nonconformity, but of being charged with sedition, for which the death penalty could be imposed.

The pressure led to the congregations from Gainsborough and Scrooby deciding to move to Holland. "By a joint consent," wrote Bradford,

> they resolved to go into the Low Countires, where, they heard, was freedom of religion for all men, as also how sundry, from London and other parts of the land, had been exiled and persecuted for the same cause, and were gone thither, and lived at Amsterdam and in other places of the land.[33]

The Gainsborough congregation led by John Smyth made their way to Amsterdam quite easily; the Scrooby congregation encountered more difficulty. In 1607, they were cheated and betrayed by the captain of the ship, many being imprisoned for a month, and Brewster, Clyfton and Robinson for longer. In 1608, they tried again but had a difficult passage. The men were on board ship, but when the captain left, fearing arrest, the women and children who had travelled separately were left behind. Eventually they were allowed to go by Robert Cecil (1563–1612), the Secretary of State and Lord Treasurer, probably because nothing seemed to be gained by keeping them in England. Brewster, Clyfton and Robinson were also able to travel to Amsterdam where they met in the autumn with much rejoicing.

Leiden
By the end of 1608, the Separatists from Gainsborough and Scrooby who were in Amsterdam started to disagree among themselves. John Smyth rejected the pattern of baptising infants and another minister decided he and his elders could dictate policy to their congregation. John Robinson decided to move, and showed, according to Philbrick's work on the history of the Pilgrim Fathers, firmness, sensitivity and judgement that came to characterise his ministry in the years ahead, as he led the majority—about one hundred in number—to settle in Leiden in 1609.[34] Clyfton stayed in Amsterdam, while Robinson was asked to become the pastor of the church in Leiden, William Brewster, its ruling elder, and William Bradford, one of its leading members.

Ecclesiology
Robinson wrote more on the nature of the church, often in response to those who opposed his views. The importance he attached to some points changed to some degree over the years.

---

[33] As quoted by Burgess, *John Robinson*, 82.

[34] Nathaniel Philbrick, *Mayflower A Voyage to War* (London: Harper Collins, 2006), 16.

The Church of England—its faults
His departure from the Church of England was opposed by Richard Bernard (1568–1641), Vicar of Workshop, John Burgess (1563–1635), probably the former Rector of St Peter Hungate, Norwich and Joseph Hall (1574–1656), Rector of Halstead, later Bishop of Norwich. In reply to these, Robinson outlines the faults he observed in the Church of England and the features he believed a church should have. He was willing to acknowledge good things within her which he and others had been grateful to receive.

Her faults, however, were many. Episcopacy—the pope, the "head" of antichrist, the "man of sin," had been removed—so also should the archbishops and bishops, its shoulders and arms, "parts of that accursed hierarchy," be taken away. The so-called "Sacred Synod" should not impose ceremonies said to be "indifferent" absolutely, unless it could determine infallibly that they edify all men at all times. Ministers of the gospel should not be appointed unless they are "apt to teach" (in line with 1 Timothy 3:2 and Titus 1:9), and to do otherwise was to break a law of the eternal God. Submitting the church to an earthly king meant disloyalty to Jesus, her real King, and so:

> we ... proclaim to all the world, separation from whatsoever riseth up rebelliously against the sceptre of his kingdom; as we are undoubtedly persuaded the communion, government, ministry, and worship of the Church of England do![35]

This view extended to St. Andrew's Church in Norwich. "St Andrew's parish in Norwich is a true church of Christ with which a Christian man may lawfully communicate in the worship of God," wrote one of Robinson's opponents, probably John Burgess, Rector of St. Peter Hungate, perhaps two-minute walk from St Andrew's. Robinson's reply was that it was a false church, not rightly constituted and involved in all the defects and corruptions of the Church of England as a whole.[36]

Faith
Robinson maintained in his response to Richard Bernard, a true church consisted of those who made a voluntary profession of faith and separated themselves, "into the fellowship of the gospel, and covenant of Abraham," even if they were only two or three in number.[37] The Church of England had been gathered "after popery ... without the preaching of the gospel, and of men and women for the most part ignorant, faithless, impenitent, disobedient" and so its constitution

---

[35] Robinson, *Works*, 3:420.

[36] Burgess, *John Robinson*, 97–98.

[37] Robinson, *Works*, 2:232.

was false.[38] However, he responded to a later claim that the visible church consisted of "penitent persons, and believing only" with the observation believers should not be opposed to their children, who might and may be in God's kingdom.[39]

Authority

Authority in the church rested, Robinson and other Separatists held, in the whole body of its membership, not in an episcopacy or a college of presbyters or elders. The Church had three polities, or forms of government: Christ the Head as its Monarch, its elders as its aristocracy and the whole body as its popular state.[40] How this worked out in practice varied in Separatist congregations, and in this Robinson displayed a considerable degree of wisdom. In 1610, there was a problem of discord in a church in Amsterdam led by Francis Johnson (1563–1618) because people put forward their complaints in Sunday assemblies. Robinson, asked for his advice, commended a "middle course" which he thought would lead to "peace and holiness," by which an issue would be referred to the elders, and if not resolved there be brought to the whole church.[41]

Robinson had a high view of the role of the minister, and held that baptism and the Lord's Supper should not be administered until a pastor or teacher was appointed. Later though, he was to clarify in a letter to William Brewster, as ruling elder in the New England church, that a church without a pastor might appoint a member, "able to teach (though out of office) to baptise" and that what he had opposed, and still seemed to, was the wild course of All-alikes who thought of themselves as another John the Baptist.[42] He did not, however, accept that the minister had a duty to conduct marriage ceremonies, objecting to the view that marriage should be viewed as a sacrament.[43] Marriage ceremonies among people from the Leiden church took place before magistrates.

Preaching was something Robinson held could be done by laymen. John Yates (*fl.*1612–1660), who had become minister of St. Andrew's, Norwich, held this should be done only by ordained ministers. Robinson's reply, printed in 1618, stated that the Bible has examples of ordinary people exercising the gift of "prophecy" (i.e., preaching) and it was not so extraordinary as Yates claimed.

---

[38] Robinson, *Works*, 2:96–97.

[39] Robinson, *Works*, 3:274.

[40] Robinson, *Works*, 2:140.

[41] Burgess, *John Robinson*, 195–197.

[42] Robinson, *Works*, 1:446.

[43] Robinson, *Works*, 3:412–413.

Baptism
On baptism, Robinson was in favour of baptising the children of believing parents. "The children of the faithful are with their parents in the visible covenant of God's love," he wrote, and having a part in it meant that they had also a part in its "seal of initiation, or entrance, baptism."[44] It was not necessary for children themselves to believe on the grounds that the gospel is about God's mercy and grace towards man "a most miserable creature … altogether unable to help himself" and the declaration of his "gracious mind of washing them, with blood and Spirit of his Son, from the guilt and contagion of sin" precedes the children's "reciprocal duties."[45] Baptism administered in the name of the Father, Son and Holy Ghost in an apostate church—and he refers to both the Church of England and of Rome—is still a spiritual ordinance, and where there is "repentance, and after the baptism of the Spirit it is sanctified, and not to be repeated."[46] This view was different to that of other Separatists, such as John Smyth and Thomas Helwys, who dismissed baptism in "false churches" as invalid, and demanded that people be rebaptised.

Despite his differences with the Church of England, Robinson clearly had a high view of what the Church should be, and his approach indicates a desire to follow what the apostle Paul wrote in 1 Corinthians14:40, that "all things should be done decently and in order."

Leiden—growth of ministry

Robinson's ministry developed over time. Leiden grew steadily. The population of 10,000, in 1575 grew to 45,000 by 1622; much of this through people coming to work in textiles, particularly the manufacture of light woollen fabrics. Among the English Separatists, William Bradford hired himself out to a French silk weaver until he was 21, and with a legacy from England did well enough to buy his own house; while William Brewster taught English at the university. Their numbers were increased by the arrival of some from England, such as Stephen Butterfield (d.1652) from Norwich, following the dissolution of Parliament by James I in 1614, and the likelihood that liberty would be denied to Separatists. The church Robinson led grew from about 100 in 1609 to 400 in 1620, which suggests he and others were a means of blessing in their day.

Robinson enrolled as a student at Leiden University in August 1615 and attended lectures in Theology. At the time there was a dispute in the Theology faculty between two groups. One led by Simon Episcopius (1583–1643) with other Arminians, also known as the Remonstrants, took the view that God might save everyone if he wished and man played a part in this by deciding how to respond

---

[44] Robinson, *Works*, 3:228.

[45] Robinson, *Works*, 1:418–419.

[46] Robinson, *Works*, 3:185.

to God's grace. A second, led by Professor Johannes Polyander (1568–1646) with other Calvinists, also known as the Counter-Remonstrants, held to the view that God predestined those who would go to heaven. William Bradford wrote that Polyander and the chief preachers of the city,

> desired Master Robinson to dispute against him [i.e. Episcopius]. But he was loath, being a stranger. Yet the other did importune him, and told him "that such was the ability and nimbleness of the adversary that the truth would suffer if he did not help them" ... When the day came the Lord did so help him to defend the truth and foil this adversary ... And the like he did a second or third time, upon such-like occasions. The which, as it caused many to praise God that the truth had so famous victory, so it procured him much honour and respect from those learned men and others which loved the truth.[47]

Robinson's time in Cambridge, and his knowledge of Latin, the language used in debate there, would have prepared him well.

Robinson continued to be involved in other debates. The Synod of Dort affirmed a form of Calvinism as the theological basis for the Reformed Church of the Netherlands, notably the doctrines of total depravity, unconditional election, limited atonement, irresistible grace and the perseverance of the saints, which together is often remembered as the "TULIP." The Synod's conclusions were opposed in a treatise by "John Murton and his associates," as mentioned above, and defended in a lengthy reply restating his Calvinist scheme of theology by Robinson. The view that only those ordained should preach, presented by John Yates, was countered by Robinson in 1618 in *The People's Plea for the Exercise of Prophecy against Mr. John Yates his Monopolie*.

Robinson's writing shows great care in the way he states the views of others, and in how he replies to them. Also noteworthy is that his assessment of people does not depend on their church affiliation. Thus, he notes the way that the Separatist Thomas Helwys and others will, in their hot zeal,

> have all, even the most zealous ministers in the Church of England, preach and pray, and do all other things by none other spirit, but the spirit of the man of sin, and that all the effects of their so preaching and praying is, but the false enlightening and heat of a false spirit.[48]

Referring to two Church of England ministers, Joseph Hall is described as a word-wise orator, "better able to feed his reader with the leaves of words, and

---

[47] Burgess, *John Robinson*, 57.

[48] Robinson, *Works*, 1:342.

flowers of rhetoric, than with the fruits of knowledge" and is contrasted with John Yates, a man of good gifts in himself, marked, "by his simple and solid dealing by the Scriptures ... giving testimony of his unfeigned love thereof."[49]

The commendation of Yates is in line with the view Robinson reached over time that contact with people in the Church of England could be of value. At one point he wished there to be a clear distance from the Separatists with him and people in the Church of England on the grounds that there should be a separation from the ungodly and from the godly who were in an unlawful church order. After further reflection, in part over the charge made by the Church of England minister William Ames (1576–1633) that Robinson had brought about "the bitterness of separation," he accepted that there could be private prayer and fellowship between Separatists and the devout from Church of England assemblies. Not all Separatists wished to follow this pattern. In his preface to the *Of Religious Communion Private and Public*, on this subject, Robinson professed himself, "always one of them, who still desire to learn further, or better, what the good will of God is" and expressed the desire to enlarge himself towards others in all things lawful.[50]

In time he was to accept also the lawfulness of hearing the ministers of the Church of England and write a treatise on the subject, arguing that hearing someone was not the same as being in spiritual communion with them—a view that others, notably Francis Johnson held—and that hearing someone was a "natural liberty," though not a substitute for being in a church with a good (in his view non-hierarchical) pattern for its life.[51] Edward Winslow (1595–1655) and John Cotton (1585–1652), writing in the 1640s, stated further that when people applied to join the Leiden church and professed their separation from the Church of England, Robinson would tell them what they needed was not separation from the Church of England, but only faith in Christ Jesus, holiness in the fear of God and separation only from the world, i.e. from what was opposed to God.[52] It is not surprising that Robinson's teaching and openness of heart were appreciated by many. William Bradford, who became Governor of the colony in New England, was in 1648 to write of his "singular virtues," noting among other things his learning and solid judgement, his hatred of hypocrisy and courtesy. Bradford stated that he:

> was ever desirous of any light, and the more able, learned, and holy the persons were, the more he desired to confer and reason with them ... He was

---

[49] Robinson, *Works*, 3:285–286.

[50] Robinson, *Works*, 3:103.

[51] Robinson, *Works*, 3:375, 378.

[52] Based on quotations in Stephen Tomkins, *The Journey to the Mayflower: God's Outlaws and the Invention of Freedom* (London: Hodder & Stoughton, 2020), 310, and in Burgess, *John Robinson*, 142.

very profitable in his ministry and comfortable to his people. He was much beloved of them, and as loving was he unto them, and entirely sought their good for soul and body. In a word, he was much esteemed and reverenced of all that knew him and his abilities—both of friends and strangers.[53]

Leaving Leiden

The blessing Robinson and the church knew in Leiden did not, however, lead them all to conclude that they should stay. Eventually about one hundred were to leave, fifty or so on the *Mayflower*, and they became the most significant group among the Pilgrim Fathers in New England. The idea of leaving seems to have come to Robinson in early 1617, and a number of different reasons lay behind this departure.

Reasons for leaving
William Bradford cited four reasons behind the venture: the hardness of life for many in Leiden, the resulting loss of morale, burdens on children, who might turn to crime or leave on ships for East Indies, and the hope of taking the gospel to the New World. It was not easy to minister to the Dutch, in part because of the language difference, and the zeal for mission found a focus elsewhere. Bradford wrote,

> They had a great hope and inward zeal of laying some good foundation, or at least to make some way thereunto, for the propagating and advancing the gospel of the kingdom of Christ in these remote parts of the world, though they should be but as stepping-stones unto others for performing of so great a work.[54]

Edward Winslow, who sailed on the *Mayflower*, gave two further reasons for departure: the fear that the people in the congregation might lose their English identity, and concern over irreligion, shown in the way greed and competition were turning Sunday into a working day.

It was relevant too that there was concern at the prospect of renewed hostilities between Holland and Spain when the ten year truce between them ended in 1621; that there was some opportunity for English colonists to go to Virginia—"Our eye," stated Winslow, "was upon the most northern parts of Virginia,"[55] and they hoped to be granted freedom of religion. Liberty was restricted, even in Holland, as William Brewster found when he published Puritan works critical of King James. Robinson held the view, developed in debate with Thomas Helwys,

---

[53] Burgess, *John Robinson*, 305.

[54] Robinson, *Works*, 1:xxxvi.

[55] Burgess, *John Robinson*, 211.

that Christians had the freedom to flee persecution depending on their strength to endure it; what would bring most good to them, and most glory to God.[56]

Faith in God
Above all there was a desire to seek the Lord in faith regarding the venture. This emerges when the idea was brought before the congregation "to the scanning of all." The answer, recorded it seems by Bradford, to those who objected because of the dangers and difficulties involved ran thus:

> it might be sundry of the things feared might never befall; others by provident care and the use of good means might in a good measure be prevented; all of them through the help of God by fortitude and patience might either be borne or overcome … Their ends were good and honourable; their calling lawful and urgent; and therefore they might expect the blessing of God in their proceeding.[57]

When the time for departure approached, Robinson drew the church together for a "Day of Humiliation to seek the Lord for his direction," speaking from 1 Samuel 23:3–4 when David sought the Lord's counsel on whether to attack the Philistines. "From which text," says Bradford "he taught many things very aptly … strengthening them against their fears and perplexities and encouraging them in their resolutions."[58]

> When the preparations for departure were completed, there was another day of Solemn Humiliation: their Pastor taking his text from Ezra 8:21: "And there, at the river by Ahava, I proclaimed a Fast that we might humble ourselves before our God; and seek of him a right way for us, and for our children, and for all our substance." Upon which [passage] he spent a good part of the day very profitably and suitable to their present condition. … And the time being come that they must depart … they left that goodly and pleasant city, which had been their resting-place near twelve years, but they knew they were Pilgrims, and looked not much on these things, but lift up their eyes to the heavens, their dearest country, and quieted their spirits.[59]

This pattern of worship was to benefit the colonists in later years.

---

[56] Robinson, *Works*, 3:161–164.

[57] Burgess, *John Robinson*, 210.

[58] Burgess, *John Robinson*, 237.

[59] Burgess, *John Robinson*, 239–240.

Preparation

Robinson's and others' faith in God's providence was complemented by diligence in preparation as far as that was possible. The venture took the form of joint stock company in which "Adventurers" made an investment by buying one or more shares costing £10 and the "Planters" travelled to the Plantation, receiving one free share, with the possibility of buying more. The arrangement was made between leaders of the Leiden church, with much of the negotiation carried out by Robert Cushman (1578–1625) as their representative, and a London merchant called Thomas Weston (1584–c.1647). Robinson took a close interest in the detail, particularly in the terms which related to the welfare of the "Planters" in the New World. He also expressed his views on the outlook the settlers should have: a person

> not content his neighbour shall have as good a house, fare, means, etc. as himself is not of good quality … and retired [unsocial] persons as have an eye only to themselves … are fitter to live alone than in any society either civil or religious.[60]

On the question of who should go, it was agreed that these should be the younger, stronger members of the congregation, and that those who went should offer themselves freely. In the event the majority stayed and, "required the Pastor to stay with them,"[61] the minority sought, and obtained, agreement that the elder, William Brewster, would travel. The two groups promised to assist each other in the future, whether this involved help to people who returned to Leiden from the Plantation, or to those who later made the journey from Leiden to it. Robinson himself hoped to travel later: a letter to his brother-in-law, John Carver (d.1621), who went on the initial journey stated "assure yourself that my heart is with you and that I will not foreslow my bodily coming at the first opportunity." Whether this happened, of course, depended on God. The conclusion of the letter looks to the Lord to guide and protect his brother-in-law, "to show you and us his salvation in the end, and bring us in the meanwhile together in the place desired (if such be his good will), for his Christ's sake."[62]

Departure and Counsel

John Robinson's desire for unity, where this was possible, commitment to prayer, and wish to learn from those wiser than himself, have already been noted. This pattern of life was one he commended to those who made the journey. On the departure of the Pilgrims from Holland at the end of July 1620, he knelt on board

---

[60] Burgess, *John Robinson*, 229–230.

[61] Burgess, *John Robinson*, 237.

[62] Burgess, *John Robinson*, 252.

the *Speedwell* at Delfshaven and "with watery cheeks commended them with most fervent prayers to the Lord and His blessing." The sense of his parting address starts with the following words written by one of the Pilgrim Fathers, Edward Winslow.

> We are now ere long to part asunder, and the Lord knoweth whether ever he should live to see our faces again. But whether the Lord had appointed it or not, he charged us before God and his blessed angels to follow him no further than he followed Christ; and if God should reveal anything to us by any other instrument of his, to be as ready to receive it as ever we were to receive any truth by his ministry; for he was very confident the Lord had more truth and light to break forth from his holy Word.[63]

In the "large letter" written to the "Planters in New England, at their first setting sail from Southampton," which included a contingent joining them from London and Essex, he commends the following. First, daily repentance especially for sins known and generally for those unknown; second, peace with others, which meant they were to avoid conflict, judging and condemning their new compatriots. Rather, they were to "stir up patience against that evil day, without which we take offence at the Lord Himself in his holy and just works." Third, they were to seek common employments for the common good, and fourth, they were to become a body politic with civil government, which involved choosing people to govern them. In choosing, "let your wisdom and godliness appear not only in choosing such persons as do entirely love and will promote the common good, but also in yielding unto them all due honour and obedience in their lawful administrations." This led to the choice, not of the overbearing governor of the *Mayflower*, Christopher Martin (*c.*1582–1621) as their governor, but of John Carver, "a gentleman of singular piety, rare humility and great condescendency," and is likely to have influenced the drafting of the *Mayflower* or Plymouth Compact, most probably by William Brewster. The pattern of joining together by a covenant as a church, which many had done back in 1606, no doubt helped to provide a precedent. This was an agreement which provided for government by civil consent, and without which the colonists could well have splintered into rival factions. The text of the Compact reads:

> Having undertaken, for the glory of God and advancement of the Christian faith and honour of our King and country, a voyage to plant the first colony in the northern parts of Virginia, do these present solemnly and mutually in the presence of God and one of another, covenant and combine ourselves together into a civil body politic, for our better ordering and preservation, and furtherance of the ends aforesaid; and by virtue hereof to enact, constitute

---

[63] Robinson, *Works*, 1:xliv.

and frame such just and equal laws, ordinances, acts, constitutions and offices, from time to time, as shall be thought most meet and convenient for the general good of the colony, unto which we promise all due submission and obedience.[64]

Contact with the Pilgrims in New England

John Robinson remained in touch with the Pilgrims through letter. One from June 1621 expressing commiseration that some have died, and commends obedience to those in government; another from the end of December 1623, telling William Brewster that he was not to administer the sacraments. One letter of particular interest, concerning their relationship with the Indians, was written to William Bradford in December 1623. In it he laments the killing of Indians who had been provoked by other settlers and threatened the Pilgrim Fathers.

> Oh, how happy a thing had it been if you had converted some before you had killed any! Besides, where blood is once begun to be shed, it is seldom staunched of a long time after. You say they deserved it. I grant it; but upon what provocations and invitements by those heathenish Christians? Besides, you being no magistrates over them, were to consider not what they deserved, but what you were by necessity constrained to inflict. Necessity of this, especially of killing so many ... I see not. Methinks one or two principals should have been full enough, according to that approved rule "The punishment to the few, and the fear to the many." It is ... also a thing more glorious, in men's eyes, than pleasing to God or convenient for Christians, to be a terror to poor barbarous people and indeed I am afraid lest, by these occasions, others should be drawn to affect a kind of ruffling course in the world.[65]

The colony survived *just* in part through help from local Indians, who gave advice on planting crops, and some of whom had learned English from earlier contact. However, in 1623 there was a severe drought, when no rain fell from mid-May to mid-July, and disaster threatened. The leaders of the colony set aside a Wednesday, a working day, as a "solemne day of Humiliation"—a pattern they knew from the days before they left Leiden, and an indication of the continuing influence of Robinson. Later the same day rain began to fall, and fell for fourteen days, interspersed with warm sunshine.[66]

---

[64] Philbrick, *Mayflower*, 42.

[65] Burgess, *John Robinson*, 280-281.

[66] Nick Bunker, *Making Haste from Babylon* (London: Bodley Head, 2010), 331-332.

Conclusion

John Robinson did not travel to New England and died of plague in Leiden in 1625. On March 4, 1625, he was buried at St. Peter's Church in Leiden. He had held to, and in time contended for, the pattern of biblical teaching he had learned as a young man. He led people who left the Church of England faithfully, yet grew to value more faithful people who remained within it, and he guided the venture to New England well. There seems to be good grounds for the tribute paid to him as he was buried when, as Edward Winslow described it:

> The University and ministers of the city accompanied him to his grave with all their accustomed solemnities, bewailing the great loss that not only that particular church had whereof he was pastor, but some of the chief of them sadly affirmed that all the churches of Christ sustained a loss by the death of that worthy instrument of the Gospel.[67]

---

[67] Burgess, *John Robinson*, 303–304.

Ss. Peter and Paul Church in Sturton le Steeple—
the foundation of this Church was laid in the 12th century
(Public Domain)

CHAPTER THREE

John Robinson's Country

ADRIAN GRAY

A Fertile Field
John Robinson did not emerge from the darkness as a solitary light but grew from a fertile landscape which had perhaps the densest network of radical puritanism outside of East Anglia. Robinson was born in the village of Sturton le Steeple, which sits just on the Nottinghamshire side of the border with Lincolnshire—a village that within a generation or two produced a major martyr of the English Reformation, two founding figures of major denominations and at least one *Mayflower* passenger.

Thomas Cranmer (1489–1556), the Archbishop of Canterbury through the crucial years of English Reformation, was born in 1489 in Aslockton in Nottinghamshire, fewer than forty miles from Sturton. Throughout his life he kept in contact with his many relatives and friends both from this county and neighbouring Lincolnshire, chief amongst them being Sir John Markham (1486–1559).[1] Markham, a friend of thirty years who probably knew Cranmer in his youth, was from a substantial family previously based at "Great" Markham and later at Cotham; Markham had been in the service of Lady Margaret Beaufort (1443–1509) and was an early adopter of "forward" religion.[2] As early as 1537 Cranmer noted that "Sir John of long season hath unfeignedly favoured the truth

---

[1] Diarmaid MacCulloch, *Thomas Cranmer: A Life* (New Haven, CT: Yale University Press, 1996), 370, refers to Markham as a boyhood friend of Cranmer.

[2] MacCulloch speculates that Gervase Markham, Prior of Dunstable where Cranmer held a hearing on Catherine of Aragon, was of this family.

of God's word," one would love to know the definition here of "long." Cranmer also spoke up for Nottinghamshire men like Anthony Neville (1508-1557) and was related through marriage to many others, such as Richard Whalley (1498/9-1583) of a family then on the rise.

The Lincolnshire and Yorkshire risings of 1536 proved a crucial turning point for gentry like Markham, who was especially prominent in serving the King loyally, and in the aftermath Thomas Cromwell (c.1485-1540) and Thomas Cranmer relied heavily on them for the dissolution of the monasteries. The dissolution of Lenton Priory involved Markham, Richard Whalley, John Babington and Markham's relative, Sir John Hercy of Grove (1499-1570). Hercy's home was barely three miles from Sturton and George Lassells of Sturton (later Gateford), who was an important assistant in the Lenton Priory dissolution, had been under his guardianship. Markham and Hercy were married to sisters.

Sir John Hercy (d.1570) is not well-known but his significance for the Pilgrims is very great. In 1536, Hercy was the childless lord of Grove near Retford, the dominant landowner in that part of the county. Through his many sisters he was related to most of the significant Protestant families, including the Markhams, Denmans, Hatfields (who were also related to Cranmer) and the Nevilles—one of this family was imprisoned as a separatist in 1608 and then fled to Holland. Hercy's father had taken on the guardianship of three Lassells children from Sturton, with whom they were also related, and which Sir John then continued.[3] Often this extended family worked together. In April 1539, the dissolution of Norwell Chantry was being handled by Hercy, Markham and Nicholas Denman (d.1561), who was Hercy's brother in law.

We could fill an entire volume with Hercy's family connections to other evangelical and Puritan families. Thomas Disney (1579-1623) of Norton Disney married, as his second wife, Elizabeth Denman of Retford, and his third Bridget Neville of Mattersey, both relatives of Sir John Hercy. These connections help to explain why it was to Beauvale, an estate owned by Disney, that John Robinson went to woo Bridget White in the early 1600s. Hercy's death in 1570 made the Denmans wealthy and Rev. William Denman became Lord of the Manor of West Retford in 1572, the title passing to his brother Francis in 1588. The Denman family systematically appointed Puritan clergy and were happy to accept those who were evidently nonconformist into their livings. They effectively protected repeat offenders such as Thomas Hancock. John Denman married the sister of Walter Travers (d.1635), a controversial radical clergyman from Nottingham who was of international prominence for many years as a pioneer of Presbyterianism. They continued Hercy's policy of bringing evangelical preachers into the area, making Babworth a Puritan church under Robert Lilley and then Richard Clifton. It was a nonconformist centre many years before Clifton was deprived in 1605, an event which began the process that eventually led to the sailing of the

---

[3] George Lassells later named one of his sons Hercye; Hercy referred to them as cousins.

Mayflower. Other families followed the same approach of appointing progressive Puritan clergy, such as the Wasteneys at Headon. In 1605, a large group of these Retford people were charged with illegally going to hear John Robinson preach at Sturton. This included several members of the extended Denman family such as the Sloswickes, whilst it was inevitably one of the Denmans who disrupted the first Easter service after Clifton had been removed from Babworth.

Yet Sturton's radical tradition includes a greater figure still.[4] We have mentioned Hercy's care for the Lassells children—George, John and Mary from Sturton. As well as being an assistant in the Dissolution, George played a major role in the downfall of Lord Darcy, the previous lord of the manor of Sturton who played a treacherous role in the risings of 1536–1537. Sir John Babington wrote to Cromwell in July 1537 to report that he had met George Lassells in London and discussed the belief that Darcy had received warning from the conspirator Aske (then in the Tower with George's cousin Christopher) to stay away.[5] Lassells told how he had been sharing a bed at Gainsborough Old Hall with Thomas Estoft, who described how Darcy had arranged with Aske, who had been invited to London for Christmas by Henry, to set post horses on the road from London to Lincoln so he could be warned if he was in danger and "again raise the people for his deliverance." Darcy was duly executed in London in June 1537 and Aske was hung in chains at York in July. In 1540, George Lassells got the manor and was able to buy himself another country seat at Gateford. However, Hercy's efforts to acquire the estate at Beauvale Priory for his other ward, John, ended in failure when it was given to Richard Disney.

A Sturton Martyr

Mary Lassells was sent off to London to spend some time in the household of the Duchess of Norfolk before getting married. In about 1536 she was living there with Katherine Howard (*c*.1523–1542), the future queen. John was found various roles in London through the support of Cromwell and Cranmer, though he lost at least one because of his strongly evangelical views. However, by 1539 he had a place in the King's household and was the leader of a radical evangelical group within it, at a dangerous time. Lassells' attempt to keep a low profile was disrupted when his sister Mary told him that she did not wish to associate with the new Queen because of Katherine's immoral behaviour before marriage; a disclosure that Lassells took to his compatriot Cranmer. This set off a cataclysm of events leading to the Queen's execution, and left Lassells a marked man, with bitter enemies.

Lassells' political vulnerability lay in his progressive faith, then far in advance

---

[4] Nick Bunker, *Making Haste from Babylon: The Mayflower Pilgrims and Their World: A New History* (New York: Alfred A. Knopf, 2010), mentions the Lassells family but misses their significance.

[5] Letters & Papers, vol XIII, part 2, item 726 (31 October 1538); Sir John Hercy of Grove confirms his cousin John Lassells as "of Sturton."

of Henry VIII's and also ahead of Cranmer's; especially on the topic of the "real presence" of Christ in the mass, which Lassells rejected. In 1546, Lassells was one of several people arrested. Also arrested was his close associate Anne Ayscough (1521–1546, often spelt incorrectly as "Askew"). She was from a family with both Lincolnshire and Nottinghamshire associations. Her sister Jane was the second wife of Richard Disney (1505–1578). Much of their correspondence has been preserved, even that written from within the Tower of London. Anne was tortured on the rack but refused to divulge names. Along with two others, they were both burnt at Smithfield, in 1546, for heresy.

The significance of this event for Nottinghamshire has been largely forgotten, but it shows that the radical gentry of the county produced one of the most important martyrs of the Reformation and specifically one who was at the centre of power supporting one of the most challenging new ideas. The BBC series, "The Tudors," left Lassells out entirely, with Anne Ayscough burnt alone, and the Church of England remembers Anne every July 16, but not Lassells. Yet Professor A.G. Dickens (1910–2001) has seen Sturton's Lassells as the leading figure, "Lascells and not Anne Askew was the leading spirit of the group."[6] Cranmer himself was to meet a similar death within a few years.

A Significant Birthplace

Some notable figures from "Robinson country" suffered persecution and death during Queen Mary's (1516–1558) reign. William Denman (1550–1587), a close relative of Hercy, was deprived of his living and fled abroad. Thomas Brumhedde of Rampton and John Willson of Dunham were similarly deprived; the "advanced" views of all three being evident in their married status. Of even greater interest, John Robinson, vicar of Hercy's home parish of Grove, was also deprived in 1554.

Such men would have looked to the new monarch, Queen Elizabeth I (1533–1603), to continue the Reformation that had first been choked by Henry VIII, and then bludgeoned by Mary. Instead they got the 1559 "Elizabethan Settlement" which drew a modest line in the sand, and then backed it by legal compulsion. The *Book of Common Prayer*, the surplice and the sign of the cross found few friends in north Nottinghamshire, but the new rules were enforced only sporadically and ineffectually. In local churches, "nonconformity" quietly multiplied.

It seems unlikely that John Robinson would have grown up at Sturton with no awareness of the story of John Lassells, given that his own family had bought their land west of the village from the Lassells family.[7] He would surely also have known of John Smyth who was perhaps six years older. Smyth was to be the most

---

[6] A.G. Dickens, *Lollards and Protestants in the Diocese of York* (Oxford: Oxford University Press, 1982), 33.

[7] Walter Burgess, *John Robinson, Pastor of the Pilgrim Fathers* (London: Williams & Norgate, 1920), 7.

mercurial of the Separatists, preceding Robinson to Cambridge and then agitating for reform and separation, before making the radical step of becoming a Baptist when in the Netherlands. Another family in the district with land at Habblesthorpe and Saundby was that of Thomas Helwys. Helwys became the great associate of Smyth in his later Gainsborough congregation and in the Baptist enterprise, until they endured a bitter split. Robinson also had family connections to the Fentons of nearby Fenton, one of whom was an overseer of his will.

There has long been a local "tradition" that Robinson lived at a house in the village known as "Crossways." This is opposite the junction to Freemans Lane. The house has been extensively altered and its original character almost impossible to comprehend, so short of a full survey we may never be able to comment on this story with any confidence.

That Sturton sent two such great figures as Smyth and Robinson to Cambridge within a few years is remarkable. In the following hundred years the village sent no one, until John Levett, who was born in 1693. Smyth and Robinson were preceded by Brian Dickons, who graduated with an M.A. from Magdalene College in 1588. So how did this happen?

Of course, we do not know. We can speculate that Dickons, Smyth and Robinson were bright young godly men who were "headhunted" by the local evangelical gentry in the way that we know Richard Bernard of Epworth certainly was. It is then unlikely to be a coincidence that Bernard ended up as Smyth's sizar at Christ's College, Cambridge, and both were indeed closely connected with Sir William Wray of Blyton and Glentworth (c.1555–1617), but there is no such trail in Robinson's life.

The next possibility is that a godly local clergyman or teacher sowed the seeds of faith and education whilst family connections provided the means. Again, we do not know where any of the Sturton graduates went to school. Several local villages had a "grammar school" which might often be just a porch or space in the church where the vicar taught lessons. Nearby Treswell had a school, and Sturton certainly had one in 1601. There is a persistent story that Robinson went to Gainsborough Grammar School, but that is seemingly based only on the erroneous assumption of it being the only school in the district.

If they had been educated at Sturton then the master would probably have been John Quippe, who was vicar from 1562 to 1602. He has tended to be dismissed as a possibility due to being involved in an altercation in 1594, but the Quippe family can claim some heritage. Another John Quipp became vicar of Littleborough, and William Quipp was removed from the churches of Morton and Torksey at the Restoration before a different William Quipp was appointed preacher at Kettlethorpe in 1684, all just across the river from Sturton.

West Burton—A Puritan Outpost
West Burton church was so isolated that it has now entirely disappeared apart

from a few bumps in the ground. But when Robinson preached there in 1603, it was a bastion of local Puritanism with a minister, James Wasteneys, who had connections into a powerful Puritan family. At that time, the bend in the River Trent, known as the "Burton Round," and famous enough to get a mention in Shakespeare, would have brought river traffic more or less up to the door of the church. Robinson was also following a well-trodden path. John Smyth had preached here without a licence the year before.

West Burton continued its nonconformist tradition for years, having resisted Archbishop Laud's attempts to enforce communion rails in the 1630s. The church was demolished in 1883 and its old font shipped to Sturton le Steeple, but the short walk from the bridge on Sturton's Common Lane is well worth the effort, as you can explore the windswept site of this "lost" village and church.

Marriage and Separation
Although Robinson clearly had the abilities for an academic career, he would have known that he could not stay on as a fellow at Cambridge if married. In 1603 he was back on home territory, preaching at West Burton church, and by 1604 he had clearly decided on marriage. Indeed, he married just a few days after resigning his fellowship. The chosen woman was Bridget White, from a family whom he had known at Sturton, though by this stage they had relocated to the former Beauvale Priory in west Nottinghamshire. Bridget's grandfather had been the manor's bailiff at Sturton, so would surely have known the Lassells family, if not Lord Darcy. By the time Robinson had come back home seeking a bride, Bridget was living at Beauvale with her brother Charles, who had leased an estate that was to become significant for coalmining. Several members of the White family went to the Netherlands and one on the *Mayflower*.

Beauvale Priory
Beauvale is in perhaps a unique position of having a great place in history both for Roman Catholics and for followers of Robinson and the Pilgrims. The priory here was founded by Carthusians in 1343 and is believed by linguistic experts to have been responsible for the famous medieval spiritual works *The Cloud of Unknowing* and *Speculum Vitae Humanae*. The Carthusians were more resistant to Henry's Reformation than other monastic orders. In 1535, Beauvale's prior Robert Lawrence (d.1535) went to see Thomas Cromwell with his predecessor John Houghton (*c*.1486–1535), and the prior of Axholme Priory, Augustine Webster (d.1535). All three were executed at Tyburn on 4 May 1535, following which the priory was surrendered to the King. Beauvale remains a place of significant annual pilgrimage for Roman Catholics and several schools are named after the three priors, who were all made saints.

The priory lands were awarded to Sir William Hussey and passed by marriage to Richard Disney, whose second wife Jane, was the sister of the famous martyr

Anne Ayscough. Disney was a noted evangelical and we can see the fellowship of Puritans in the arrival at Beauvale of the White family from Sturton to help manage the estate. The interconnections flow from here to the *Mayflower* itself for Thomas Disney, who was MP for Boroughbridge, married Katherine Smith, née Porter, the grandmother of the White girls who married John Robinson and John Carver. Thomas Disney (1579–1623) married, as his second wife, Elizabeth Denman of Retford, and his third Bridget Neville of Mattersey, both relatives of Sir John Hercy and members of prominent Nottinghamshire puritan families.

It is likely that by this time significant coal working had begun in the area. Charles White of Sturton took a lease on what was, however indirectly, a connected family estate, and began to sink mines. Because of the Whites, John Robinson himself came calling to secure the hand of Charles' sister Bridget, whom he married at Beauvale's parish church of Greasley.

The Beauvale site is now being gradually restored to provide pleasant walks and a good lunch or tea in the old monastic buildings. It is a place of unique spiritual history to be treasured as a place of both sacrifice and romance. You might care to walk around the grounds and read from *The Cloud of Unknowing*—for example some words that seem still appropriate in the age of social media:

> Let each man take care that he does not presume to take upon himself the task of blaming and reproving other men's faults, unless he feels truly that he is stirred up by the Holy Spirit within to do this work; or else he may very easily err in his judgements. So beware! Judge yourself if you wish; that is a matter between you and your God, or you and your spiritual director. But leave other men alone.[8]

Here again we see hints of the connections that sustained the faithful fellowships. The mother of the White family, Eleanor Smith, was related through marriage to the Disneys who had held Beauvale; through them she was related to the Denmans of Retford and the Nevilles of Mattersey.[9] Members of the Denman family were among those charged for going illegally to Sturton to hear John Robinson preach. By the time Robinson had come back home seeking a bride, Bridget was living at Beauvale, with her brother Charles who had leased the estate. Several members of this family went to the Netherlands and one on the *Mayflower*.

The parish church for Beauvale was at Greasley, which is where the wedding took place. Some suggestions have been made that Robinson's own mother was herself from Greasley, which was itself a notable centre of radical Puritanism for many years from at least 1574, when its minister, Elias Oakdene, had been the

---

[8] Robert Way (trans), *The Cloud of Unknowing* (Wheathampstead, 1986), 52.

[9] Genealogists seem to agree she was born in Sturton in 1545, although links to Greasley have also been suggested. The surname is interesting given John Smyth's origins in the district.

first in Nottinghamshire to be cited for not wearing a surplice.

Greasley

Nowadays Greasley is deceptively rural. The church stands on a beautiful hilltop close to a site which once boasted a castle. Nature and modern buildings are now covering the remains of the coalmining that once scarred this landscape, at a time when novelist D.H. Lawrence roamed the fields and woods. The church appears as "Greymede Church" in *The White Peacock* and "Minton Church" in *Sons and Lovers*. However, the church itself was largely rebuilt in 1896 after subsidence from coal mining caused it to start falling apart. But before this, Greasley attained a special status as a puritan and flagrantly nonconformist church of some significance—a fitting place for Robinson to marry Bridget White.

Aside from Robinson's marriage, Greasley is significant because of its depth of Puritan history. In February 1607 John Smyth, the future separatist and Baptist, preached here without a licence, probably when he was staying with Thomas Helwys nearby at Broxtowe or Basford. One of his friends, Richard Jackson, also preached here without authority. It is also likely that Brian Barton, the perpetually nonconformist vicar of South Collingham, preached here also illegally, as did John Darrell in 1607—best known for the exorcisms with which he was involved. All were radical Puritans and no doubt all were favoured by the churchwardens. Rebel preaching continued after Smyth, Helwys and Robinson had gone to Amsterdam in 1608. John Herring preached here in 1609. He had been linked with Smyth in a "riot" at Marnham church and had got the living of Basford instead.

Lemuel Tuke was ordained in 1623 and then appointed as vicar of Greasley in 1628. A later critical account, perhaps not to be entirely believed, alleged that he was a weaver with no university education and "had intruded into a cure of souls in Nottinghamshire, for which ever since the Parliament began he has been a non-resident."[10] He was cited for Prayer Book issues repeatedly and suspended in 1638 and 1639. The same account alleges that his parishioners accused him of "battery, drunkenness and whoredom."[11] One offence was administering communion to "strangers" while they were sitting—two Puritan offences at once! We do not know how long he was at Greasley after that, but by about 1641 he was down in Essex and preaching at Bocking where he was cited for being "derogatory" about the Prayer Book.

When the Civil War broke out, Tuke was in the right place. He preached against the King and he "laboured to poison his people with sedition and rebellion, affirming openly that in some cases it was lawful not only to resist but (which I tremble to relate) to kill the King."[12] Tuke secured the living at Rayne.

---

[10] Bruno Ryves, *Mercurius Rusticus* (London, 1642), 19.

[11] Ryves, *Mercurius Rusticus*, 19

[12] Ryves, *Mercurius Rusticus*, 20. This is a strongly pro-Royalist booklet.

The previous vicar, Edward Simmons, had been ejected in 1642 for his Royalist views, somehow having then ousted Thomas Atkins who was intended for the living. Tuke moved North, in about 1650, to Sutton-in-Ashfield, just a few miles from Greasley. He seemingly ran the parish and also a "gathered congregation" at the tail end of a long Puritan career. Inevitably, he was ejected in 1662, when said to have been "old and blind." He died in 1670.

The influential Robert Smalley, a "winning preacher" was forced out of Greasley in 1662 and took refuge in Mansfield, known as the "Zoar" of Nottinghamshire. He still managed to develop an independent congregation here. It was fertile ground and there had been an Independent chapel at Moor Green since 1652. In 1669, meetings of around a hundred Presbyterians were taking place at a tanner's house in nearby Newthorpe, addressed by Smalley. He also held meetings in his own house in Mansfield. Smalley had a "presage" of his own imminent death and so met other godly men in Mansfield to pray, apparently dying later the same day.

During the period of his courtship and marriage, Robinson sought employment in Norwich but failing to secure it, came home to his roots. In May 1605, he preached at Sturton and attracted a crowd of "gadders" from Retford, seventeen of whom were charged for failing to attend their own churches. Their names were a roll-call of north Nottinghamshire's Puritan families, including plenty of Denmans, no doubt still smarting after Richard Clifton had been deprived from his living at Babworth a few weeks earlier. Perhaps by this time Robinson had renewed acquaintance with Smyth, and probably also with Clifton and his circle, which came to include William Brewster and William Bradford.

The journey to separation of any of the Separatists from this region is still little known, especially as many contradictory accounts were written. Robinson certainly returned to Cambridge to discuss the issue and probably attended the "summit meeting" in Coventry where many of the leading Puritans from across the Midlands discussed what to do. The hostess on this occasion was Lady Isabel Bowes, the sister of Sir William Wray and patroness of Smyth and Richard Bernard. Most accounts place Robinson's fellow Sturton man, Smyth, as the main instigator.

We have only sketchy details of what else Robinson did at this time. He had a child baptised in Norwich in early 1607, and at that time he preached at South Leverton and Treswell churches, both of which had strong Puritan traditions. However, it is clear from all his subsequent actions that he aligned with Clifton's congregation and Scrooby rather than Smyth's group at Gainsborough, despite it being nearer to his original home. We do not know where Robinson lived. Perhaps he did not like being second to Smyth, who was much more established in the district. Later, Bishop Joseph Hall referred to the two Sturton preachers as "Mr Smyth and his shadow."

Treswell: Robinson's Last Pulpit in England?
Robinson's sermon at Treswell in February 1607, is the last occasion when we know that he preached from a church pulpit in England, and we only know of it because the churchwardens were cited for allowing it to happen. But why here?

Treswell was a little odd in being one church with two rectors. In 1603, the wardens reported that their minister was a "preacher"—a good sign of a Puritan. John Robinson was permitted to preach here and in 1608, a Mr Edwards also preached here without a licence. In 1610, twenty-seven parishioners of Treswell refused to attend the sermons of a new rector and were fined one shilling each, but the West Rector appointed from 1610, was clearly of a Puritan inclination. Henry Langley had been one of the successors as curate at Epworth to the famous Puritan writer Richard Bernard, and was probably another Christ's College, Cambridge man, like Bernard and John Smyth. In 1612, the wardens reported that "our parson Mr Langley does all things fitting for God's glory and his place."Langley appears twice in interesting documents. In a famous exorcism case involving the charismatic preacher Richard Rothwell and a "possessed" man named Fox, Rothwell sought advice by letter from Langley and Richard Bernard, vicar of Worksop.

Before the Archdeaconry Court in 1613, the churchwardens' evidence reflected the existence of the two ministers of whom Langley was clearly the most "godly":

> We cannot tell that the canons have been read according to the first article; we have no service on Wednesdays and Fridays; he does not ordinarily wear the surplice, but he does sometimes; he omits the litany because he preaches twice every Sunday; he uses the words of the sign of the cross; Willm Lincolne, parson, is not resident with us, but is in Lincolnshire; one Mr Edwardes preached on a workday, Mr Langley knew his name; he [Langley] does not read christenings and burials in the church; our minister is a preacher ... Originall Gilbie is our schoolmaster, he came from Worksope and has a licence to help Mr Langley to read ... John Stirtiuant has entertained a separatist for one night or so, but he himself is a very honest man and comes duly to the church.[13]

Of exceptional interest here is the visit of a "separatist" (and indeed the use of that word) five years after the migration of Smyth, Robinson, etc., to the Netherlands. "Gilby" had been a member of Bernard's congregation but even more remarkable is that Treswell had a school!

Langley and Gilby must have known the young John Viccars (1604–1660) who was born in Treswell. "Vicars" was mentioned in correspondence between Ed-

---

[13] Nottingham Archdeaconry Court Presentment Bills, Easter 1613, although the individual document is not dated.

ward Reyner (a Puritan in Lincoln) to John Cotton in 1627, along with Langley, but the actual issues have been lost. Langley died in about 1636. Viccars became vicar of St. Mary's Stamford in 1627, where he attracted huge attention by forming a separate congregation within his parish and denouncing his enemies from the pulpit, causing a huge legal case, as the weight of Church power was brought down upon him. Then he set out on a massive project to examine manuscript versions of the Psalms in as many eastern languages as he could find, including spending many weeks in libraries across Italy, including the Vatican. On his return, he and his brother Samuel funded the printing of "Decapta in Psalmos," which looked at ten languages and for which he had to pay to have Arabic and Syriac typeface created.

Viccars was related by his sister Helen's marriage to Obadiah Grew, an Anglican on the Puritan wing, who debated with Hanserd Knollys (1599–1691), the famous Lincolnshire Baptist leader who travelled to New England and back again. Grew spent six months in prison for nonconformity and their only son Nehemiah became a famous botanist.

Edmund Calamy the younger's account of persecuted godly ministers included one at Treswell seemingly brought down by his wife's desire for a comfortable life:

> Mr Rainbow, of Triswell, in this county, upon the Restoration, was vehemently urged by his wife to conform; but he told her it was against his conscience. When the Act took place, the clerk of the parish brought the Common Prayer Book to his house, at which he was troubled, and shook his head, saying, "Hast thou brought this gear?" He was very thoughtful about reading it, and his wife was very pressing: but he fell ill on the very Lord's day morning, when he was obliged to read it, if he kept his living; and he died in a few days after, saying to his wife, "If thou couldst have trusted God, thou mightiest have had a living husband, and a livelihood for thyself and children; but now art like to lose both."[14]

Thomas Rainbow of Treswell is known to have been presented at Retford for not reading the Prayer Book in January 1661.

We know that Robinson was among those who stayed behind as the move to the Netherlands began and it is because of Robinson that we know some details of how Helwys paid for some of the escape of May 1608. Once in the Netherlands, Robinson had several of his wife's family to remind him of home and one of these, Katherine, married for the second time to John Carver, and went on the *Mayflower*. Carver's origins have been a mystery, but it is interesting that

---

[14] Edmund Calamy the Younger, *The Nonconformist's Memorial: Being an Account of the Lives, Sufferings, and Printed Works*, ed. Samuel Palmer (London: Button, Son & Hurst, 1803), III, 110.

Robinson later chose him to be the leader of the Pilgrims. There were indeed Carvers from Sturton le Steeple, but the parish records have been lost, so we are left to wonder whether Sturton's radical tradition included yet another influential figure. This was indeed Burgess' conclusion in his pioneering study of 1920, but since then other views have proliferated based on slender name evidence only in the vacuum created by the absent Sturton records. It is worth noting that Katherine's first husband was George Leggatt, another Sturton man, although the latest research points to Carver as being from Suffolk.

The influence of Sturton itself went far beyond this. Smyth, even more radical than Robinson, became a Baptist whilst in the Netherlands, and his erstwhile friend Thomas Helwys returned to England to start an English-speaking Baptist tradition that can now be found all over the world. Sturton, therefore, has several sons and daughters who shaped the development of Christianity worldwide. Can any other place of similar size claim such an impact?

William Bridge

CHAPTER FOUR

William Bridge, A Norfolk Puritan

MICHAEL A.G. HAYKIN

The Mayflower Pilgrims were children of the Reformation, proponents of which had first appeared in England during the reign of Henry VIII (r. 1509–1547). But it was not until the reign of his son Edward VI (r. 1547–1553) and that of his daughter Elizabeth I (r. 1559–1603) that the Reformation got a firm footing in English soil. After Elizabeth I ascended the throne there was clearly no doubt that England was firmly in the Protestant orbit. The question that arose, though, was to what extent the Elizabethan church would be reformed. It soon become clear that Elizabeth was content with a church that was "Calvinistic in theology, [but] Erastian in Church order and government [i.e. the state was ascendant over the church in these areas], and largely mediaeval in liturgy."[1] In response to this ecclesiastical "settledness," there arose the Puritan movement in the 1560s, which sought to reform the Elizabethan church after the model of the churches in Protestant Switzerland, especially those in Geneva and Zürich.

Within twenty years, however, some of the more radical Puritans, despairing of reformation within the Church of England, began to separate from the state church and organize what historians term Separatist congregations. The "clarion-call" of this Separatist movement was *A Treatise of Reformation without Tarrying for anie* (1582) by Robert Browne (*c*.1550–1633) or "Troublechurch" Browne, as one of his opponents nicknamed him.[2] Browne came from a family

---

[1] Robert C. Walton, *The Gathered Community* (London: Carey Press, 1946), 59.

[2] B.R. White, *The English Separatist Tradition from the Marian Martyrs to the Pilgrim Fathers* (Lon-

75

of substance and was related to Robert Cecil (1520–1598), Lord Burleigh, Elizabeth I's Lord Treasurer and chief minister. During his undergraduate years at Cambridge University, Browne had become a "thoroughgoing Presbyterian Puritan." A few years after graduation, though, he had come to the conviction that each local congregation had the right, indeed the responsibility, to elect its own elders.[3] These convictions were hammered out by Browne in Norwich, where he had come to live in 1580 due to the presence of a Cambridge friend by the name of Robert Harrison (d.1585?), who was the Master of the Great Hospital in Norwich from 1580 to 1582.

By 1581 Browne and Harrison were both of the opinion that the establishment of congregations apart from the Established Church and its parish churches was a necessity for, as Browne wrote that year, "God will receive none to communion and covenant with him, which as yet are at one with the wicked."[4] The two men decided to transform the hospital chapel, St. Helen's, into a Separatist congregation of sorts. Matters of doctrine and practice were decided by Browne and Harrison in consultation with the church members though the church was still technically a parish church.[5]

Not surprisingly, state authorities sought to shut them down, and Browne, Harrison, and their Norwich congregation left England in 1582 for the freedom of the Netherlands. The Netherlands was attractive to the Separatists because of its geographical proximity to England, its policy of religious toleration, its phenomenal commercial prosperity—the early seventeenth century witnessed such a flowering of Dutch literary, scientific and artistic achievement that this period has often been called "the golden age of the Netherlands"—and the Reformed nature of its churches. It was there that Browne published *A Treatise of Reformation without Tarrying for anie*.

In this influential tract, Browne set forth views that, over the course of the next century, would become common property of all the theological children of the English Separatists, including Independents/Congregationalists like William Bridge (1600–1671). First of all, Browne willingly conceded the right of civil authorities to rule and to govern. However, he drew a distinct line between their powers in society at large and their power with regard to local churches. As citizens of the state, the individual members of these churches were to be subject to civil authorities, but, he rightly emphasized, these authorities had no right "to

---

don: Oxford University Press, 1971), 42. On Browne, see Joyce Reason, *Robert Browne (1550?–1633)* (London: Independent Press, 1961); White, *English Separatist Tradition*, 44–66; Michael R. Watts, *The Dissenters: Volume I: From the Reformation to the French Revolution* (Oxford: Clarendon, 1986), 27–34. For more on Browne, see below, Chapter 7.

[3] White, *English Separatist Tradition*, 45–48.

[4] White, *English Separatist Tradition*, 48–49.

[5] Ted Doe, "Nonconformity in Norwich," *Norwich Heart* (http://www.heritagecity.org/research-centre/churches-and-creeds/noncomformity-in-norwich.htm; accessed February 15, 2017).

compel religion, to plant Churches by power, and to force a submission to ecclesiastical government by laws and penalties."[6]

Then, Browne conceived of the local church as a "gathered" church, that is, a company of Christians who had covenanted together to live under the rule of Christ, the risen Lord, whose will was made known through his Word and his Spirit. Finally, the pastors and elders of the church, though they ultimately received their authority and office from God, were to be appointed to their office by "due consent and agreement of the church ... according to the number of the most which agree."[7]

Browne had seen clearly that the kingdom of God cannot be brought about by the decrees of state authorities and that ultimately Christianity is "a matter of private conscience rather than public order, that the church is a fellowship of believers rather than an army of pressed men" and women.[8] Although Browne later recanted these views, he had started a movement that could not be held in check.[9] His writings had led to the adoption of Separatist principles by a significant number in the English capital, London. As the English Baptist historian B.R. White has noted, "For many it was but a short step from impatient Puritanism within the established Church to convinced Separatism outside it."[10]

William Bridge: A Puritan within the Church of England

One of those in the seventeenth century who took this step from Puritanism within the Church of England to Independency outside was the main subject of this chapter, William Bridge (1600/1601–1671). His thinking about the church and the Scriptures were essentially that of many of those who emigrated to the New World in the 1620s and 1630s, and this quick study of his thinking in these areas can help illuminate the worldview of those who left England for America.

Born in Cambridgeshire in either 1600 or 1601, Bridge went up to Emmanuel College, where a multitude of Puritan leaders received their theological education, in the summer of 1619.[11] He graduated with a B.A. in 1623, and then ob-

---

[6] White, *English Separatist Tradition*, 59.

[7] Cited Watts, *The Dissenters*, 30.

[8] Watts, *Dissenters*, 34.

[9] See the brief overview of Browne's later career by Doe, "Nonconformity in Norwich."

[10] White, *English Separatist Tradition*, 84.

[11] For this biographical sketch, Richard L. Greaves, "William Bridge," *Oxford Dictionary of National Biography*, ed. H.C.G. Matthew and Brian Harrison (Oxford: Oxford University Press, 2004), 7:559–561 has been enormously helpful. See also James Reid, "William Bridge, A.M.," in his *Memoirs of the Lives and Writings of those Eminent Divines, who convened in the Famous Assembly at Westminster, in the Seventeenth Century* (Paisley, [Scotland]: Stephen and Andrew Young, 1811), 137–145 and the sole book-length biography by H. Rondel Rumburg, *William Bridge: The Puritan of the Congregational Way* (n.p.: Xulon Press, 2003).

In the "Memoir" of the 1845 edition of Bridge's works, the editor noted that "materials for a length-

tained an M.A. three years later in 1626. During his studies at Emmanuel, he also found the time to ride down to Dedham in Essex, a Puritan stronghold, where he would listen to the preaching of John Rogers (1570–1636), who was by all accounts an extraordinary preacher. Bridge may well have been present on the occasion in the mid-1620s when, during one of Rogers' sermons, Rogers took the part of God, angry with his people for not prizing and reading the Scriptures. He threatened to take away the Bible from such an ungrateful people. Rogers then impersonated the people, falling to his knees in the pulpit and pleading with God not to give them a famine of hearing the Word of God: "Lord, whatsoever thou dost to us, take not thy Bible from us; kill our children, burn our houses, destroy our goods, only spare us thy Bible, take not away thy Bible." The sermon's impact was electrifying. Many of the people in the church were smitten in their consciences, reduced to copious weeping in repentance, and converted.[12]

Bridge was made a priest in the Church of England just before Christmas, 1627. Like many Puritans of his day, he initially refused to wear the white surplice and academic hood that was expected of those leading worship, in his first charge at Saffron Walden, Essex. In 1631, upon the recommendation of some London Puritan leaders, he was appointed to the living of St. Peter Hungate in Norwich.[13] From there he was licensed the following year as a curate and lecturer at St. George Tombland, also in Norwich. During his four years of ministry at St. George's, from 1632 to 1636, Bridge brought in various Puritan preachers to also lecture, men such as Jeremiah Burroughs (1600–1646), whom Bridge had met at Emmanuel College and who, like Bridge, became a key leader of the Congregationalists.

Bridge soon ran into opposition, though, and that from Matthew Wren (1585–1667), who became Bishop of Norwich in 1635. Wren, the uncle of the famous church architect Christopher Wren (1632–1723), was firmly opposed to Puritanism and its perspectives on theology and worship. Bridge had already been under fire for attacking Arminian theology, which was favoured by Wren and by William Laud (1573–1645), the Archbishop of Canterbury, and also for espousing particular redemption. When Bridge refused to answer fresh charges that Wren brought against him, the Norwich bishop not only removed Bridge from

ened Memoir of William Bridge do not exist" (*The Works of the Rev. William Bridge, M.A.* [London: Thomas Tegg, 1845], 1:xi).

    For the larger ecclesiological context into which Bridge must be placed, see especially Geoffrey F. Nuttall, *Visible Saints: The Congregational Way 1640–1660* (Reprint; Weston Rhyn, Oswestry, Shropshire: Quinta, 2001).

[12] This story was related by John Howe, *The Principles of the Oracles of God*, Lecture X in *The Whole Works of the Rev. John Howe, M.A.*, ed. John Hunt (London: F. Westley, 1822), 6:493–494. For a brief overview of Rogers' ministry and thought, see Michael A.G. Haykin, "A Boanerges and a Barnabas," *Tabletalk*, 36, no.3 (March 2012): 32–33.

[13] This church has not been in use as a place of worship for nearly a century.

his ministry at St. George's, but also excommunicated him in 1636.

After Bridge left England that summer for the Netherlands, William Laud, in an annual report that he gave to the king, Charles I (1600–1649), noted "Mr. Bridge of Norwich rather than he will conform, hath left his lecture and two cures [i.e. parishes], and is gone into Holland." Opposite this statement, in the margin of this annual report, Charles I wrote, "Let him go: we are well rid of him."[14] Bridge ended up in Rotterdam, where, for the next five years, he was involved as the minister of an English-speaking church in that city. He was joined by Jeremiah Burroughs and another Emmanuel College graduate Sidrach Simpson (c.1600–1655).[15] These three men would all return to England around the onset of the English Civil War (1642–1651), and all three of them would become key leaders in the Congregationalist movement, along with Thomas Goodwin (1600–1680) and Philip Nye (c.1595–1672), both of whom had also been in exile in the Netherlands.[16] Bridge's time in the Netherlands cemented his commitment to Congregationalism, and he was actually re-ordained as a Congregationalist minister in Rotterdam.[17] His views on church government during this time period are well captured in a letter he had written in 1637 to friends in Norwich that Anglican church government, being episcopal, was "papal and romish," and that they had a duty to seek out that "form of government left by Christ and his Apostles," namely one in which church has "the power within itself, and is not subject to one officer, or to another congregation."[18]

Supporting the Puritan Cause in the Civil War

When Bridge returned to England in the spring of 1641, the country was on the verge of war. Charles I had governed England without Parliament throughout the 1630s, having prorogued Parliament in 1628. To many Puritans, this time of Charles' personal reign was nothing less than a species of tyranny. Moreover, Charles' Archbishop of Canterbury, William Laud, was a zealous advocate for Arminian theology, as well as the divine right of kings which asserted that the king was ultimately responsible for his conduct to God alone. Laud also believed that the Reformation had gone too far in getting rid of certain aspects of medieval worship. Thus, on one occasion in 1637, Laud had argued that parish church altars were

The greatest place of God's residence upon earth. I say the greatest, yea

---

[14] Reid, "William Bridge" in his *Memoirs of the Lives and Writings of those Eminent Divines*, 139.

[15] Thomas Edwards, *Antapologia: Or, A Full Answer to the Apologeticall Narration of Mr Goodwin, Mr Nye, Mr Sympson, Mr Burroughs, Members of the Assembly of Divines* (London: John Bellamie, 1644), 35, 142–144; Watts, *Dissenters*, I, 64–65.

[16] Goodwin and Nye were in Arnhem. See Edwards, *Antapologia*, 35; Watts, *Dissenters*, I, 64–65.

[17] Nuttall, *Visible Saints*, 12.

[18] Cited Edwards, *Antapologia*, 45.

greater than the pulpit. For there 'tis *Hoc est corpus meum*, This is my body. But in the pulpit, tis at most, but: *Hoc est verbum meum*, This is my word. And a greater reverence (no doubt) is due to the body, than to the Word of our Lord.[19]

To Puritan ears this would have sounded like a return to medieval Roman Catholic perspectives on worship, which highlighted the mass as the central aspect of worship instead of preaching. Laud was also insistent that his perspectives on worship be adopted throughout the length and breadth of the Church of England, and actually used force to create a uniform liturgy.

An attempt by Charles, at the urging of Laud, to impose Anglican worship as well as episcopacy upon Scotland had resulted in two wars with England's northern neighbour, the Bishops' Wars of 1639 and 1640, in both of which England was the loser. Charles consequently had to recall Parliament to help raise funds to pay reparations to the Scottish. This led to a show-down between Parliament and the king over the governance of England and Laud's religious policies, and eventually the outbreak of civil war in the late summer of 1642 when Charles declared war on Parliament.

Returning in 1641, Bridge was not slow to make his strong stance on the side of Parliament known. Asked to preach before the House of Commons on April 6, 1641, he spoke on Revelation 14:8, which speaks of the fall of Babylon and which Bridge interpreted to be the imminent collapse of the Church of Rome.[20] He urged his hearers to engage in helping forward that fall by removing from local churches in England "all the relics and remains of Babylon." Bridge especially admonished the members of Parliament, whom he considered totally "fitted for the service and work of God" to

> see that all the ordinances of Jesus Christ, be rendered to the churches in their native beauty ... True marble needs no painting. And God's ordinance is all marble, no chalk. True beauty needs no colouring; and the most deformed of God's ordinances to a gracious eye, is most beautiful.[21]

When the Civil War did break out in the summer of 1642, Bridge published a sermon he had preached in Norwich to volunteers for the Parliamentary army. Taken from 2 Samuel 10:12 (AV), the sermon urged these soldiers to

---

[19] William Laud, *A Speech delivered in the Starr-Chamber ... at the Censure, of John Bastwick, Henry Burton, & William Prinn; Concerning pretended Innovations in the Church* (London, 1637), 47. This text has been modernised in terms of punctuation and capitalization.

[20] William Bridge, *Babylons Downfall* (London: John Rothwell, 1641), 6–10.

[21] Bridge, *Babylons Downfall*, 21, 13.

be courageous in the face of "vaunting, bragging, boasting Cavalierism."[22] Bridge emphasized what a mercy it was to have peace, but not at the expense of allowing tyranny to enslave Englishmen, have one's "wife and daughters … abused," one's "poor children … massacred," one's "house … plundered," and one's "country … betrayed."[23] Near the sermon's end Bridge raised the issue of the lawfulness of taking up arms against one's sovereign and sought to make a distinction between rebellion against the monarch and defence of the realm:

> I know it is objected, "They take up arms against their King." I am persuaded there is not such a thought in the bosom of any of you all, and God forbid there should; but there is much difference between taking up arms against the King's person, and taking up for the defence of the Kingdom, without the King's command. David though he were God's anointed, yet he was a subject unto Saul his King, and he took up arms to defend himself… David's example is our practice… So that when you consider the law of the land, or the law of God, or the law of nature, which is for a community to defend itself, your way and course is very warrantable, your cause is good.[24]

This military defence of the cause of Parliament was absolutely critical, Bridge was further convinced, for even as these volunteer soldiers were "the bulwarks of England," England itself was "the bulwark of the Protestant religion."[25]

A longer defence of the legality of Parliament's cause was necessitated when Henry Ferne (1602–1662), one of Charles' personal chaplains who later became Bishop of Chester after the restoration of the monarchy in 1660, argued forcefully in a 1642 publication that Parliament had no legitimate grounds, from either Scripture or human reason, to oppose the king by military force. Men like Bridge who argued otherwise, he described as "hellish spirits, enemies to peace and quietness." And as for those who followed Bridge's advice, they ran the risk of damnation for the sin of unlawful resistance against divinely-mandated authorities—a reference to Paul's statement about obedience to political authorities in Romans 13:2.[26]

Bridge replied the same year with *The Wounded Conscience Cured, the Weak*

---

[22] It is noteworthy that for this sermon Bridge used the AV. William Bridge, *A Sermon Preached unto the Volunteers of the City of Norwich and also to the Volunteers of Great Yarmouth in Norfolk* (London: Ben Allen, 1642), 6.

[23] Bridge, *Sermon Preached unto the Volunteers*, 12.

[24] Bridge, *Sermon Preached unto the Volunteers*, 17–18.

[25] Bridge, *Sermon Preached unto the Volunteers*, 15.

[26] Henry Ferne, *The Resolving of Conscience, upon this Question, Whether upon such a Supposition or Case, as is now usually made (The King will not discharge his trust, but is bent or seduced to subvert Religion, Laws, and Liberties) Subjects may take arms and Resist? and Whether that Case be now?* (Cambridge: Edward Freeman and Thomas Dunster, 1642), 46, 50–51.

One strengthened, and the doubting satisfied, in which he argued again for the right of the people to defend themselves against tyrannical governments. He also rightly noted that Ferne had misinterpreted Romans 13:2—the passage had nothing to do with damnation but the "punishment of the magistrate in this life."[27] Bridge insisted that the king had violated the trust of his people, and this annulled any political obligations they had towards him, even as in a marriage when there was unrepentant adultery, the marriage was at an end.[28] And whereas Ferne had argued that a monarchy was the best type of government known to man, Bridge asserted that "the best government is such, when the people have the free choice of their governor."[29] The following year, 1643, Bridge wrote a further tract against Ferne entitled *The Truth of the Times Vindicated*. By this point in time, the civil war was in full swing and Bridge admitted, "if war be the worst of all miseries, civil war [is] the worst of all wars."[30]

This first stage of the civil war lasted till 1646 and resulted in the defeat of the king's forces and the king's capture. Charles, refusing to accept the demands of Parliament to establish a constitutional monarchy, was instrumental in re-igniting the civil war which broke out afresh in 1648. A number of key Parliamentary leaders, including Oliver Cromwell (1599–1658), were now convinced that the king was a traitor to his coronation oath to protect the English people and determined to put him on trial. The trial took place during the month of January 1649 and issued in the condemnation of the king to death. Charles was executed on January 30 and a republic declared in which there was a substantial amount of religious liberty. We do not know how Bridge viewed the death of the king—though his friend John Owen (1616–1683) viewed it as necessary.

An "eminent teacher"

In 1642 Bridge had been appointed as a preacher in Great Yarmouth, and the following year, as the civil war began to rage in earnest, he helped form a Congregationalist church in the town. The members, who lived in both Yarmouth and Norwich, drew up a covenant in which they stressed that they would seek to walk in God's "ways and ordinances according to his written word," and that they considered it their "duty at all times to embrace any further light or truth that shall be revealed to us out of God's word."[31] For about ten months, from November 1643 to August 1644, Bridge had an assistant by the name of John

---

[27] William Bridge, *The Wounded Conscience Cured, the Weak One strengthened, and the doubting satisfied* (London: Benjamin Allen, 1642), 14.

[28] Bridge, *Wounded Conscience Cured*, 30–31.

[29] Ferne, *Resolving of Conscience*, 27; Bridge, *Wounded Conscience Cured*, 40–41.

[30] William Bridge, *The Truth of the Times Vindicated* (London: Ben. Allen, 1643), 1.

[31] Cited John Browne, *History of Congregationalism and Memorials of the Churches in Norfolk and Suffolk* (London: Jarrold and Sons, 1877), 211.

Oxenbridge (1608–1674), who eventually would go to Surinam in South America after being silenced by the Act of Uniformity in 1662 and where he sought to engage in evangelism till 1667.[32]

For much of 1643 and 1644 Bridge was actually in London, where he was involved in the Westminster Assembly (1643–1653) as one of the five so-called "Dissenting Brethren"—Jeremiah Burroughs (1600–1646), Sidrach Simpson (c.1600–1655), Thomas Goodwin (1600–1680), Philip Nye (c.1595–1672), and Bridge—who argued for congregational church government.[33] These five Congregationalists presented a brief to Parliament, *An Apologeticall Narration* (1643), in which they stressed that their convictions about church government were grounded ultimately in the fact that their consciences were "possessed with that reverence and adoration of the fullness of the Scriptures, that there is therein a complete sufficiency as to make the man of God perfect, so also to make the churches of God perfect."[34] During the latter half of the 1640s, Bridge was frequently in London, and despite his opposition to Presbyterianism, his preaching was obviously regarded with esteem in the capital since he preached a number of times before Parliament.[35] The Quaker, George Whitehead (1636–1723), who wrote against Bridge's theology, cited a public perception of him in the 1650s and 1660s as an "eminent teacher."[36] His prominence is also evident from the fact that collections of his sermons began to be published from 1649 onwards.[37]

The Rise of Quakerism

Now, among the works that led to this high esteem of Bridge were three sermons that he preached on 2 Peter 1:19 ("We have also a more sure word of prophecy, whereunto ye do well that ye take heed, as unto a light that shineth in a dark place, until the day dawn, and the day star arise in your hearts" [KJV]) and

---

[32] Browne, *History of Congregationalism*, 212. Browne cites a statement by the Calvinistic Baptist Samuel Pearce (1766–1799) about Oxenbridge's ministry: "the time [for such evangelism] was not come—both wise and foolish virgins then slumbered and slept" (Browne, *History of Congregationalism*, 212).

[33] Greaves, "William Bridge," 560. See also Rumburg, *William Bridge*, 117–141.

[34] Thomas Goodwin, Philip Nye, Sidrach Simpson, Jeremiah Burroughs, and William Bridge, *An Apologeticall Narration, Humbly Submitted to the Honourable Houses of Parliament* (London: Robert Dawlman, 1643), 9.

[35] See, for example, his signature to *The Reasons Presented by the Dissenting Brethren Against Certain Propositions concerning Presbyteriall Government* (London: Humphrey Harward, 1648), 40. See also the discussion by Watts, *Dissenters*, I, 99–102. Greaves, "William Bridge," 560.

[36] George Whitehead, *The Law and Light Within* ([London, c.1656]),1. Whitehead was in Norwich in 1654 and 1655 as a Quaker evangelist. See his *The Christian Progress of that Ancient Servant and Minister of Jesus Christ, George Whitehead* (London: J. Sowle, 1725), 24–59, *passim*.

[37] Greaves, "William Bridge," 560.

that he later published in 1656 as *Scripture Light, the Most Sure Light*.[38] In them, Bridge defended the Puritan movement's great emphasis on the Scriptures as the touchstone of all doctrine and practice. Such a defence was needed in light of the emergence of various religious movements in the 1640s and 1650s, like the Quakers, who relied heavily on visions and so-called revelations.[39] Bridge himself was thoroughly convinced that Quaker principles were "destructive to the gospel."[40]

The Quaker movement, an especial challenge to the Puritans, essentially took its rise from George Fox (1624–1691), a Leicestershire-born shoemaker and part-time shepherd, who began to win converts to a perspective on the Christian faith in the late 1640s and early 1650s that rejected much of orthodox Puritan theology. Fox and the early Quakers proclaimed the possibility of salvation for all humanity, and urged men and women to turn to the light within them to find salvation. Fox and the Quakers had a deep conviction that the Spirit was speaking in them as he had spoken in the apostles. In practice, this often led to an elevation of their experience of the indwelling Spirit over the Scriptures. Thus, when some Baptists in Huntingdonshire and Cambridgeshire became Quakers and declared that the "light in their consciences was the rule they desire to walk by," not the Scriptures, they were simply expressing what was implicit in the entire Quaker movement.[41]

George Whitehead, who critiqued Bridge's sermons on 2 Peter 1:19, similarly argued:

> [T]he inward Light both discovering sin, and inclining and enabling man to that which is good, it must be the rule of their [i.e. believers'] lives, for the Spirit of Truth leadeth into all truth, John 16:13, which is more than the Scriptures will do, though we truly own the Scripture in its place as it testifies of the Truth, and against sin in the general. Yet the Light within must be the more sure rule, for it shows unto particular men their particular sins, and shows unto them wherein they are guilty, and opens their eyes and showeth them the way to Life which is Christ, who enlightens every man coming into the world,[42] and this is more than all outward words or writings.[43]

---

[38] William Bridge, *Scripture Light, the Most Sure Light* (London: Peter Cole, 1656).

[39] For other Congregationalist responses to Quakerism, see Nuttall, *Visible Saints*, 125.

[40] Cited Rumburg, *William Bridge*, 169.

[41] Cited Barry Reay, *The Quakers and the English Revolution* (New York: St. Martin's Press, 1985), 34.

[42] An allusion to John 1:9, a key theological verse for the Quakers.

[43] Whitehead, *Law and Light Within*, 7.

While Whitehead appreciated the Scriptures, he was adamant that "the Light within," which is none other than the indwelling Spirit, was to be regarded as the supreme authority when it came to direction for Christian living and thinking, since it could speak to each man personally and individually.[44]

Scripture Light, the Most Sure Light

In the first sermon Bridge maintained that the light referred to by the apostle Peter in 1 Peter 1:19 is none other than holy Scripture, "the most excellent, safe and sure light: it is the light of lights; the most excellent light of all under God in Christ."[45] As such, Bridge argued, "it is a full and sufficient light, able to make the man of God perfect unto salvation," a reference to 2 Timothy 3:17. And if Scripture does this, it must be considered the definitive "rule of life" for the believer.[46]

Bridge was well aware that there were other sources of guidance that people in his day heeded:

> 1. Revelations or visions. 2. Dreams. 3. Impressions made upon the heart, with or without a word. 4. Experience. 5. The law and light within. 6. Providence. 7. Reason. 8. Judicial Astrology.[47]

While Bridge was adamant that the last of these, the use of astrology, was not at all appropriate for a Christian, he was prepared to concede that some of these—in particular, impressions, experience, providence, and reason—were useful, though limited.[48] Impressions, for example, "though good, are not our daily food."[49] Or consider human reason:

> Though human reason be a beam of divine wisdom, yet if it be not enlightened with an higher light of the gospel, it cannot reach unto the things of God as it should… Though the light of reason be good, yet it is not a saving light. How many are there in the world, who have strong reason, yet shall go to hell, and miscarry to all eternity? But the light of the Scripture, gospel light, is saving light.[50]

---

[44] See also the helpful analysis of Quaker thinking about the Spirit and the Word by Richard Dale Land, "Doctrinal Controversies of English Particular Baptists (1644–1691) as Illustrated by the Career and Writings of Thomas Collier" (DPhil thesis, Regent's Park College, Oxford University, 1979), 205–211.

[45] Bridge, *Scripture Light, the Most Sure Light*, 12.

[46] Bridge, *Scripture Light, the Most Sure Light*, 13–14.

[47] Bridge, *Scripture Light, the Most Sure Light*, 14.

[48] Bridge, *Scripture Light, the Most Sure Light*, 35–38, 23–27, 30–35.

[49] Bridge, *Scripture Light, the Most Sure Light*, 23.

[50] Bridge, *Scripture Light, the Most Sure Light*, 32 and 33.

As for the first two of these alternate sources of knowledge and guidance—revelations and dreams—Bridge admitted that God is indeed able to employ such to guide his people since the closure of the canon of the Scriptures, but essentially the written Word of God has replaced them, and they are to be viewed with great wariness.[51] He cited examples from the history of the church of people being deceived by so-called revelations, from Muhammad in the seventh century to the Zwickau Prophets of Luther's day. Thus, he asked, "if Luther had hearkened to revelations and visions, and not kept close to the Scripture, what had become of his reformation?"[52] Thus Bridge averred with reference to a saying by an earlier Puritan leader, Richard Greenham (c.1540/45–1594):

Though God may sometimes lead a man in extraordinary ways, and work by ways and means extraordinary; yet if a man's heart be drawn off from the ordinary means by what is extraordinary, it is not right. Mr. [Richard] Greenham, famous for resolving cases of conscience, being once asked, … Whether there might now be visions, agreeable to the word? He said, there might be such extraordinary; but, saith he, whoso is moved with them, and not with the word, wherewith he is charged to be moved, and is not drawn the more by the vision to the true means, that man's faith is suspicious.[53]

Bridge tackled the Quaker view of divine guidance in the middle of his second sermon under the source he termed "the law and light within."[54] He helpfully summed up the heart of the Quaker perspective thus: "if the Spirit that is in me, be the same Spirit with that which did write the Scripture, what need I wait on or be ruled by the word without, or the Scripture, any longer?"[55] He then answered this objection to the Puritan focus on the Scriptures:

When the Spirit comes, it takes of the things of Christ, and opens them to

---

[51] Bridge, *Scripture Light, the Most Sure Light*, 14–23.

[52] Bridge, *Scripture Light, the Most Sure Light*, 16–17.

[53] Bridge, *Scripture Light, the Most Sure Light*, 19. Richard Greenham has been rightly identified as the pioneer of Puritan pastoral care (O.R. Johnston, "Richard Greenham and the Trials of a Christian," in J.I. Packer, ed., *Puritan Papers. Volume 1 1956-1959* [Phillipsburg, NJ: P&R Publishing, 2000), 71]. Some years after his death, he was reckoned to be among the three or four most important figures of the Elizabethan church, renowned for his skill as spiritual guide. And, yet, as Eric Josef Carlson has noted, "for centuries he has almost vanished from the historical record, thanks to his decision to labor in the relatively obscure rural Cambridgeshire parish of Dry Drayton" (Eric Josef Carlson, "Book Reviews: *Richard Greenham: Portrait of an Elizabethan Pastor*. John H. Primus," *The Sixteenth Century Journal*, 30, no.1 [Spring, 1999]: 239–240; Kenneth L. Parker and Eric J. Carlson, *'Practical Divinity': The Works and Life of Revd Richard Greenham* [Aldershot, Hampshire: Ashgate, 1998], 5).

[54] Bridge, *Scripture Light, the Most Sure Light*, 27–30.

[55] Bridge, *Scripture Light, the Most Sure Light*, 28.

you. It is sent to open the Scripture to you, not to take away the Scripture from you; it is not sent to be your rule, but to be your help to understand the rule. Because, although ye have the same Spirit which did write the Scriptures, yet you have not the same inspiration of the Spirit. All believers in Paul's time had the same Spirit that Paul had, but not the same inspiration of the Spirit; that is very diverse. The apostle speaking of diversities of gifts, 1 Cor 12:11, "But (saith he) all these worketh that one and the self-same Spirit, dividing to everyone as it pleaseth him." So that though a man have the same Spirit wherewith the Scripture was written, yet he may not have the same inspiration. But because people understand not this, therefore they think that if they have the same Spirit, they may lay by the Scripture as to their rule.[56]

Basing his thoughts on John 16:14, Bridge argued here that the Holy Spirit has been sent by the Lord Jesus to help us understand the Scriptures, not replace them. The core reality of being indwelt by the Holy Spirit, a basic fact of life in Christ since the apostolic era, does not mean that Paul's experience of the Spirit within him, for example, inspiring the letters that he wrote to the churches was the same as other believers in his day. They were indwelt by the Spirit—and this enabled them to understand the Word of God—but they did not experience the Spirit inspiring their words as holy Scripture. Proof for this diversity of spiritual experience Bridge rightly found in 1 Corinthians 12:11.[57] The Spirit-wrought Scriptures have a unique authority by which all other spiritual experience is to be tried an examined.

By way of conclusion, Bridge therefore maintained:

> [T]his light of Scripture is the best light, the most excellent light; more excellent than that of revelations and visions; more excellent than that of dreams and immediate voices; more excellent than that of impressions; more excellent than that of the law and light within; more excellent than that of Christian experience, or that of divine providence, or that of human reason; more excellent than this pretended light (but in truth, darkness) of judicial astrology. Surely therefore it is the most excellent, safe and sure light in the world.[58]

And if the Bible be indeed this most excellent guide for the Christian, then,

---

[56] Bridge, *Scripture Light, the Most Sure Light*, 28–29. Bridge's use of a Roman numeral to identify the chapter of his citation from 1 Corinthians has been changed to an Arabic number.

[57] It is noteworthy that Bridge's Quaker opponent George Whitehead has a similar interpretation of this text. See his *Christian Progress*, 55–56.

[58] Bridge, *Scripture Light, the Most Sure Light*, 38.

as Bridge in typical Puritan fashion applied this truth in his third sermon on 2 Peter 1:19, believers ought to cleave to it as "the only rule" of their lives, prize it above all earthly treasures, have their hearts "affected with love to every truth" they know, and

> let it be your continual companion, going where you go; if you go into the fields, oh! let the word go with you; if into your calling, oh! let the Scripture and the written word of God be with you. Thus shall you take heed unto it, as to a light shining in a dark place.[59]

Final Years

In late September, 1658, Bridge was once again in London, this time as a delegate at the Savoy Conference that drafted the statement of faith known as the Savoy Declaration. Oliver Cromwell, the leading political power in England during the 1650s when England had been a republic, had just died and there was deep uncertainty about the future of the nation. The men who drew up this confession—of whom Bridge was one along with Thomas Goodwin, John Owen, and Philip Nye and two or three others—were hopeful that the religious liberty that they had enjoyed throughout the 1650s would continue.[60] But it was not to be. In 1660 the monarchy was restored in the person of Charles II (r. 1660–1685), and within two years, the vast majority of Puritan ministers in England—Congregationalist as well as Presbyterian—were expelled from their churches and forbidden to engage in ministry at the risk of imprisonment. Among them was Bridge.

Ejected from his Yarmouth congregation in 1661, Bridge moved to Clapham in Surrey, on the outskirts of London, where he pastored a Congregationalist church.[61] A goodly number of his extant sermons date from this period of Bridge's life, including a series of nine sermons he published as *Seasonable Truths in Evil-Times* (1668).[62] In one of these sermons Bridge sought to encourage his hearers who were in the midst of persecution:

> Beauty raises persecution, and persecution raises beauty. ...Persecution you shall find doth always fall upon the beautiful piece of religion ... So long as Christ our Saviour liv'd, persecution lay upon him, and not upon the Apostles: when Christ was dead, then the Apostles were the most beautiful piece of religion, and then the persecution lay upon them especially. When the

---

[59] Bridge, *Scripture Light, the Most Sure Light*, 41, 56.

[60] Rumburg, *William Bridge*, 159–160.

[61] Greaves, "William Bridge," 561.

[62] See Greaves, "William Bridge," 561.

Apostles were gone off the stage, in the primitive times, the persecution always fell upon the most eminent saints. Persecution always falls upon the beauty of religion.[63]

On the other hand, Bridge emphasised that

> as beauty raises persecution, so persecution raises beauty. A man's never more beautiful in the eyes of God, than when he is persecuted for the name of Christ, and when he doth leave and forsake a worldly interest upon the account of Christ.[64]

Bridge himself narrowly escaped imprisonment not long after he preached these sermons. He had returned to Yarmouth to preach in 1668 and had been arrested under the Five-Mile Act, which had been passed three years before and which specified that a minister who had been ejected from a church could not come within five miles of the town where the church was. Only after being threatened that he would be forced to comply with this law did Bridge promise that he would not come within five miles of Yarmouth.[65]

Bridge died three years later in 1671 in Clapham. A quintessential Puritan, his life had been devoted to the exposition of the Word of God. As he had said nearly thirty years earlier in the *Apologeticall Narration*, his conscience was captive to a "reverence and adoration of the fullness of the Scriptures," words that the Mayflower Pilgrims could easily have echoed.

---

[63] William Bridge, *Seasonable Truths in Evil-Times* (London: Nath. Crouch, 1668), 68–69. Bridge went on to argue this point from an exegesis of Song of Songs 1:5–6a.

[64] Bridge, *Seasonable Truths in Evil-Times*, 69.

[65] Greaves, "William Bridge," 561; Rumburg, *William Bridge*, 192–193.

A TREATISE
Of the Ministery of the Church of England.

Wherein is handled this question,
Whether it be to be separated from, or ioyned vnto.

Which is discussed in two letters, the one written for it, the other against it.

Wherevnto is annexed, after the preface,
A brief declaration of the ordinary officers of the Church of Christ.
And, A few positions.

Also in the end of the treatise,
Some notes touching the Lordes prayer.
SEVEN QVESTIONS.
A table of some principal thinges conteyned in this treatise.

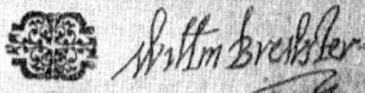

Trie all thinges: keep that which is good. 1 Thes. 5. 21.

If (the Prophets) had stood in my counsell: then should they have caused my people to heare my vvordes, and have turned them from theyr evil vvay, and from the vvickednes of theyr inventions.
Ierem. 23. 22.

Lord, who hath beleeved our report? and to whom is the arme of the Lord reveled?
Esa. 53. 1. Ioh. 12. 38. Rom. 10. 16.

Title page from *A Treatise of the Ministry of the Church of England*, written by Arthur Hildersham and Francis Johnson, c.1595, publisher and place of publication unknown (Netherlands?) (Public Domain).
As the signature bears witness, this book was owned by William Brewster.

CHAPTER FIVE

Francis Johnson
Life, Controversies, and Freedom

TOM NETTLES

The Early Life of Francis Johnson
England
Francis Johnson, whose father was one-time mayor of Richmond in Yorkshire, was born about 1562. In April of 1579 he matriculated at Christ's College, Cambridge, and received his B.A. early in 1582. His brother, George, entered the same college in December of 1580 and graduated in 1585. By then Francis had been elected to a fellowship at Christ's College.

On January 6, 1589, Johnson and Cuthbert Bainbridge, another Fellow, preached militant Puritan sermons in the University Church. The text for Johnson's sermon was 1 Peter 5:1–4. Reflecting on Peter's address to "the elders who are among," and Peter's own position as a "fellow elder," Johnson advocated a presbyterial form of church government. It was unfortunate for Johnson that such boldness had been outlawed by the new university statutes of 1570. Clause 45 of the statutes provided that any man preaching or lecturing "anything against religion, or any part of the same as received and established by public authority" could be ordered to recant "and publicly confess his error or rashness" or, if not done properly, "be for ever expelled from his college and banished the university [sic]."[1] The Vice-Chancellor with the assent of the majority of the heads of colleges pronounced the sentence.

---

[1] H.C. Porter, *Reformation and Reaction in Tudor Cambridge* (Cambridge: Cambridge University Press, 1958), 56.

Several ideas expressed by Johnson in his sermon were offensive to the authorities: that the Church of God ought to be governed by elders, that this form of government is prescribed and commanded by the word of God, and no other form is to be allowed. Johnson also asserted that neglect of this commanded government was the cause of ignorance, idolatry, and all disobedience. He stated there should be an equality among ministers and elders.[2] He was committed to the town jail along with Bainbridge.

The authorities prepared recantations for both men. Bainbridge, ready to comply, read his and gained freedom. Johnson proved to be too captive to his conscience and refused to conform. Porter records the recantation prepared for Johnson:

> I do not think that there is set down by the word of God any precise form of eternal regiment of the Church which must of necessity be observed in all times and places without exception; but am persuaded that for the better government of particular congregations, her Majesty may establish such orders, as by her godly wisdom with the advice of her godly and learned prelates she shall find to be most expedient for the state of her country, according to her Majesty's pre-eminence in church government established by the laws of this realm, and expressed in her most just title, which is both agreeable to the word of God, and conformable to the example of most ancient churches, which have been ruled by Christian magistrates.[3]

As a result of his refusal to read the recantation, Johnson was expelled from the University. He refused to go, appealed the decision, was rejected, still remained at Cambridge, and finally was imprisoned again. From prison he appealed to Lord Burleigh to act as King Zedekiah had acted when Jeremiah was in prison, but deliverance from Burleigh did not come. The situation was finally resolved when Johnson was dismissed to Middelburg in the Netherlands, where he became pastor of the Congregation of English Merchants. It was there that the tendencies of his thought crystallized into Separatism.

Middelburg

In the spring of 1591, Johnson discovered Barrowe's and Greenwood's *Plaine Refutation of M. Giffards Booke intituled, A short treatise against the Donatistes of England* in process of printing at Dort. Governor Bradford records the story.[4] Johnson supervised the burning of the books. He retained two copies, one

---

[2] Porter, *Reformation and Reaction in Tudor Cambridge*, 141–142.

[3] University Archives, Registry Guard Books, vol. 6 (1), no. 18, quoted by Porter, *Reformation and Reaction in Tudor Cambridge*, 144–145.

[4] White concludes that this is the time of the printing rather than spring of 1592 or late in 1591 thus preceding the October 1591 action at his church in Middelburg. See Barrington Raymond White, *The*

for himself and one for a friend, in order that he might acquaint himself with the errors propagated by Greenwood and Barrowe. Johnson read the pages superficially until he "met with something that began to work upon his spirit."[5] He resolved to read the entire book more carefully, "which he did once again."[6] Being impressed with what he read, he crossed the sea and came to London, according to Bradford, where he conferred with the authors and joined the Separatists immediately.

However, if the chronology of Barrington White is correct, Johnson's journey back to England was not as immediate as Bradford implies. In October of 1591 Johnson created considerable surprise and substantial opposition by demanding that all the members of his congregation sign a covenant. One article of the covenant read,

> Wee doe acknowledge, that God in his ordinarie meanes for the bringinge us unto and keepinge of us in this faythe of Christe, and an holie Obedience thereof, hath sett in his Churche teachinge and rulinge Elders, Deacons, and Helpers: And that this his Ordinance is to continue unto the ende of the worlde as well under Christian princes, as under heathen Magistrates.[7]

The church led by Thomas Ferrers opposed Johnson in his attempt. Because of this opposition, Johnson decided to seek a conference with Barrowe and Greenwood. The details concerning this meeting are unclear. However, Johnson was elected as pastor of the Barrowist congregation in September of 1592.

In March of 1593, fifty-six members of the congregation were arrested and placed in several London prisons. They wrote an appeal to the High Court of Parliament complaining of their treatment, defending their manner of worship, and proclaiming their loyalty to and prayers for the Queen and Parliament. The appeal did little good, for within a few weeks, Greenwood, Barrowe, and Penry were executed.[8]

English Separatist Tradition (London: Oxford University Press, 1971), 93. William Bradford, "Governor Bradford's First Dialogue," *Plymouth Church Records, 1620-1859* 22 (Boston: Publication of the Colonial Society of Massachusetts, 1920), 121f, quoted by White, *English Separatist Tradition*, 93. See also Champlin Burrage, *The Early English Dissenters in the Light of Recent Research (1550-1641)* (New York: Russell & Russell, 1912), 1:140, and Henry Martyn Dexter, *The Congregationalism of the Last Three Hundred Years as Seen in Its Literature* (New York: Harper and Bros., 1880), 264.

[5] Burrage, *Early English Dissenters*, 1:140.

[6] Burrage, *Early English Dissenters*, 1:140.

[7] Burrage, *Early English Dissenters*, 1:138.

[8] Burrage, *Early English Dissenters*, 1:149–52, for testimonies of contemporaries concerning their martyrdom.

The Move to Amsterdam

The Conventicle Act of 1593 was the stimulus for the immigration of the church to Amsterdam. The people had experienced a rigorous imprisonment but toward the end of 1593 most of the church made their way across the sea to Campen, moving later to Naarden.[9] Thus, for four years they were separated from their pastor and they celebrated neither baptism nor the Lord's Supper in his absence.[10]

Johnson arrived in late September or early October of 1597 accompanied by Daniel Studley, a church elder; George Johnson, Francis' brother; and John Clerk, former mayor of St. Albans and protector of Penry. Their travel was circuitous and hazardous involving some piracy and shipwreck, but, in the eyes of George Johnson, guided by "the wondrous providence of God."[11]

Controversy Over Dress

However, the new arrivals also brought contention to the church. While imprisoned, Francis had married a wealthy widow, Mrs. Thomasine Boys. Her husband had been a Separatist and had died in prison. George objected violently because Mrs. Johnson dressed too ostentatiously.

There was immediate uproar in the congregation when Mrs. Boys visited her new husband dressed more elegantly than ever. George took it upon himself to point out the immodest nature of Mrs. Johnson's dress.[12] The controversy between George and Francis became bitter and George applied Jeremiah 3:3 to the pastor's wife: "thou hadst a whore's forehead, thou refusedst to be ashamed." Daniel Studley managed to reconcile the two brothers and Mrs. Boys seemed more discreet in her dress. The turmoil ceased temporarily.

In Amsterdam, the first communion was held in the early spring of 1597. George partook with his brother and sister-in-law, but soon fellowship was broken again as the turmoil reoccurred. Francis was too comfortable while George was in poverty, and the apparent worldliness of Mrs. Johnson reappeared, inflaming George.

---

[9] J.H. Shakespeare, *Baptist and Congregational Pioneers* (London: Kingsgate Press, 1907), 107.

[10] Burrage, *Early English Dissenters*, 1:156. Whether or not the church was in Amsterdam by the time of Johnson's arrival in September or October of 1597 is unclear. They were in Amsterdam within two weeks after his arrival. See Burrage, *Early Dissenters*, 1:156–57.

[11] G. Johnson, *A Discourse of Some Troubles in the Banished English Church at Amsterdam* (Amsterdam [?], 1603), 100, quoted by Walter H. Burgess, *John Smith, the Se-Baptist* (London: James Clarke, 1911), 40. Johnson's book is the major source for the inner life of the congregation from 1594 to 1600. It is incomplete, printed before it was finished, and written from a highly partisan stance. George felt himself victimized by his brother and Daniel Studley.

[12] The listing of offenses in apparel included "the wearing of a long busk after the fashion of the world ... Whalebones in the bodices of peticotes Contrary to the former rules, as also against nature, being as the Phisitians affirme hinderers of conceiving or procreating children ... Foure or five gould rings at once ... A copple crowned hatt with a twined band, as yong Marchants wives, and yong Dames use. Immodest and toyish in a Pastors wife" (Johnson, *Discourse of Some Troubles*, 135–137, quoted by Burrage, *Early English Dissenters*, 1:160).

In November of 1597, George was disregarded in the election of elders because of his abusive attitude toward the pastor's wife. Asked to apologize for applying Jeremiah 3:3 to Mrs. Johnson, George replied that it was not an unfit comparison at all.

The controversy continued, and eventually the entire church examined and voted concerning Mrs. Johnson's hat. At a later meeting one of her dresses was scheduled for examination by the congregation but the pastor and elder Studley refused to permit it. George Johnson then described the dress for the church and, in passing, severely criticized the deportment of Mrs. Johnson.

During the controversy, the pastor and the elders tried to limit the discussions to as small a group as possible. George Johnson protested, "Ye elders end and determine matters, yet they will pretend that ye church doth it, whereas, in truth, they give the church the title and name, but they usurpe the power."[13]

In 1599 George Johnson was excommunicated; the father of the two brothers, seeking their reconciliation, was excommunicated in 1602. In George's case, Francis was accuser, judge, and the one who pronounced the sentence of excommunication.

Attempts at Recognition

The Ancient Church, as Johnson's church was eventually called, attempted to secure the sympathy of the Dutch theologians. They sent a Latin translation of their Confession to a number of universities defending their own position and criticizing the Church of England. Francis Junius of Leyden replied that they had been indiscreet in publishing abroad the difficulties of the English Church. He did not criticize their views, however, and they interpreted his silence as endorsement. Such was not the case, and after three letters of Junius they were given to understand that he had no desire to debate with exiled sectaries of whom he knew nothing. Also, he had heard that the Englishmen in exile were highly critical of the Reformed congregations of Amsterdam.[14]

In 1603 Johnson and his followers attempted to gain legal recognition in their own country. They petitioned James three times, sending him their Confession of Faith, a list of fourteen points of differences between their church and the Church of England, and an exposition of these points. They finally condensed their appeal to seventeen lines. The first paragraph contains the essence:

Our humble suit to the Kings Majesty is, that it would please his Majesty,

---

[13] Johnson, *Discourse of Some Troubles*, 145–146, quoted by Dexter, *Congregationalism*, 291.

[14] White, *English Separatist Tradition*, 103–106. Dexter, *Congregationalism*, 229–306. The Separatists delineated eleven things of which they disapproved in the Dutch Reformed community. The points were entirely in line with Separatist thought and dealt with the nature of discipline, sacraments, ordination, worship, size of churches, and reception of unworthy people as members.

that we may be suffred to live here in peace, professing and practicing the truth of the Gospell by us now witnessed, without molestation; as the French and Dutch Churches are, not withstanding the differences from the hierarchy & worship of the church of England: we carying ourselves as loyall subjects, and leaving the suppressing abolishing or reforming of the abuses that we witnesse against, to his Maiestyes discretion.[15]

James rejected their appeal and the Ancient Church remained in Amsterdam.

Differences with Other Separatists
Further trouble came to Johnson from outside attacks of men who were compatriots and had been of his persuasion. Thomas White came to Amsterdam and received the hospitality of Johnson and took communion with the Church. However, probably because of unfulfilled ambition, he formed his own church with thirteen others who had come to Amsterdam with him. He published a virulent attack on Johnson in 1605, *A Discovery of Brownisme*. Johnson answered him in 1606 with *An Inquirie and Answer of Thomas White*, and, by this, Johnson appears to have silenced the critics for a short time.[16]

John Smyth, upon arriving in Amsterdam in 1608, immediately found differences between his group and Johnson's. He published a work under the title *The Differences of the Churches of the Separation* which set forth six points of difference between the churches. Therefore, he did not join with Johnson and eventually moved into Anabaptism.[17]

Despite this, Johnson's church in 1609 had over three hundred communicants including John Robinson and the Scrooby Church.[18] However, in February, Robinson, perhaps fearing what transpired with Smyth and foreseeing coming division in the Ancient Church, sought and received entrance to Leyden.

Christopher Lawne, one-time member of Johnson's congregation, published

---

[15] Henry Ainsworth, *An Apologie or Defence of Such True Christians as Are Commonly (but Uniustly) Called Brownists* (Amsterdam, 1604), 82.

[16] Burrage, *Early English Dissenters*, 1:167; Dexter, *Congregationalism*, 310–11; and White, *English Separatist Tradition*, 106–109.

[17] The move into Anabaptism was not new to Johnson. Part of his congregation had done it in 1594 before his arrival in Holland. He records that "divers of them fell into the heresies of the Anabaptists (which are too common in these countreys)." See *An Inquirie and Answer of Thomas White* (Amsterdam, 1606), 63, quoted by Burrage, *Early English Dissenters*, 1:156.

[18] This number was attained probably in 1606. By November of 1606 they had purchased a site on which to build a structure that would serve for dwelling and worship. A hurricane destroyed the unfinished building, a certain sign to the Reformed community of God's displeasure, but the building was eventually finished and used for many years. J. De Hoop Scheffer, *History of the Free Churchmen Called the Brownists, Pilgrim Fathers and Baptists in the Dutch Republic, 1581–1701*, ed. William Elliot Griffis, trans. J. De Hoop Scheffer (Ithaca, NY: Andrus & Church, 1922), 96–101.

in 1612 a violent attack on the church.[19] He charged it with injustice, cruelty, and lewdness. A second attack came from his pen called *Brownisme Turned Inside Outward*. Collaborating with Lawne were John Fowler, Clement Saunders, and Robert Bulwarde. Despite the scathing accusations they made, their hostility did not inflict as much damage upon the church as did the division between Johnson and the teacher, Henry Ainsworth, in 1610.

Johnson and Ainsworth

Disciplinary matters in the church provoked another quarrel, perhaps the most debilitating of all. Charges of scandalous behavior had been levelled at some members of the church. No steps of purgation were taken for several months. When Johnson finally began to broach the matter, he indicated preference for limiting its discussion to the elders. Johnson suspected that malice was the source of the complaints and believed that such cases could be more wisely handled by a small group. Ainsworth objected to the suggested procedure of Johnson and retorted that Johnson was violating the principles upon which the church was founded.

The matter became more complicated and personal when Daniel Studley was accused of immorality, and fifteen brethren insisted on his dismissal. Studley feared that this was the beginning of popular government, a nemesis to all good order in church and commonwealth.[20]

For a full year, the controversy continued. On December 15, 1610, Ainsworth and his followers withdrew fellowship and were excommunicated. Ainsworth was deposed from his position as teacher and Richard Clyfton replaced him in Johnson's congregation.

The "Ainsworthians," as Ainsworth's followers were called, took up residence on the same street only one door removed from Johnson, who retained the original building. Before the schism there had been several efforts at arbitration and several plans of coexistence proposed and rejected. Now a new question arose as to the legal ownership of the building.

Although Ainsworth's group per se did not enter into litigation to obtain the property, three of the members as private persons desired to submit their claims to the judgment of impartial arbitrators. They corresponded with contributors in England and explained the situation to them so that if consulted by the civil authorities of Amsterdam their testimony would favor the Ainsworthians.

The legal basis of their claim to the church was that they truly represented the original church contemplated in the erection of the building. They gave as evidence a list of specific points in which the "Franciscans," as Johnson's followers

---

[19] Christopher Lawne, et al., *The Prophane Schism of the Brownists or Separatists, With the Impietie, Dissensions, Lewd and Abominable Vices of that Impure Sect* (London, 1612), passim.

[20] Scheffer, *History of the Free Churchmen Called the Brownists*, 124–125.

were dubbed, had violated the Confession of Faith.[21]

The accusations were recorded by Christopher Lawne.[22] Articles 23, 24, 29, 31, 32, 33, and 38 had been violated by Johnson's group, according to the Ainsworthians. They had abridged the rights and powers of the brotherhood; Clyfton was installed as teacher without further imposition of hands; they had defended the Church of England, yea of Rome, as true churches in violation of article 31; and they had refused "counsell and helpe" of a church of like faith.

The magistrates ruled in favor of the plaintiffs, not as a congregation but as private citizens, and they reassumed ownership in 1612. In May of that year Johnson and his followers left Amsterdam for Emden.

He returned to Amsterdam shortly before his death on January 10, 1618. In his last writing he styled himself the "Pastor of the ancient English Church, now sojourning at Amsterdam in the Low Countreyes." Among the verses quoted on the title page was Isaiah 50:5, 6, "The Lord hath opened myne eare; and I was not rebellious, neyther turned away back. I gave my back to the smiters, and my cheeks to them that plucked off the haire: I hid not my face from shame & spitting."[23]

He also graced the title page with the testimony of Paul, "I have fought a good fight, I have finished my course, I have kept the faith" (2 Timothy 4:7). Johnson knew his death was near. He had nothing to recant and nothing of which to repent. He was quite satisfied that his way was that way absolutely delineated in Scripture.

Baptism

With the defection of John Smyth to the Mennonites, Francis Johnson wrote a treatise on baptism. It was entitled *A Brief Treatise Conteyning Some Grounds and Reasons, Against Two Errours of the Anabaptists*. The two errors were the rejection of infant baptism and the rebaptism of older people. In the preface Johnson states that schism within the church is the greatest of trials, but that it must come so that the truth will be further cleared and that the faith once given to the Saints will stand stronger against any opposition or delusion.[24]

The last writing of Johnson, *A Christian Plea*, contains a treatise against the Anabaptists also.[25] In this, he duplicates much of the material in *A Brief Treatise* and augments it with several additional sections, although the argument is

---

[21] Dexter, *Congregationalism*, 336; Scheffer, *History of the Free Churchmen Called the Brownists*, 130–131.

[22] Lawne, *Prophane Schism*, 78–80, quoted in Dexter, *Congregationalism*, 336.

[23] Francis Johnson, *A Christian Plea Conteyning Three Treatises* (Amsterdam [?], 1617), title page.

[24] Francis Johnson, *A Brief Treatise Conteyning Some Grounds and Reasons, Against Two Errours of the Anabaptists* (Amsterdam, 1609), 3–7.

[25] Johnson, *A Christian Plea*, 1–220.

materially the same. The difference lies in the intention of the writings. *A Brief Treatise* sets forth a positive presentation of the Reformed position against the two alleged Anabaptist errors. The treatise in *A Christian Plea* attempts a point-by-point refutation of the entire Anabaptist argument.

Baptism in *A Brief Treatise*

Johnson defends infant baptism on the strength of seven propositions. The first is that God has commanded that his people and their seed be given the "signe and seale of his covenant of grace."[26] The seed are to receive this seal in their infancy. Since the covenant was made with the faithful and their seed forever, this ordinance has never been repealed.[27]

Second, Christ confirmed this perpetual covenant when he sent his Apostles forth to make disciples and to baptize them. To make disciples is to bring people by the gospel into the covenant that God made with Abraham and his seed. Thus, the new converts and their seed are to receive baptism which "did now succeed and seale it [the covenant] instead of Circumcision."[28] Apart from this, the Gentiles should not be made coinheritors with the Jews.[29]

The third proposition is that the Apostles actually baptized those that believed and their households also. The cases in Acts 16 and 1 Corinthians 1 are used as examples, and Johnson observed that mention of a house, family, or household in Scripture implies the presence of children.[30]

Fourth, the children of believers are holy, are Abraham's seed, and heirs of the promise. Since they are promised baptism of the Spirit and the blessing of Abraham to an inheritance everlasting in the heavenly kingdom, Johnson implies it would be presumptuous to deny baptism to infants.[31]

Fifth, baptism "is the Lord's signe of his washing away of our sinnes, receiving of us into the church, his death and resurrection."[32] Not only adults, but the children of believers possess these benefits. Moreover, the subject of baptism is entirely passive in its ministration and so infants are fully capable of meeting all requirements for baptism. Johnson contrasts the active role of the recipient of the Lord's Supper, to take, eat, drink, remember, show forth, and examine, with the inactive role of the recipient of baptism and concludes "the truth of this point

---

[26] Johnson, *A Brief Treatise*, 9.

[27] Johnson, *A Brief Treatise*, 9.

[28] Johnson, *A Brief Treatise*, 9.

[29] Johnson, *A Brief Treatise*, 9–10.

[30] Johnson, *A Brief Treatise*, 11.

[31] Johnson, *A Brief Treatise*, 11.

[32] Johnson, *A Brief Treatise*, 12.

[infant baptism] yet further is cleared and confirmed unto us."³³

The sixth proposition concludes that since there is one baptism and one mediator to the faithful and their seed, the same baptism pertains to the children and the faithful together just as they have the same mediator.³⁴

The final proposition employs a lesser-to-greater argument. The lesser is the inclusion of the children in the covenant; the greater is the promise to children since Christ's coming. Unless the grace of God, since the coming of Christ, is to be "lessened and straitned more then it was before," and unless the comfort and confirmation of the faithful for themselves and their children is less than it formerly was, then infants of believing parents must be included in baptism.³⁵

In the next section of *A Brief Treatise*, Johnson gives seven reasons for holding that the rebaptism of adults is an error. His basic proposition is "that Baptisme received in apostatical Churches of Christians, as of Rome and the like, is not to be renounced and a new to be repeated againe."³⁶

Johnson begins by stating there is neither precept nor example in the Old or New Testament of rebaptizing. It is therefore the invention of men and not the ordinance of God.³⁷

Further, there is only one baptism as there is only one circumcision. Circumcision was valid even when performed in an apostate Israel, and thus, baptism is valid even if received from Rome.³⁸

Next, the covenant of God's grace is an everlasting covenant. Since it pleases God to deal mercifully with his people, even when they are in apostate churches, so should we deal with them in consideration of their baptism.³⁹

Also, Christ died to sin once and was raised from the dead. In baptism, one is buried with him and grafted into him in the similitude of his resurrection. Thus, Johnson claims, all that are baptized into his name can no more be baptized again than can Christ's death and sacrifice, once offered, be repeated.⁴⁰

In addition, the baptism of Rome was instituted in the days of the apostles with the rest of Christ's ordinances, and the church was espoused to Christ. Therefore, notwithstanding the adulteries and apostacies she has committed, the ordinances

---

³³ Johnson, *A Brief Treatise*, 12, 13.

³⁴ Johnson, *A Brief Treatise*, 14.

³⁵ Johnson, *A Brief Treatise*, 15.

³⁶ Johnson, *A Brief Treatise*, 16.

³⁷ Johnson, *A Brief Treatise*, 16.

³⁸ Johnson, *A Brief Treatise*, 16, 17.

³⁹ Johnson, *A Brief Treatise*, 17, 18.

⁴⁰ Johnson, *A Brief Treatise*, 18, 19.

received from her are to be held in due respect.[41]

Furthermore, when God calls his people from the Romish Babylon he calls them to leave her abominations and adulteries. However, since baptism is not one of the adulteries, but a pure ordinance of Christ, all who have received it are to retain it.[42]

Finally, if men are allowed to renounce their baptism received in the Roman Church, why could they not also renounce the articles of faith, the learning of Scripture, and proceed to dissolve marriages performed by its ministry? Johnson holds that a rejection of Rome's baptism could logically be followed by these and "other as strange consequences that by like manner of reasoning would be inferred thereupon."[43]

Johnson concludes that rebaptizers are erroneous in three points. First, they add to the word of God by rebaptizing and take from it by prohibiting infant baptism. Next, they bring themselves into a state of persons unbaptized by renouncing their former, and holding to an unscriptural baptism. Last, by their actions, they show their own lack of faith in God's promise and remove themselves from under God's covenant.[44]

As recently as 1608, one year previous to these assertions, Johnson had soundly disparaged the validity of sacraments received at the hands of the ministry of the Church of England. He had used virulent language to describe the position of these ministers as a "false Ministery ... erected by Sathan" and "reteyned by Antichrist for the subversion of the Church." He concludes that "none can heare the word, receive the Sacraments, or learne the truth" from the English Church.[45]

John Smyth advocated believer's baptism soon after the publication of *Certayne Reasons*. The next year, 1609, Johnson testified to the validity of baptism received in the Church of England. Clearly his shift was prompted by Smyth's action. This is still evident at the time of his last writing, *A Christian Plea*.

Baptism in *A Christian Plea*

The first treatise of *A Christian Plea* is entitled "Touching the Anabaptists." For 220 pages, Johnson discussed his position on points especially related to the objections of the Anabaptists. Section one duplicates most of *A Brief Treatise*. Johnson then answers eight objections the Anabaptists propose to infant

---

[41] Johnson, *A Brief Treatise*, 19.

[42] Johnson, *A Brief Treatise*, 20.

[43] Johnson, *A Brief Treatise*, 21.

[44] Johnson, *A Brief Treatise*, 22, 23.

[45] Francis Johnson, *Certayne Reasons and Arguments Proving it is not Lawfull to Heare or Have any Spirituall Communion with the Present Ministers of the Church of England* (Amsterdam [?], 1608), 63–69.

baptism.⁴⁶ He adds no new arguments to his defense of infant baptism but does engage in a more laborious discussion of the different points and more extended exegesis of critical passages. Section two presents a brief discussion of original sin in which he seeks to refute the Anabaptist conviction on the innocence of children by advocating the Augustinian concepts.

In chapter three, Johnson defends the baptism received from Rome and other "apostatical" churches. Seven objections are presented to which he gives answer. Again, his arguments are elaborations of the basic position taken earlier in *A Brief Treatise*. There are remnants of true Christianity in the Roman Church, mainly baptism; and salvation is possible within it because elements of the covenant remain. If this is true of Rome, then how much more is it true for the Church of England "which is already purged (by the mercy of God) from the apostasie, iniquitie; & abominations of the church of Rome"?⁴⁷

Chapter four of "Touching the Anabaptists" contains another group of replies concerning churches in apostasy and the Church of Rome. Johnson is redundant in his defense of these churches, but his verbal arrows this time are aimed specifically at Henry Ainsworth. Ainsworth, in line with traditional Separatist thought, maintained that "the church of Rome is acknowledged by all that fear God to be the throne of Antichrist."⁴⁸

Johnson sought to reject this assertion. His motivation, however, is less than absolute. He rejected some of Ainsworth's interpretation, not as false, but as leading to Anabaptism:

Secondly, although that this being but generally spoken, and in a good understanding, might be admitted [Ainsworth's interpretation of 2 Thessalonians 2:4]: yet ... we must take heed how we admitte it, considering what consequences follow thereupon, for the upholding of Anabaptistrie and other erroneous opinions thereabout.⁴⁹

---

⁴⁶ The eight objections he deals with are: (1) that there is not in the New Testament mention of any child so baptized; (2) out of Acts 16:32, 34 that the jailer with his household believed in God; (3) out of Matt. 28:18, 19 that Christ commanded the apostles first to teach, and then to baptize; (4) of the reasoning from circumcision to baptism; (5) of the difference between the Jews' estate and ours, their ministration of circumcision to the males only, and on the eight day; (6) of the Jews and Proselytes, that were both circumcised and baptized; (7) that Christ was not baptized until he was about thirty years old; (8) that children not understand the mystery of baptism. See Johnson, *A Christian Plea*, n.p. ("A Table of some principal things").

⁴⁷ Johnson, *A Christian Plea*, 119.

⁴⁸ Henry Ainsworth, *An Animadversion to Mr. Clyftons Advertisement* (Amsterdam [?], 1613), 76, quoted by Johnson, *A Christian Plea*, 140.

⁴⁹ Johnson, *A Christian Plea*, 140. Although often attributed to Ainsworth, because of the conjecture by Dexter, *The Congregationalism*, 270, some scholars now believe that the Confession of 1596 was the work of Francis Johnson or someone intellectually dependent upon him (Burrage, *Early English Dissenters*, 1:163). The Preface to this confession states that the Church of England is "false and counterfeit, deceyving hir children with vaine titles of the word, Sacraments, Ministrie, &c. having indeed none of

Johnson referred to Ainsworth's view of Rome and its ordinances as "erroneous and Anabaptisticall" on several occasions. These phrases occur: "What miserable assertions are these, and merely Anabaptisticall?" "Whiles he would shun the gulf of Poperie, runs his leak bark upon the rocks of Anabaptistrie." "Erroneous also it is and Anabaptisticall, that he saith..." "And againe extreemely erroneous and Anabaptisticall it is, that he said the 'Church of Rome hath not the true baptisme, the one baptisme, spoken off, Ephes. 4, 5.'"[50]

Johnson offered the same option to Ainsworth that Joseph Hall offered to John Robinson.[51] Johnson chides: "They must needs become Anabaptists, and get another outward baptisme then that they have, if they will walk conscionably: ... So eyther they must leave their Anabaptistical opinions, or admit of Anabaptistical courses."[52]

However, Johnson's position was no less awkward than Ainsworth's. His purpose was to "bring men more soundly to separation from the apostasie of Antichrist," but the logic of his position was at least as untenable as that of Ainsworth, who denied that Rome had true baptism yet would not rebaptise.[53] Johnson claimed that the baptism of Rome is the Lord's baptism, the sign and seal of his covenant, the ordinance of God, and so is true baptism from heaven and not from men. Although he maintained Separatist nomenclature, his final position on the validity of his baptism was like that of the Independent Puritans who sought to maintain sacramental continuity by officially remaining within the established church while worshipping apart from its "Popish superstitions."

Thus, Johnson defended infant baptism as a continuation of God's covenant with the faithful and their physical seed. The Christian Church should practice the ordinance exactly as the Israelites practiced circumcision. He also took special pains to defend Roman Catholic baptism; to do less would be to yield to the Anabaptists.

Difference in the Testaments

The fundamental difference, however, between Johnson and the Anabaptists is seen in their respective hermeneutics. Johnson essentially defends infant

---

these in the ordinance and powre of Christ emongst." See Williston Walker, *Creeds and Platforms of Congregationalism* (Boston: Pilgrim Press, 1960), 51. Johnson moved from this position.

[50] Johnson, *A Christian Plea*, 174, 179.

[51] Joseph Hall, upon becoming aware of John Smyth's baptism said: "Either you must go forward to Anabaptism or come back to us. All your Rabbins cannot answer that charge of your rebaptized brother: if we be a true Church you must return, if we not (as a False Church is no Church of God) you must re-baptize. If our baptism be good then is our Constitution good" (Henry Ainsworth, *An Animadversion to Mr. Clyftons Advertisement* [Amsterdam, 1613], xi, quoted by Burgess, *Early English Dissenters*, 156–57).

[52] Johnson, *A Christian Plea*, 179.

[53] Johnson, *A Christian Plea*, 180.

baptism by assuming that it is scriptural. All of his refutations of the Anabaptists are rooted in one presupposition: infants are proper candidates for baptism. His argument centers on the relationship between the Old and the New Testaments. For Johnson, the Old Testament is only relatively different from the New Testament. The New Testament does not at all replace the Old Testament but merely adds to it in several unique ways. Thus, those things not abrogated, if they are "morall and perpetuall," are to be continued in the same manner as before.[54]

Among the "special things" declared in the New Testament are the "exhibiting of the Messiah in the flesh" for the redemption of his people and the revealing of the mystery of the incarnation of the Son of God and his humiliation and exaltation. Also, the shadows and ceremonies of the law were fulfilled never to be shaken but to endure to the end. Other special additions are the spreading of the gospel abroad in the world and the calling of the Gentiles.[55]

Among the items remaining unchanged is the necessity of "sealing the children of beleevers."[56] Remaining unchanged also is the essence of church government. The types of church officers are anticipated in the Old Testament and remain essentially the same in the New Testament as do the "ordinarie Sacraments and seales of God's covenant."[57] The Passover as well as circumcision has its direct New Testament answer. In short, Johnson concludes quoting Ainsworth's *Defence of the Scripture*. "What one thing have we in the worship of God, which Israel had not before us?"[58] Everything in the ministry, worship, and government of the church is in its essence in the Old Testament.[59]

Johnson does affirm, as previously stated, that the shadows and ceremonies of the law are fulfilled in the New Testament. However, much of this involves merely a name change and a backward rather than a forward look. For instance, the Passover and sacrifices have now become the Lord's Supper. The former was to lead to Christ in the future; the latter leads to Christ in the past by way of remembrance. The priest offered the sacrifices formerly, the pastor performs the celebration of the Supper. Many other specific elements of Israel's organization coincide exactly with the New Testament specifications for the church according to Johnson.

Thus, the difference between the Testaments is of time, degree, and nomenclature, not of essence. In the Old Testament one finds both foundation and superstructure. The New Testament adds ornamentation to change the appearance

---

[54] Johnson, *A Christian Plea*, 4.

[55] Johnson, *A Christian Plea*, 5.

[56] Johnson, *A Christian Plea*, 5.

[57] Johnson, *A Christian Plea*, n.p. ("To the Christian Reader").

[58] Johnson, *A Christian Plea*, n.p. ("To the Christian Reader").

[59] Johnson, *A Christian Plea*, n.p. ("To the Christian Reader").

while leaving the construction intact.

The Constitution and Order of the Church

In 1593 Thomas Bilson wrote a treatise entitled *Perpetual Government of Christes Church* in which he claimed that episcopacy was the only scriptural method of church government, and apostolic succession was absolutely essential to the existence of the church. However, he hardly claimed that the many offices and rites of the Church of England were warranted by Scripture. Johnson believed that the situation should be otherwise. In 1595 he stated that the church should observe the "Ministry, Worship, and Government prescribed in his [Christ's] Testament, and no other." The Apostles had "planted in this way and order, as being the onely true way and order appoynted by Christ, and to be observed to the end of the world."[60]

In 1603 Johnson sent to King James a petition listing fourteen points of difference between the Ancient Church and the Church of England. The first point of difference was this:

> That Christ the Lord hath by his last Testament given to his Church, and set therein, sufficient ordinary Offices, with the maner of calling or Entrance, Words, and Maintenance, for the administration of his holy things, and for the sufficient ordinary instruction guydance and service of his Church, to the end of the world.[61]

In 1617 he still contended that the officers of the church were to fulfill their ministry and perform all things pertaining to their office "according to the word of God" and not according to the "Statutes or Edicts of Princes and States; the Canons of Prelates" or any other way imposed by men.[62]

Johnson believed the Scripture gave four basic components for a true church. The first was people. They should be a "company of faithful people" separated from the world and the ways of antichrist. These people should be gathered and

---

[60] Francis Johnson, *A Treatise of the Ministry of the Church of England. Wherein Is Handled this Question, Whether It Be to Be Separated From, or Joyned Unto* (London, 1595), n.p.

[61] Ainsworth, *An Apologie*, 36. When James became king in 1603 the hopes of the Separatists were heightened and they sent James a petition along with a copy of their creed in Latin. This was ignored. They sent a second appeal along with the fourteen points of difference. The Separatists then prepared a third petition and included a recapitulation of the fourteen points with an elaborate defense. All of this was to no avail. Then some "honourable personage" asked them to condense their appeal to its essence and he would personally present it to the king. This they also did to no avail. All of these documents were then printed together, the Confession of Faith in English, in 1604. Henry Ainsworth appended a defense of the petitioners' position against some accusations of Oxford men and included a letter of Henry Barrow. The result was this book.

[62] Johnson, *A Treatise of the Ministry*, 73.

joined together in a holy covenant and fellowship of the gospel. They should make a "voluntary publick profession of … faith and purpose to live and walk together in the obedience of Christ according to his word."[63]

The "free and voluntary election" of the proper scriptural officers composed the second ingredient for a true church. These officers, as stated below, are pastors, teachers, elders, deacons, and widows and helpers.[64]

The third element, according to Johnson, was proper worship, which consisted of prayer, preaching of the word, administering the sacraments, exercise of prophecy, and use of the censure. All of this was to be done "not according to the inventions, book worship, canons, or constitutions of any men whatsoever but only according to the Testament of Christ."[65]

The final mark of the true Church Johnson listed was the scriptural and loving exercise of discipline. The scriptural support for this in 1595 was almost exclusively New Testament and it was expressed simply and transparently. However, although he still supported the practice of censure and discipline, by 1617 the scriptural support is based on an obscure and garbled treatment of Old Testament passages.[66] The years of controversy with the Anabaptists, with his brother George, and with Henry Ainsworth had driven him to the Old Covenant for an elaborate support of positions indefensible from the New Testament. He thus felt compelled to find scriptural justification for even the simplest church matters in the Old Testament either by direct statement or by sophistry.

Although he rejected any practice or office not found in Scripture, he resorted to a subtle pragmatic shift in authority when his situation deemed it necessary.

Church Government and Discipline
Francis Johnson's offence in 1589 at Cambridge was his belief that the church should be governed by elders. He remained consistent in this belief. In 1595 he wrote in prison and had published a small quarto volume, 143 numbered pages, entitled *A Treatise of the Ministry of the Church of England. Wherein is handled this question, Whether it be to be separated from or joyned unto.*[67] He states that there are five ordinary officers in the church: pastors, teachers, elders, deacons,

---

[63] Johnson, *A Treatise of the Ministry*, 73.

[64] Johnson, *A Treatise of the Ministry*, 73.

[65] Johnson, *A Treatise of the Ministry*, 74.

[66] Johnson, *A Treatise of the Ministry*, 74, and Johnson, *A Christian Plea*, 300–306.

[67] Johnson, *A Treatise of the Ministry*. This treatise was prompted by Arthur Hildersham's letter to a "Mrs. A. a Gentlewoman" in which he defends the ministry of the Church of England. "Mrs. A.," who "would not partake with the publick ministery" of the Church of England and was imprisoned, submitted Hildersham's letter to Johnson. Johnson answered it section by section seeking to show the unscriptural nature of the ministry, worship, and government of the English Church and the exclusively Christian nature of his own.

and widows or helpers.[68] He claims that to the elders is committed "the oversight and guydance of the Church together with the pastors and teachers."[69] This is clearly a Barrowist emphasis in government.

However, at this point Johnson had not given the elders as much power as he later would entrust to them. He discussed their method of discipline emphasizing the passage in Matthew 18 on which he would later write a treatise:

> Finally, we all of us labour to build up one another in our most holy faith; and when any of us fall… if the sinne be private, the party is admonished thereof by such as are privy unto it: whom if he heare not then taking one or two witnesses, they admonish him agayn and seek to draw him from his sinne: If he heare not them, as also if the sinne be publicke, then is it brought before the whole Church, whose voyce if he despise, he is cast out from among them.[70]

This procedure is done for the protection of the church, the honor of God's name, and the good of the sinner. A significant aspect of this quote is the simplicity of Johnson's mention of the "whole Church." He evidently considers the words to refer to all the covenanted people and not just the elders as he later interpreted the phrase.

He presented his final stance on the question in the third part of *A Christian Plea*, virtually duplicating the material found in the treatise of 1611 entitled *A Short Treatise Concerning the Exposition of Those Words of Christ, Tell the Church &c. Matt. 18, 17*. Johnson highlighted Barrow's emphasis upon the authority of the elders which may have been influenced by the narrative reporting the troubles of the Marian exiles in Frankfort.[71] Even so, Johnson's increasing accent upon the elders was probably due to the numerous internal difficulties his church had experienced. He was not willing that matters as trivial as those concerning his wife be aired and enlarged before the entire congregation.

The biblical support with which he buttresses his view of church government is entirely consistent with his view of the relation between the two covenants. Johnson first asks whether Christ's words in Matt. 18:17 can be understood to refer to the Sanhedrin or Congregation of elders in Israel. He concluded from studying the Greek and Hebrew texts that the words could definitely refer to the elders as in Israel. Contextually, it must have that meaning, since Jesus was speaking to Jews, and they would understand the word "church" in its Old Testament sense. Logically, the elders are the church since they are selected "out

---

[68] Johnson, *A Treatise of the Ministry*, n.p., 73.

[69] Johnson, *A Treatise of the Ministry*, 73.

[70] Johnson, *A Treatise of the Ministry*, 74.

[71] Burrage, *Early English Dissenters*, 1:130.

of the people, by the people, and for the people."⁷² No power is taken from the people by this process; rather it is confirmed and established. Biblically, no other understanding of the word can be admitted than that which agrees with Moses and the Prophets since Christ came not to destroy the Law and the Prophets but to fulfill them. Thus, Christ used the word "church" in Matthew 18:17 to refer to the Sanhedrin.⁷³

Next, Johnson asked if the verse can be applied to the Christian presbytery and congregation of elders. He cited eight reasons why it must be so. The climactic reason is that the office of Elder or Governor is "morall and perpetual; not first and newly begun in the time of the Gospell; but continued and derived from Israel to the churches of the Gospel."⁷⁴ To have another form of government would violate the second and fifth commandments as it would bring in a strange and new government not ordained by the Lord.

Finally, Johnson stated that the word "church" could possibly mean the elders in conjunction with the congregation. However, if it is not "rightly understood" that the liberty of the people does not disannul or weaken the authority of the elders, "divers errours, abuses, and erroneous courses" might be "gathered, received, pleaded for, and urged earnestly hereabout."⁷⁵ Johnson lists thirty-six of these errors and credits all of them to Ainsworth and his followers. All that love the truth should avoid such people, according to Johnson, and seek the conversion and amendment of them.⁷⁶

In short, although Johnson was congregational in that he believed each particular church was a self-contained political unit, he was aristocratic and presbyterial in his view of each individual congregation. The locus of authority was in the elders. Richard Clyfton summarised the position of Johnson thus,

> Whether ye elders power be not ministeriall under the Lord, in and for the Church, so as it is the Lord's primarily, the churches secondarily, & ye Officers ministerially, or instrumentally, for the Lord and ye Church, whose officers they are; & that therefore there is no weight in their obietions about ye Elders power, as if it were not the churches, & that which perteyneth to ye bodie of ye congregation, but that in deed it is the churches, & so to be ministred by ye Officers whome ye Lord hath set in his church, to minister in His name for ye Churchs use & benefit.⁷⁷

---

⁷² Johnson, *A Christian Plea*, 306–310.

⁷³ Johnson, *A Christian Plea*, 306–310.

⁷⁴ Johnson, *A Christian Plea*, 12.

⁷⁵ Johnson, *A Christian Plea*, 313–314.

⁷⁶ Johnson, *A Christian Plea*, 316.

⁷⁷ Richard Clyfton, *An Advertisement Concerning a Booke Published by C. Lawne* (Amsterdam [?],

The Magistrate and the Church

Not only did Johnson differ with Robert Browne on church government, he never considered developing Robert Browne's thought on the place of the magistrate. Desiring to reform the church "without tarying for anie," Browne wrote the magistrates should "doo nothing concerning the Church, but onelie civilie."[78] Johnson did nothing to advance that thought.

The earliest confession of faith with which his name is connected is "A True Confession of the Faith, and Humble Acknowledgement of the Alegeance, which We Hir Maiesties Subjects, falsely called Brownists, doo hould towards God, and yield to hir Majestie."[79] This was written in 1596 while Elizabeth reigned and was sent to James at his accession to the throne in 1603. Their desire was that they be allowed to worship without molestation in their own country.

However, while asking for personal religious liberty, they did not extend it to anyone else. Negatively, the confession states it is the duty of the magistrates to suppress and root out all false ministries, voluntary religions, and false worship of God. Positively, the magistrate, God's lieutenant on earth, should establish and maintain by law pure religion and the true ministry and enforce all his subjects to "do their dutyes to God and men."[80] If the magistrates were to protect the true religion, the godly would account it a happy blessing that God had granted such nursing fathers and nursing mothers to his church. However, if God should withhold the magistrate's permission, the godly still would proceed together in Christian covenant in obedience to Christ despite all opposition and danger to their lives, "remembering always that wee ought to obey God rather then man."[81]

Scheffer claims that most of the Separatists later altered their opinions and became advocates of "complete separation of Church and State and a full religious toleration."[82] While this is true of John Smyth and Thomas Helwys in their journey toward the baptism of believers only, as well as of Roger Williams in America, the statement is misleading. The Separatists ardently sought freedom for themselves, but still hesitated to grant it to others. They were willing to suffer for their own freedom before God, but still needed many complex provocations to apply such freedom to the population in general. Johnson certainly did not

---

1610), 34, quoted by Dexter, *Congregationalism*, 326.

[78] Walker. *Creeds and Platforms*, 12. See also Dexter, *Congregationalism*, 101–102. C. Norman Kraus, "Anabaptist Influence on English Separatism as Seen in Robert Browne," *Mennonite Quarterly Review* 34 (1960): 5–19. Kraus concludes there was little if any Anabaptist influence in Browne's statement and that, in context, it represents little more than the normal Puritan position on church-state relations.

[79] Walker, *Creeds and Platforms*, 49–74.

[80] Walker, *Creeds and Platforms*, 71–72, Articles 39, 40.

[81] Walker, *Creeds and Platforms*, 73. Articles 41, 42.

[82] Scheffer, *History of the Free Churchmen Called the Brownists*, 35.

complete that journey.

In 1617 his views toward the magistracy had not changed. In discussing the maintenance of ministers and other church officers, Johnson advocated that primary support should come from each congregation. At times, a well-established congregation may help a poor congregation maintain its officers and its poor people. However, it is also the duty of kings and all other magistrates to care for the estate of the ministers and churches under them "after the example of Hezekiah king of Judah, and Nehemiah the Prince."[83]

In another section dealing with "the remnants and monuments of idolatrie or superstition" Johnson asks rhetorically "whether it be not the duty of the Magistrate, to take away and demolish all remnants and monuments of Idolatrie and superstition … with all maner of false worship whatsoever."[84] Johnson indicates an amazing liberal-mindedness in this chapter as he allows men lawfully to use the remnants of Roman Catholicism including images, altars, and temples so long as "they shall not themselves personally offend, and pertake with other mens sinnes."[85] Thus, the negligence of the magistrates becomes to a degree the permission of God. Johnson closes, "And sundry things and persons there are, which being not taken away by the Magistrates (as they ought to be) men have a good & Lawfull use of them, so long as they are suffered to remayn."[86]

Johnson never wavered in his advocacy of magisterial reform after the manner of the Old Testament kings. In a section entitled "Of the general duty of all churches and people (in these parts) concerning religion" he writes that the gospel would be less demanding than the Old Covenant if kings did not now do at least that which they were commanded to do in Israel.[87] Princes and magistrates are to submit themselves to the Prince of the kings of the earth and "to see the truth of God mainteyned, and his ordinances observed, in all things." If not, the judgments of Ahaz, Jeroboam, and Ahab will fall upon them. If so, they will receive the blessings of David, Hezekiah, and Josiah.[88]

Johnson was sure that the magistrate should support and cause his subjects to support the true church. If the magistrate neglected his obligation, God's people must be willing to suffer banishment, confiscation of goods, and death itself, for the sake of the truth. This was not just his belief, it was his way of life.

---

[83] Johnson, *A Christian Plea*, 317.

[84] Johnson, *A Christian Plea*, 318.

[85] Johnson, *A Christian Plea*, 319.

[86] Johnson, *A Christian Plea*, 319.

[87] Johnson, *A Christian Plea*, 320–323.

[88] Johnson, *A Christian Plea*, 320–323.

Summary

The career of Francis Johnson was seldom free of controversy. From the time of his Fellowship at Cambridge until his death in 1617 he was involved in polemical speaking and writing. He became a Separatist in 1592 and was elected pastor of the Barrowist congregation. Part of the congregation moved to Holland in 1593 leaving Johnson and several members in England. Both segments of the church experienced dissension, and Johnson's arrival in Amsterdam in 1597 did not long bring peace to the troubled church. A series of problems arising from within and without culminated in the schism between Johnson and the church's teacher, Henry Ainsworth. The bitter struggles served to mold Johnson into a paradoxical figure. Making subtle shifts within the confines of Separatism, he became clearly Presbyterian in his view of church government and surprisingly tolerant of certain elements of Roman Catholicism. Despite the controversy that plagued his ministry, he died, not as a disillusioned man, but as a man convinced that he held the truth.

If we are to look for a doctrine that promotes liberty of conscience, endorses separation of church and state, and excludes the magistrate from determining the religion of the country, we must look beyond Francis Johnson and find a more consistent application of the New Covenant elsewhere. Johnson, nevertheless, forms a vital and energetic part of the ecclesiological discussion—with John Robinson, John Smyth, Thomas Helwys and others—that eventually led to the freedoms embedded in the Constitution of the United States.

The Mayflower at sea —painting by
Granville Perkins (1876)
(New York Public Library Digital Collections)

CHAPTER SIX

The Voyages of the Pilgrims

FRANCIS J. BREMER

As we commemorate the voyage of the *Mayflower* four hundred years ago, a central theme in the story of the Pilgrims is an understanding of the sacrifices these men and women made and the sufferings they endured for their faith. These include how they responded to the growing pressures to conform to the restriction that England's church authorities applied to those who sought further reform in the Church of England; the difficulties of adjusting to a foreign culture and a different economy during their years in the Netherlands, and the hardships of settling a New World. While the voyage from England to America is a critical part of the story, too often we neglect the dangers of travelling from England to the Netherlands and from Delfshaven to Plymouth.

While many of their fellow Puritans in the first years of the seventeenth century continued to hope that it would be possible to remain in their parish churches and work for reform of the national church from within, some concluded that they could no longer make the compromises demanded of them while waiting for further reformation. In 1602 or within the next few years, one such group, centered in the neighborhood of Scrooby, Nottinghamshire, separated from their parishes and formed a new church by agreeing to a covenant "to walk with God, and one with another, in the enjoyment of the ordinances of God, according to the primitive pattern in the Word of God."[1] They chose the deprived clergyman

---

[1] *Of Plimoth Plantation by William Bradford. The 400th Anniversary Edition*, edited by Kenneth P. Minkema, Francis J. Bremer, and Jeremy D. Bangs, with a special introduction by Paula Peters (Boston: Colonial Society of Massachusetts and New England Historic and Genealogical Society, 2020), 98–99; hereafter cited as *Plimoth Plantation*. For a recent history of the congregation in England, Leiden, and

Richard Clyfton as their pastor, but within a few years benefited also from the membership of John Robinson, who had been removed from a clerical post in Norwich for preaching against practices of the established church.

By absenting themselves from their parish churches, the members of the new congregation were in violation of English civil and ecclesiastical laws. Following the appointment of Tobias Matthew as Archbishop of York, pressures on the congregation intensified. As one of the members, William Bradford, later recalled, "they could not long continue in any peaceable condition, but were hunted & persecuted on every side," with some "taken and clapped up in prison" while "others had their houses beset & watched night and day."[2]

The first voyages of the Scrooby congregation involved efforts to cross the North Sea in search of refuge in the Netherlands, a land where other English separatists had found toleration. Since the 1540s a variety of restrictions had been placed on Englishmen travelling abroad, requiring authorization for such journeys. The Scrooby refugees would have to evade those laws. An attempt to leave from the vicinity of Boston in 1607 failed, with passengers "stripped of their money, books and much other goods" and handed over to the authorities. After about a month's confinement the majority were released.[3] Undeterred, the believers tried again in May of 1608 from along the Humber River. Again they were betrayed, though some were able to make their escape. Eventually, the members of the congregation were reunited in Amsterdam, from which they soon moved on to the town of Leiden.

The experience of crossing to the Netherlands was not what we might enjoy crossing on a modern ferry. William Bradford recorded how the ship he sailed on encountered "a fearful storm at sea" that lasted two weeks or more, during which "they neither saw sun, moon nor stars, and were driven near the coast of Norway."[4] Preparing food was impossible. Passengers became violently ill as the ship was tossed in the waves. The crew were terrified, and we can imagine, the Pilgrims were as well. At one point the waves crashed over the ship and "the water ran into their mouths and ears, and the mariners cried out we sink, we sink!"[5] But eventually the storm weakened, and "the lord filled their afflicted minds with ... comforts."[6]

One can imagine that those who survived such a journey would never wish to

---

America see Francis J. Bremer, *One Small Candle: the Plymouth Puritans and the Beginning of English New England* (New York: Oxford University Press, 2020).

[2] *Plimoth Plantation*, 100–101.

[3] *Plimoth Plantation*, 103

[4] *Plimoth Plantation*, 105.

[5] *Plimoth Plantation*, 105.

[6] *Plimoth Plantation*, 105.

set foot on a ship again. Yet when, after a decade in the Netherlands, the members of the congregation came to believe that while their situation was better than it had been in England, their goal of living godly lives was frustrated in their new home as well, and they faced the necessity for another voyage. Refugees in a different land, they struggled to make their livings in a more commercial economy than they had been used to. The cultural norms of the Dutch threatened to lead their children astray. And the probable resumption of warfare between the Netherlands and Spain might well embroil them in a conflict which was not theirs. So, they began to explore the prospect of emigration yet again, this time with their focus on the New World.

Such a voyage would be much more challenging than their relocation in the Netherlands. For while they had faced challenges in that country, it was a European nation with most of the civilized amenities to which they were accustomed. In America, as a later traveler to New England pointed out, "once parted" from Europe, "you shall meet neither with taverns nor alehouses, nor butchers nor grocers, nor apothecaries' shops to help what things you need … Here are neither markets nor fairs to buy what you want."[7]

Rather than fellow Protestants, some of them fellow English refugees who had welcomed them in the Netherlands, the New World in which they would settle was inhabited by those whom Bradford referred to as "savage and brutish men, which range up and down little otherwise than the wild beasts" of the land.[8] Though such generalizations mischaracterized the Natives of America, the men and women who contemplated this new journey found plenty of accounts that described the Indians as "cruel, barbarous, and most treacherous, being most furious in their rage, and merciless when they overcome; not being content only to kill and take away life, but delight to torment men in the most bloody manner that may be."[9]

Equally daunting were the tales of failed ventures. They would have been familiar with the story of the "Lost Colony" on Roanoke Island. They knew of the horrors of the "Starving Time" of 1609–1610 in the Jamestown settlement. Closer to home, they knew of two failed attempts to settle in America by English separatists. Francis Johnson, who was a leader of the "Ancient Church" in Amsterdam that had provided the initial welcome to the Pilgrims in the Netherlands, had attempted to establish a separatist refuge in Newfoundland in 1597. But his colony of Ramea in the St. Lawrence River had failed, and Johnson had returned to Europe. In 1618, just when the Leiden Pilgrims were reaching a

---

[7] Francis Higginson, quoted in Francis J. Bremer, *First Founders: American Puritans and Puritanism in the Atlantic World* (Hanover, NH: University Press of New England, 2012), 33.

[8] *Plimoth Plantation*, 120. A good overview of English attitudes towards Natives of the Americas is Karen O. Kupperman, *Indians and English: Facing Off in Early America* (Ithaca: Cornell University Press, 2000).

[9] *Plimoth Plantation*, 121.

decision, Francis Blackwell, who had been an elder of the Ancient Church, set forth with 180 fellow passengers to plant a settlement in the Virginia colony. "Packed together as herrings," they experienced "the flux [dysentery] and also want of fresh water," with the result that 130 of them, including Blackwell, died before reaching America.[10]

Despite such concerns, the congregation committed itself to trust in God and establish a new home in America. The search for a patent and the struggle to find financing has been told many times. By the summer of 1620 preparations were complete. Only a minority of the congregation would initially depart. Pastor John Robinson remained with the majority in Leiden for the time being, though all hoped to eventually join the colony. Elder William Brewster would provide spiritual leadership to those who were going first. Two ships had been secured— the *Mayflower*, chartered by the colony's investors to carry the settlers to the New World, and the *Speedwell*, which had been purchased to carry passengers and then remain in America for the use of the colonists. Following a day of fasting and prayer by the entire congregation to invoke God's aid, those departing embarked on the *Speedwell* in Delfshaven and sailed for Southampton, England to join up with the *Mayflower* for the transatlantic voyage.

The crossing of the North Sea revealed problems with the *Speedwell* that became more troublesome when the two ships sailed west from Southampton into the English Channel on August 5. After a week at sea the *Speedwell* began to leak and the two ships put in to the port of Dartmouth to make repairs. The journey resumed on August 21, but after about three hundred miles at sea it became evident that the *Speedwell* could not continue. Both ships turned back to Plymouth, where it was determined that the *Mayflower* would have to proceed alone. Some of those who had been on the *Speedwell* were moved to the *Mayflower*, while others, perhaps discouraged by the misadventures, remained behind. Cargo had to be shifted and the *Mayflower*, already heavily laden with passengers and goods, became more crowded. Furthermore, some of the supplies intended for the voyage had been depleted by the delays.

The ships that brought Englishmen to America at this time were not designed for comfort, or even for passengers. They were converted from the purposes of commerce. The *Mayflower*'s exact dimensions are unknown, but judging from Bradford's estimate that she had a capacity of seventy tons, she probably measured about 100 feet from the beak of her prow to the tip of her stern, and was about 25 feet at her widest point. There were fore- and aft- "castles," the latter of which was thirty-foot-high and contained the captain's cabin, crew quarters, and the steerage room. Its height made it difficult to sail against the wind. In the bow was the gun deck, where the passengers travelled, so named because there were cannon that could be run out to defend the ship against privateers. It was a

---

[10] Robert Cushman to John Robinson and others, 8 May 1619, included in *Plimoth Plantation*, 135–136.

space measuring about 50 by 25 feet, with a five-foot ceiling. This was where the 102 passengers would spend most of their time on the ship, crowded in a space smaller than a modern gymnasium floor. The deck below was where most of the colony's supplies were stored.

Unless faced with an enemy, the gun ports remained closed, cutting off light and the circulation of air. The atmosphere was made more close and gloomy when the passengers erected partitions to provide some privacy, but that was minimal and must have been particularly challenging for the women. The few lanterns offered little light, and during foul weather these were extinguished and the hatches opening to the main deck were closed. There were no tables or benches, so meals were eaten sitting on the floor. Rats and other pests plagued the passengers. Buckets were used as chamber pots. In calm conditions these would be taken to the main deck and emptied over the side. In bad weather, the passenger quarters would be befouled by the contents of overturned buckets as well as the vomit of seasick men, women and children.

Crew members mocked the seasick passengers. One in particular—a "proud and profane young man" wrote Bradford—"would always be contemning the poor people in their sickness and cursing them daily."[11] He told them he hoped he would have the pleasure of dumping half of their bodies overboard before they reached the New World. But, providentially as the Pilgrims saw it, their tormentor was seized with "a grievous disease, of which he died in a desperate manner, and so was himself the first that was thrown overboard."[12]

Once the *Speedwell* had been left behind, the voyage began smoothly for the *Mayflower*. But the travelers soon experienced "cross winds, and met with fierce storms."[13] Everyone knew of ships that had perished in such storms while attempting to cross the Atlantic. During some of the storms, "the winds were so fierce and the seas so high as they could not proceed forward towards their destination."[14] Winds shredded some of the sails and passengers joined the crew in manning pumps to rid the ship of incoming water. When the storms were particularly strong the *Mayflower*'s captain, Christopher Jones, was forced to furl sails and ride the tempest out, the ship often being driven back towards England. The colonists in essence endured a "long imprisonment as it were" in the ship.[15] During one particularly bad storm, one of the main midship beams cracked, raising the prospect of the ship breaking up and sinking. But the passengers had brought with them "a great iron screw," a house jack that was used to push the

---

[11] *Plimoth Plantation*, 175.

[12] *Plimoth Plantation*, 175–176.

[13] *Plimoth Plantation*, 176.

[14] *Plimoth Plantation*, 176.

[15] *Plimoth Plantation*, 176.

beam back in place and secure it.[16]

During the sixty-six days that the *Mayflower* was crossing what Bradford called the "vast and furious ocean," Elder William Brewster comforted the colonists and led them in prayer and the singing of psalms.[17] He preached on occasion—lay prophesying being a characteristic of this congregation—and sought to keep them focused on their mission. But the journey did not end when land was sighted. Having arrived off Cape Cod they sailed south towards their intended destination, the region around the mouth of the Hudson River where the patent, granted by the Virginia Company, authorized them to settle. But dangerous shoals forced them to reverse course and consider the Cape. With no legal basis for settling there, they drew on their congregational practices to bind themselves together in a self-governing covenant that would be known as the Mayflower Compact.

After many days of exploration, they settled on the site of the former Native village of Patuxet as their new home, giving it the name of Plymouth. In the bitter late December weather, they began to cut down trees and erect a common house, in the meanwhile spending their nights on the *Mayflower*. Supplies had been largely depleted because of the false starts and long voyage. Faced with cold, sharp winds, and snow, many sickened and died—half of their number in the first two or three months. While some of the sick were nursed in the newly erected common house by William Brewster and Myles Standish, others remained on the ship. Crew members likewise became ill and were assisted by those passengers capable of helping. As the number of colonists shrank, their fears of Native attacks grew.

The *Mayflower* finally departed in April 1621, leaving the surviving colonists to their own devices. The voyages of the Pilgrims were over, however their struggles to build a godly commonwealth continued.

---

[16] *Plimoth Plantation*, 176.

[17] Because John Robinson had remained in Leiden to minister to members of the congregation who remained behind, Elder William Brewster would supervise the religious life of the colonists on the *Mayflower* and in New England.

> · TO THE MEMORY OF ROBERT BROWNE, A
> FOUNDER OF THE BROWNISTS, OR INDEPENDENTS
> · RECTOR OF THORPE ACHURCH, 1591-1631 ·
> WHO WAS BURIED IN THIS CHURCHYARD 8ᵀᴴ OCT. 1633
> A TRIBUTE TO A LIFE WHEREIN, AMONG MANY
> THINGS OBSCURE, ONE THING SHONE BRIGHTLY, THAT
> CHRIST WAS BY HIM EXALTED AS HEAD ABOVE ALL.
>
> ERECTED BY CONGREGATIONALISTS IN CONNECTION
> WITH THE VISIT TO NORTHAMPTON, OCT. 1923, OF THE
> CONGREGATIONAL UNION OF ENGLAND AND WALES.

A commemorative plaque to Robert Browne
in the churchyard of St. Giles, Northampton,
where Browne is buried.

CHAPTER SEVEN

Robert "Troublechurch" Browne and the "Brownist Emigration"

GARY BRADY

The actor Sir John Gielgud (1904–2000) once observed that Shakespeare's *Twelfth Night*, first performed in 1602, is full of "archaic and difficult" jokes. An example appears in Act 3, Scene 2, where the character Sir Andrew Aguecheek says, "I had as lief be a *Brownist* as a politician." This can be glossed, "I'd rather be a heretic than a schemer with fancy plots." Reaching for a word for a *heretic*, Shakespeare chose one not then archaic or difficult though it may be today.

Brownist is a word the Mayflower Pilgrims knew well. At one time people referred to the *Mayflower* sailing as the "Brownist emigration."[1] This reflects the fact that the founders of the Plymouth Bay Colony, unlike those of the later Massachusetts Bay Colony, were not simply English Puritans but English Puritan Separatists. Like many in England in the early seventeenth century, they had taken the "short step from impatient Puritanism within the established Church to convinced Separatism outside it."[2] Not only did they believe that the Church of England was impure, as did all Puritans, but also that it could be right to separate from it and form independent local churches. Separatism, the black sheep of Puritanism, was vilified in many quarters as "Brownism."

Brownist is a sort of theological swear word; a term the Mayflower pilgrims repudiated. William Bradford (*c.*1590–1657), whose story will be told

---

[1] See Alexander Young, *Chronicles of the Pilgrim fathers of the colony of Plymouth, from 1602–1625* (London: E.P. Dutton & Co., 1923), vi.

[2] Barrington Raymond White, *The English Separatist Tradition* (Oxford: Oxford University Press, 1971), 84.

subsequently, after being in New England many years, felt the rising generation did not really understand the Separatist roots of the Plymouth plantation. In 1648, he wrote *A dialogue or the sum of a conference between some young men born in New England and sundry ancient men that came out of Old England and Holland*, insisting in the strongest terms that the nickname Brownist was unacceptable. He says of his generation in New England that "they did as much abhor Browne's apostasy, and profane course, and his defection, as the disciples and other Christians did Judas's treachery."[3]

In view of this, it is useful to know what happened in Norwich some forty years before the pilgrims sailed, especially with regard to this man Browne, from whose name the term comes. Students of the pilgrims know that in 1604 their pastor, John Robinson (1576–1625), probably took charge at St. Andrew's, Norwich, but was suspended, then ejected for his radical views. From there he went on to form a small Separatist congregation, eventually falling in with the Scrooby Separatists. About twenty years or so before that however, Norwich had been the scene of equally significant events. These events concern two men. Most importantly, the enigmatic and perplexing Robert Browne (c.1550–1633).

Much has been written about Browne, much of it incorrect, misleading or confusing. It is said that few terms, positive or negative, have not at some time or other been applied to him. It has been maintained on the one hand, that he had one of the keenest minds of his day and, on the other, that his vagaries and vacillations can be accounted for only on the supposition that he was mentally unstable—a hypothesis which appears in both contemporary and modern estimates. He is held to have been a pioneer in the field of religious liberty, but even those who have accepted his views have hastened to repudiate his name. Alongside Browne was Robert Harrison (died c.1585) who "never emerges into the full light of day" but "is shrouded in mist."[4] Whatever view is taken of the pilgrims, their story needs to be known.

Browne, Early Years c.1550–1580

Browne can be thought of as a firework lighting up the sky in a blaze of glory only to quickly fizzle out and practically disappear. In the early 1560s, Joyce Reason said he was like "an angry young man."[5] To call him "father of the pilgrims" or "forefather of the American nation" even is to go much too far, but his significance should not be underestimated.

---

[3] William Bradford, *Governor Bradford's First Dialogue: A Dialogue, Or the Sum of a Conference Between Some Young Men Born in New England and Sundry Ancient Men that Came Out of Holland and Old England, Anno Domini 1648* (Boston: Directors of the Old South Work, 1896), 7.

[4] Leland Carlson and Albert Peel, ed., *The Writings of Robert Harrison & Robert Browne* (London: Routledge, 1853), 4:1.

[5] Joyce Reason, "Robert Browne (1550?–1633)," *Heritage biographies* (London: Independent Press, 1961), 3.

Born around 1550, the third of seven children, he grew up in comfortable circumstances in Tolethorpe Hall, the Manor House at Little Casterton, Rutland, near the historic market town of Stamford, Lincolnshire. In Henry VIII's time, his grandfather was granted the right to appear bareheaded in the royal presence. Browne's parents, Anthony Browne (*c*.1515–*c*.1591) and Dorothy Butler (d.1602), daughter of Sir Philip Butler of Watton-at-Stone, Hertfordshire, were "responsible, respected people, whose social standing and general reputation in the community must have been assured."[6]

In 1570, Browne traveled 45 miles south to study in Cambridge, gaining a B.A. two years later from Corpus Christi (Benet's, as Protestants called it). Cambridge would become a centre for Puritanism in the 1580s but even in Browne's time the trend had begun. Puritan polemicist William Fulke (1538–1589) was master at Pembroke. At Corpus Christi, Thomas Aldrich (1530–1576) was master and Thomas Robardes (d.1596) was a fellow—both Puritans. The Lady Margaret Professor of Divinity, Thomas Cartwright (*c*.1535–1603), was lecturing on the Book of Acts and publicly advocating Presbyterianism, unflatteringly comparing the hierarchy and constitution of the contemporary church with the early church. He clashed fiercely with Cambridge Vice-Chancellor and later Archbishop, John Whitgift (1530–1604). In 1572, Cartwright supported the anonymous *Admonition to Parliament*, a Puritan manifesto calling on Elizabeth to restore the "purity" of New Testament worship and eliminate remaining Romanist elements. It demanded not only faithful preaching and administration of the sacraments but proper church discipline too.[7]

Impatient by nature, even as a student, Browne tangled with the authorities as he threw himself into religious life. He was among a handful of men eager to see deeper reforms than those implemented to that time. Cambridge peers included Harrison, his brother, William Harrison (*c*.1550–1630), Browne's own older brother Philip, and Robert Barker, later part of the Middelburg congregation formed by Browne and Harrison.

At the end of his studies, instead of taking orders, Browne became a school master. Was it in Stamford, Islington, Southwark, East Anglia or Oundle, Northamptonshire? All are suggested. Wherever it was, his willingness to discuss the Puritan ideas fermenting in his head with pupils and friends led shortly to his dismissal. He continued tutoring privately for a while but in order to escape the ravages of a local plague, at the urging of his father, he returned to home for six months.

We next find him living with a man who has been referred to as the architect of Puritan pastoral piety. The hugely influential Richard Greenham (*c*.1535–*c*. 1594) ministered at Dry Drayton, five miles north west of Cambridge, presiding

---

[6] Dwight C. Smith, "Robert Browne (*c*.1550–1633) as Churchman and Theologian" (PhD thesis, University of Edinburgh, 1936), 84.

[7] Written by the London clergymen John Field (1545–1588) and Thomas Wilcox (*c*.1549–1608).

over a veritable school of the prophets that attracted a number of young men including Browne.[8] Browne apparently preached for Greenham, though unlicensed. Browne went on to accept a charge at St. Benet's Church, next door to Corpus Christi, but encountered a sticking point. He had come to the opinion that bishops were unbiblical and so refused episcopal ordination. At this point his brother Philip, a clergyman himself, stepped in, obtaining a preaching license and permission for Robert's ordination. But Robert burned these; conveniently lost replacements, and returned a third set unopened. This was typical of Browne's behaviour. Meanwhile, he carried on preaching, not slow to reveal his radical views or disparage the church hierarchy. This period came to a close when he fell seriously ill and another Archbishop-to-be, Richard Bancroft (1544–1610) served an injunction on him from the Privy Council. Whether Browne was at this point or ever a Separatist is debated. He was certainly being encouraged in that direction by the church. He was convinced that the Church of England was not a New Testament church. Corrupt and ill-disciplined, it needed purifying.

Browne and Harrison, Norwich 1580–1581
At this time Browne's old friend, Robert Harrison, returned from Norwich to Cambridge, intending to prepare for ordained ministry. He had previously studied, at his own expense, at St John's, transferring in 1564 to Corpus Christi. He graduated with a B.A. in 1567 and an M.A. in 1572. As he discussed matters with Browne, he became disinclined to enter the ministry. Associating with a known radical, of whom the church authorities were already weary, meant he probably would have been refused ordination, even had he sought it.

Harrison returned to Norwich and, when he was well, Browne joined him. At the time, Norwich was England's second city, a major trading centre and England's richest provincial city. It was the county town of Norfolk, England's most populous county. Its wealth came chiefly from textiles. Just before this time many weavers had come from the continent, fleeing religious persecution. They say the refugees brought the canaries with which Norwich has ever since been associated. They also brought Calvinism, where it was welcomed by many such as mayor and MP John Aldrich (1520–1582), father of Thomas, already mentioned. A virtually Separatist congregation existed at St Andrew's under Yorkshireman John More (d.1592), "the Apostle of Norwich" and, from 1574, Thomas Robardes, also mentioned, at St Clement's. Norwich was experiencing a reformation at this time as it deliberately sought to "become an English Geneva, and England's premiere city of reforming Calvinism. It was indeed hailed as the model of social reform" and other cities sought its help to reform.[9]

---

[8] Including Richard Rogers (c.1550–1618), Henry Smith (c.1560–1591), and Arthur Hildersham (1563–1632).

[9] Francis J. Bremer and Tom Webster, ed. *Puritans and Puritanism in Europe and America: A Comprehensive Encyclopedia* (Santa Barbara, CA: ABC-CLIO, Inc., 2006), 1:483. As with Cambridge,

Harrison briefly served as a school master in Aylsham Free School, twelve miles north of Norwich, where he married in 1573. He lost his post when he tried to alter a baptismal service but went on to become head of a Norwich almshouse or hospital, where he and Browne lodged. Founded in 1249, the hospital, previously known as St. Giles or the Old Men's Hospital, was run by the city council and was called the Great Hospital or God's House.

Harrison was drawn to the Puritanism of men like More and Robardes, but as discussion continued with Browne, his more radical arguments began to hold sway. As others joined them, a small community formed early in 1581. At first, only a group of like-minded Christians, it was later constituted as an independent church. Browne attracted large crowds whenever he preached but it is difficult to know how many joined the group he formed. Several were deterred by persecution.[10]

In the spring of 1781, 46 people eventually covenanted together as a gathered church, being convinced, in Browne's words, that they should "forsake and deny all ungodliness and wicked fellowship" and "refuse all ungodly communion with wicked persons."[11] Their goal was to make one another "obedient to Christ" and judge all things by God's Word.

On April 19, 1581, Browne was arrested for the first time while preaching in Bury St. Edmunds, 40 miles south of Norwich.[12] Many Puritans were unhappy with him and complained to the Bishop of Norwich, Edmund Freke (*c.*1516–1591). Freke, in turn, corresponded with Lord High Treasurer William Cecil (*c.*1520–1598), Lord Burghley, about Browne. Burghley, a powerful man, distantly related to Browne and a Stamford neighbor, was keen to support him if he could and throughout his remaining years showed concern for him. Freke explained how "many godly preachers" had complained about Browne's "corrupt and contentious doctrine."[13] He says, "his arrogant spirit of reproving was such as it was to be marvelled at: the man being also to be feared, lest if he were at liberty, he should seduce the vulgar sort of the people, who greatly depended on

---

Norwich's Puritan heyday came after Browne. In the 1630s William Bridge (*c.*1600–1670) served in Norwich and Jeremiah Burroughs (1599–1646) near Diss. See above, Chapter 4 on William Bridge.

[10] It was probably in 1580 that a petition later sent from Norfolk to the Queen was readied, seeking further reform on Presbyterian lines. The fact 175 signed, including Browne and Harrison, shows how common such thinking was.

[11] Robert Browne *A true and short declaration: both of the gathering and ioyning together of certaine persons, and also of the lamentable breach and division which fell amongst them* (1583).

[12] This was part of the "Bury stirs" religious controversies and disorders involving, among others, Freke and Calvinist politicians like Sir Robert Jermyn (1539–1614) of Rushbrook Hall and Sir John Higham (*c.*1540–1626) of Barrow.

[13] See Benjamin Hanbury, *Historical Memorials Relating to the Independents Or Congregations Lists: From Their Rise to the Restoration of the Monarchy A.D. MDCLX, Volume 1* (London, Congregational Union of England) 2.

him: assembling themselves together, to the number of an hundred at a time, in private houses and conventicles, to hear him, not without danger of some evil event."[14]

Browne and Harrison, 1581–1585

Burghley did what he could to mitigate for Browne, suggesting his error was "of zeal rather than of malice." He had him brought to London and imprisoned, not for the last time. In his absence, Browne's followers discussed fleeing to Scotland, knowing Presbyterianism held sway there. The Channel Islands were also considered for the same reason. From prison, Browne sought to dissuade them. On returning to Norfolk a short while later, he was again arrested and imprisoned with other church members. By this time, it was generally agreed that migration to Holland was wisest and a short while later they regrouped in Middelburg, the Netherlands. There they covenanted together as a church and became more of a Congregationalist assembly.[15]

Middelburg

The Dutch experiment was short lived; dissension soon dissolving the gathered community. By this time, Browne had married Alice Allen (d.1610) possibly a sister of Harrison's wife, though Alice is said to be from Yorkshire not Norfolk. Alice may have been a focus for disagreement in the church. Browne was often sick and resigned as pastor several times before leaving Middelburg. No doubt there was fault on both sides but "Browne was undoubtedly an overbearing and an exceedingly difficult person."[16]

In 1582, in Middelburg, Browne published, at Harrison's expense, three separate works bound in a single volume: *A Treatise of Reformation without tarrying for any*, the best known, pressed for immediate reformation of the church and condemned any who evaded this responsibility; *A Book which Showeth the Life and Manners of All True Christians and how unlike they are unto Turks and Papists and Heathen folk* was a kind of catechism for the spiritually uninstructed and a guide to daily religious life, and *A Treatise upon 23 of Matthew* denounced the empty self-serving preaching of many contemporary clergy.

Browne was clearly loyal to Queen and country but argued that the state should not have authority over the church. Unlike those who despaired of change from within, he seems to have expected it and only later does he appear to have given up this hope. On June 30, 1583, a royal proclamation was issued against Browne and his writings. They found an eager readership, however. Just

---

[14] See the Freke and Burghley correspondence in the Lansdowne Collection in The British Library.

[15] The suggestion that Browne first preached to the Dutch or in the merchants' church led by Cartwright is unfounded.

[16] Smith, *Robert Browne*, 115.

before the proclamation, in Bury, Freke had John Coppin(g), a cobbler, and Elias Thacker, a tailor, brought before attorney general Sir John Popham (1531–1607) and hanged for distributing Browne and Harrison's writings, and forty books were publicly burned.[17] Copping had been imprisoned for preaching Separatist views seven years before and converted fellow prisoner, Thacker. No doubt Browne's better connections and loyalty to the crown saved him from a similar fate. Ten years later, in 1593, Separatists John Greenwood (c.1560–1593), Henry Barrowe (c.1550–1593) and John Penry (1559–1593) would be martyred in London, despite efforts by Burghley and others to save them. All three were hanged for "devising and circulating seditious books."[18] By then, as we shall see, Browne had made his apparent recantation.

Browne on the move
Following Middelburg, in 1584 Browne and some other families sailed to Dundee, Scotland. Moving on to Edinburgh via St. Andrews, they attempted to join the kirk but Browne's views proved unacceptable, as did his "arrogant manner." He appealed to the state and found a surprising ally in James VI (1566–1625), later James I of England, as James wanted to spite the Presbyterians.

Browne traveled extensively in Scotland, it seems, but found it no better than England, perhaps worse. Returning to England he probably settled his expectant wife in Stamford then went overseas again, where he published *A true and short Declaration, both of the joining together of certain persons, and also of the lamentable breach and division which fell amongst them* outlining the development of his views up to the Middelburg years. "Although not directly so intended" it is "in the nature of a spiritual autobiography, covering the ten most important years of his life, during which his views on church matters were taking shape, and growing firm."[19] He later answered a letter to Harrison from Cartwright, probably in 1585. Published in London, he later sought to distance himself from it.

Back home, in February 1584, his daughter Joan was baptized, apparently against his wishes. Shortly after, his son Anthony was also baptized. His movements are then unclear but, not surprisingly, he was imprisoned again. He appears to have been imprisoned over thirty times altogether, weakening, no doubt, his already poor constitution. His sufferings and growing despair at ever finding the church he desired must have left him in a fragile state of mind. Burghley continued to do what he could. Browne's aging father was also

---

[17] One copy survived and is in Langham Place Library, where Bancroft's "stately handwriting records its origin" (Nick Bunker, *Making Haste From Babylon: The Mayflower Pilgrims and Their World: A New History* [New York: Alfred A. Knopf, 2010], 92).

[18] See entry for Barrowe in *Encyclopedia Britannica* (Cambridge: Cambridge University Press 1911).

[19] Henry Martin Dexter, *The Congregationalism of the last three hundred years* (New York: Harper & Brothers, 1880), 62.

concerned for him.

Harrison dies in Middelburg
Meanwhile in Middelburg, following Browne's departure, Harrison became congregation leader. In 1583 he published three catechisms and a work on Psalm 122:1. Mayflower pilgrim William Brewster (1568–1644) later republished the latter, in Leyden in 1618.[20]

Like Browne, Harrison was eager for reform and emphasized the present rule of the risen Christ in the midst of his people by means of biblical discipline. Browne's idea of the church as a covenanted community is not found in Harrison's writings.

Cartwright led another congregation in Middelburg and efforts were made to unite the two churches but these failed. Harrison appears to have died in Middelburg about 1585. But for his untimely death, he may have been a much more significant figure in the Separatist movement.

Browne, Final Years 1585–1633
As for Browne, in 1585 he was closely examined by Whitgift, now Archbishop, and strongly warned against his prevailing trajectory. Never physically strong, his health was now broken. He speaks of being poor enough and broken too much with former troubles and needing no more affliction. With concern for his family, ideological fatigue and pressure from his father and Burghley combined, on October 7, 1585 he made a full and abject apology for his previous conduct. It is this apparent climb down that has earned Browne the opprobrium that clings to his name. At the age of 35 he had apparently sold his soul. Are we right to assume dissimulation, however? It is more likely that he simply gave Whitgift what he wanted—a commitment to outward conformity.

Stamford and Southwark
At first, he lived with his father but within a few months had moved to Stamford. Despite his capitulation, the authorities continued to be suspicious, perhaps rightly. Church attendance was sporadic and for this he was taken to task. In November, 1586, he became schoolmaster at St. Olave's, Southwark, under a strict state church regime, though when signing the regulations, he made clear his reservations. Almost inevitably neighbors sought him out and when asked he was not slow to state opinions found in his published works. That made for tensions. He was attacked from two sides. Puritan physician Stephen Bredwell (*c*.1563–1624) charged him with hypocrisy and inconsistency in his collection of their correspondence *The Razing of the Foundations of Brownism*.

---

[20] In 1572, he had translated a book on ghosts and spirits, exposing Romanist superstition by Swiss Reformer Ludwig Lavater (1527–1586). He also wrote a work on church and kingdom, unpublished until 1920.

In an extended debate Bredwell dubbed him "Troublechurch," a name that stuck. On the other hand, Browne also disputed with the Separatists Barrowe and Greenwood.[21]

At the end of 1588 Browne corresponded with his uncle, a Mr. Flower.[22] Flower passed the letter to Whitgift and others. In February, 1589, Bancroft, now Bishop of London, preached in the open air at Paul's Cross quoting the letter and other writings by Browne. He liked his arguments against Presbyterianism and the Barrowists. This exposure won Browne no favors.

In this period Browne came up with a Bible-centred educational system in which he tried to interest Burghley without success. His father probably died in 1591 and the inheritance, including the right to appoint the local rector, fell to the oldest brother, Francis Browne (died c.1608). Browne was briefly installed but by the year's end was replaced by Philip Browne, deprived for nonconformity in 1604. Robert was then installed in the place in the Nene Valley, where he would spend the rest of his days.

Achurch

From 1591 almost until he died Browne was rector of St. Giles, Achurch-cum-Thorpe, Northamptonshire. At that time, the parish was in the gift of the crown and was assigned by Burghley. "Although the remaining forty years were not without conflict they were, comparatively, quiet and uneventful. So far as the main stream of English civil and religious life were concerned, Browne was practically buried in Achurch."[23] The family grew in this period. There were eight or nine children. Some married in due time and there were over twenty grandchildren before Browne died. He apparently loved music and was "a singular good lutenist" and taught his children music.[24] While outwardly conforming, Browne probably did not completely abandon his previous views. Champlin Burrage believed he organized the parish church on gathered church lines, as did many Puritans.[25] F. Ives Cater suggests he kept his duties to a minimum and served a nearby Brownist congregation.[26]

In 1610 Alice Browne died and in 1613 Browne remarried. His marriage to

---

[21] Champlin Burrage published a work by Browne in 1907 as Browne's *Retraction*. It is supposedly his work against Barrowe and Greenwood but is more likely to be Cartwright's work, copied out by Browne in order to counter it.

[22] Browne's letter was published in 1904 as *A New Years Gift*.

[23] Smith, *Robert Browne*, 164.

[24] See the anonymous, *A Threefold Discourse between Three Neighbours* (London, 1642).

[25] Champlin Burrage, *The Early English Dissenters in the Light of Recent Research (1550–1641)* (Cambridge: Cambridge University Press, 1912), 2:114.

[26] F. Ives Cater, *Congregational Historical Society Transactions 1901-1918* (London: Congregational Historical Society, [n.d.]), 3:305.

Elizabeth Warrener, a widow from Stamford St. Martin's, Northamptonshire, was unhappy. By late 1615, he appears to have moved out of the parsonage, where his wife remained. There is evidence that in his absence she sought the company of other men but in October 1623 she sued for restitution of conjugal rights. There may have been a measure of reconciliation.[27] In 1617, he was suspended and stopped holding parish services. These abruptly began again in 1626. Local tradition suggests that from 1616 to 1626 he met with a gathered church at his new home in Thorpe Waterville. In 1627, he was before the authorities for non-conformity and in 1631 was excommunicated, his living being sequestrated in 1632. Throughout this period Browne may have been involved in a long running battle with parishioners he deemed schismatic.

Sadly, when over eighty years old, the parish constable, his godson, Robert Greene visited, brusquely demanding a statutory payment. He and Greene clearly had history and a by now corpulent and feeble Browne struck Greene in temper with a stick. This was reported and Browne proving intransigent was arrested and carried to prison one last time. There he remained until he died in 1633. The date of his burial is recorded in the parish book as October 8. His burial place is unknown.[28]

"It has been usual—almost universal—to brand Robert Browne as an ambitious bigot in his earlier, and a contemptible sneak in his later years; with the easy if not inevitable inference that he must have been a hypocrite through all."[29] Such harsh judgments are wide of the mark. It is unlikely that he was wholly deceitful in advocating the radical views he did, nor wholly honest when he apparently moved from being a dissenter to being a churchman. Dexter is not the first to see the answer lying in Browne's mental state. Bredwell, a physician who knew him well took the same view but is a hostile witness. It is unlikely that this explains Browne. Rather, Browne was a convinced Separatist or Semi-separatist who endeavored to live out his beliefs as best he could in none too easy circumstances.

Brownists

Shakespeare was not the only dramatist to refer to Brownism. Thomas Middleton, Ben Jonson and others do also. The Oxford English Dictionary says the earliest printed reference is 1583, in *Anatomy of Abuses* by Philip Stubbes (1555–1610) which warns against "newfangled fellows sprung up of late as Brownists."[30] In 1593, debating the Conventicle Act in Parliament Sir Walter

---

[27] Claims by Robert Baillie (1602–1662) that Browne beat his wife and was a Sabbath breaker are unsubstantiated.

[28] In 1923, the Congregationalists raised a memorial to Browne at St. Giles, Northampton.

[29] Dexter, *Congregationalism*, 87.

[30] See Benjamin Hanbury, *Historical Memorials Relating to the Independents or Congregationalists* (London, 1844), 3:34.

Raleigh (1552–1618) claims Brownists are "worthy to be rooted out of the commonwealth," fearing there were 20,000 of them. The previous year Sir Francis Bacon (1561–1626) was much more sanguine, opining that Brownists, "were at the most, a very small number of very silly and base people, here and there in corners dispersed," and had now been suppressed and scattered.[31] As stated, Brownist is really a theological swear word, a pejorative term used chiefly by opponents of Separatism.

Brownist emigration?
Facts about Browne are often mangled and misrepresented and he is not helped by the fact that he has been disparaged not only by the established church, to which he latterly belonged, but also by the dissenting one, which has always found him unattractive and incoherent. Many Puritans wrote against Browne and Brownism. In 1617 John Darrell (b.1562) published *A treatise of the Church. Written against them of the separation, commonly called Brownists*. In 1590 George Gifford (d.1620), lumping them in with a sect opposed by the church fathers, wrote "against the Donatists of England, whom we call Brownists."[32] Anabaptist was another term often hurled at Separatists. It is understandable then that even Separatists wanted to distance themselves from the term *Brownist*.

The Westminster Assembly was famously Presbyterian but included five Dissenting brothers.[33] In *An Apologetical Narration*, a sort of manifesto for Congregationalism or Independency, they say they believe the truth is "in a middle way, betwixt that which is falsely charged on us, Brownism, and that which is the contention of these times, the Authoritative Presbyterial Government."[34] A few years later, in 1648, John Cotton (1585–1652) in New England, answering Baillie in *The Way of Congregational Churches Cleared*, similarly denies a Brownist label. He traces Separatism back to 1567 "many years before Browne" and says that the backsliding of Browne from that way of Separation is a just reason why the Separatists may disclaim denomination from him, and refuse to be called Brownists, after his name; "and to speak with reason if any be justly to be called Brownists, it is only such as revolt from Separation to formality, and from thence to profaneness."[35]

---

[31] See Hanbury, *Historical Memorials*, 3:34. The Lord Bacon quotation is from "Certain Observations" in Carlson and Peel, ed., *Writings of Robert Harrison & Robert Browne*, 2:294.

[32] George Gifford, *A short treatise against the Donatists of England, whom we call Brownists* (London: Cooke, 1590).

[33] Thomas Goodwin, Philip Nye (c.1595–1672), Sidrach Simpson (c.1600–1655), Jeremiah Burroughs, William Bridge.

[34] Thomas Goodwin et al, *An apologeticall narration, hvmbly submitted to the honourable houses of Parliament* (London: R. Dawlman, 1643), 24.

[35] John Cotton, *The way of Congregational churches cleared: in two treatises* (London: Matthew Simmons, 1648), 5.

As early as 1596, Separatist exiles in Amsterdam were adamant that they were not Brownists. In *A True Confession of the Faith and Humble Acknowledgement of the Allegiance, which we her Majesty's Subjectes, falsely called Brownists, do hold towards God, and yield to her majesty and all other that are over us in the Lord, etc* they happily identify with Barrowe, Greenwood and Penry but not with Browne. It is no surprise then that in his *Dialogue* Bradford takes a similar line. At one point, reference having been made to Penry, Barrow and Greenwood, he has the young men say "But these were rigid Brownists, and lie under much aspersion, and their names much blemished and beclouded, not only by enemies, but even by godly and very reverend men."[36] Bradford's ancient men reply that it is no more just to call them Brownists than to call the disciples Judasites.

A little later the young men ask whether "Browne that fell away and made apostasy" was "the first inventor and beginner" of Separatism? Bradford is adamant:

> No, verily; for, as one answers this question very well in a printed book, almost forty years ago, that the prophets, apostles and evangelists have in their authentic writings laid down the ground thereof; and upon that ground is their building reared up and surely settled. Moreover, many of the martyrs, both former and latter, have maintained it, as is to be seen in *The Acts and Monuments of the Church*. Also, in the days of Queen Elizabeth there was a separated church, whereof Mr. Fitz was pastor, and another before that in the time of Queen Mary, of which Mr. Rough was, etc.[37]

For Bradford and his ancient men, Browne is only someone who later wrote about Separatism. Just as people pinned the name Puritan on the godly who desired reformation so they did the same with the term Brownist to people "that never would own it, nor had reason so to do."[38]

Bradford quotes Cotton in support. The young men will not leave it, however:

> but if we mistake not, Mr. Browne is accounted by some of good note to be the inventor of that way which is called Brownism, from whom the sect took its name. Moreover, it is said by such of note as aforesaid, that it is not God's usual manner of dealing to leave any of the first publishers or restorers of any truth of his to such fearful apostasy.[39]

---

[36] William Bradford, *Governor Bradford's First Dialogue:* ... (Boston: Directors of the Old South Work, 1896), 7.

[37] Bradford, *First Dialogue*, 17.

[38] Bradford, *First Dialogue*, 18.

[39] Bradford, *First Dialogue*, 19.

Bradford comes back: "Possibly this speech might arise from a common received opinion."[40] He then quotes Cotton denying Brownism and adds, "it is very injurious to call those after his name, whose person they never knew, and whose writings few if any of them ever saw, and whose errors and backslidings they have constantly borne witness against."[41] Bradford says they got their truths, "from the light of God's sacred word, conveyed by other godly instruments unto them."[42] He has to admit that Browne "may sometimes have professed some of the same things" but he has now "fallen from the same, as many others have done."[43] Again, Barrowe, Greenwood, Penry, John Smith (1554–1612), Richard Clyfton (d.1616), Francis Johnson (1563–1618), Henry Ainsworth (1571–1622) are all acceptable but Governor Bradford insists on blackballing Browne. Wonderfully inconsistent, he praises Copping and Thacker, mentioned above, even though they died for distributing Browne's books!

Bradford's unhappiness with Browne is understandable given the common view of his career but it was quite unnecessary and probably unjust. If not a thoroughgoing Separatist, Browne was at least on his way and deserves to be remembered as a Separatist founder, despite any black marks against his conduct. As it has been put, he was "the first Englishman of strong intellectual gifts to win distinction as a preacher of Separatism and as the bold author of works which directly encouraged separation from the Church of England." The influence of his predecessors is insignificant when compared with his. From 1582 to the present his name "has been a landmark in English church history" in England and beyond.[44] Yes, "some authorities claim Richard Fitz and the Plumbers' Hall Congregation" as the first Separatist group, though more an independent, Puritan inspired gathering not a Separatist one, but Browne appears to have been "the first influential true Separatist thinker and leader."[45] In Nick Bunker's words, "Browne was not the first Separatist … but he gave the movement its title because he was articulate … energetic, and at the outset … fearless."[46]

---

[40] Bradford, *First Dialogue*, 19.

[41] Bradford, *First Dialogue*, 20.

[42] Bradford, *First Dialogue*, 20.

[43] Bradford, *First Dialogue*, 21.

[44] Champlin Burrage, *The Early English Dissenters in the Light of Recent Research (1550–1641)* (Cambridge: Cambridge University Press, 1912), 2:94.

[45] Noel Dean Vanek, "Congregationalism Against the Background of the Radical Reformation: A Study of Influences and Differences" (Essay, Union Theological Seminary, 1979), 17.

[46] Burrage, *Early English Dissenters*, 2:94; Noel Dean Vanek, "Congregationalism Against the Background of the Radical Reformation: A Study of Influences and Differences" (Essay, Union Theological Seminary, 1979), 17; Bunker, *Making haste*, 77.

Conclusion

In 1630 William Bradford sat at his desk and began his "scribbled writings."[47] For another twenty years he "pieced up at times of leisure" what amounted to 270 folio pages.[48] Known as *Of Plymouth Plantation*, it was lost for a period but rediscovered in 1855 in London. In it he writes of how, back in England, people "became enlightened by the word of God" and "saw further into things by the light of the word of God."[49] This is the very thing that Browne claimed to have done. The Pilgrims may have rejected the name Brownist, but they and Browne were singing from the very same psalter and headed in the very same direction even though separated first by time and then by space. There is every reason to speak of the pilgrims as a Brownist emigration.

---

[47] William Bradford, *Bradford's History of the Plymouth Settlement, 1608-1650* (Massachusetts: E.P. Dutton, 1920) 6, 11.

[48] Bradford, *History of the Plymouth* Settlement, 6, 11.

[49] Bradford, *History of the Plymouth* Settlement, 6, 11.

The statute of William Bradford in
Pilgrim Memorial State Park,
Plymouth, Massachusetts,
by Cyrus Edwin Dallin (1861–1944).

CHAPTER EIGHT

Stepping-Stones on the Congregational Way: The Ecclesiological Legacy of the Pilgrim Fathers

NATHAN TARR

By 1648, events in both New and old England had placed Governor William Bradford (1590–1657) in a reflective mood. In formulating the *Cambridge Platform*, Puritans from the Massachusetts Bay colony had asserted their prerogative to define and defend the congregational polity that co-author John Cotton (1585–1652) termed the New England Way.[1] Congregational practice had arrived in New England with the Pilgrims in 1620. But Puritan hegemony, escalating after 1630 across ecclesial, financial, political, and social sectors, made it unlikely that the Old Colony would exercise influence over any future discussions.[2]

---

[1] Responding to Presbyterian pressures, the Massachusetts General Court called the synod in 1646 to provide a constitution for Congregational churches in the colony. For a discussion of the debate surrounding the synod, see James F. Cooper Jr., *Tenacious of Their Liberties: The Congregationalists in Colonial Massachusetts* (Oxford: Oxford University Press, 1999), 1–45; David D. Hall, *The Faithful Shepherd; A History of the New England Ministry in the Seventeenth Century* (Cambridge, MA: Harvard University Press, 2006), 93–120.

[2] Bradford did briefly attend the conference at Cambridge in 1647, but only as an observer. The contrasts that had emerged between Plymouth and Boston by the mid-1630s were striking. The Plymouth colony was, by 1630, no longer undergoing active colonization. Politically, they were a colony without a proper charter for the land they occupied; even the charter procured in 1630 was suspect, lacking the Great Seal. Financially, they did not turn a profit for their Company, lacking the finances to supplement their population after 1623 (none of the 14 ships arriving from 1624–1629 held colonists for Plymouth).

Voluntarily or otherwise, the baton of New England polity had been passed.³

Meanwhile, news reached Bradford from across the Atlantic that had been unthinkable short years before; Oliver Cromwell's (1599–1658) Parliamentary army had defeated the forces of Charles I (1600–1649) and Archbishop Laud (1573–1654), liberating the national church from her "tyrannous bishops."⁴ The impetus for the Pilgrim exodus, first to the Netherlands and then to the new world, had arisen from the "papisticall prelates" who persecuted non-conformity and whose hierarchy cast the legitimacy of the Church of England into doubt. Their sudden removal reinvigorated the great work of church reformation. But, as it was Parliamentary initiative backed by New Model muscle that opened the door, the center of gravity for effecting change had shifted three-thousand miles away, to the very counties the Pilgrims had fled in 1609.⁵

Both the *Cambridge Platform* and Cromwell's alliance with Parliament codified aims that had inspired Bradford's pilgrim band to venture toward "those vast unpeopled Countryes of America."⁶ Yet, as neither the Bay Puritans nor the British Parliament acknowledged any ongoing need for the Old Colony in their work, Bradford was moved to reflect on Plymouth's legacy within the project of church reform. What contribution could the Pilgrims claim toward a process

Spiritually, pressured by their economic position, they admitted significant numbers of Strangers to their original company. Necessity pressed even many of the Saints to farm at increasing distance from the town, prohibiting them from gathering for worship. Having been deprived of the hope of receiving John Robinson as minister by his death in 1626, and confronted with unsatisfactory ministers thereafter, the Pilgrims endured a sacramental drought from their founding through 1629. In sharp contrast, the Massachusetts Bay colony not only received a charter for the territory they occupied but, much to the chagrin of Charles I and William Laud, had managed to bring it with them. This meant, with the entirety of their government located in the New World, that they could function practically as an autonomous territory. They did so during the Commonwealth. Financially, the Bay colony was comprised primarily of middle-class families who benefitted from connections to the gentry behind in Britain. As a result, to take one example, thirteen ships entered Massachusetts Bay in 1630 alone, carrying over one-thousand settlers. This was three times as many as had come to Plymouth in a decade. Spiritually, where Plymouth struggled to find a serviceable minister, three of England's most eminent ministers arrived in Boston aboard a single ship.

---

³ Bradford used the image of Plymouth as mother whose children have grown up and moved away. The Pilgrim church was now, "an ancient mother, grown old and forsaken of her children" (William Bradford, *Of Plymouth Plantation*, ed. Samuel Eliot Morrison [New York: Alfred A. Knopf, 1952], 333).

⁴ Bradford, *Plymouth Plantation*, 351. Bradford admitted, "Full little did I think that the downfall of the Bishops ... had been so near, when I first began these scribbled writings." Bradford had not been alone in his pessimistic appraisal of the church's prospects in the face of increased Laudian pressure. Thomas Hooker preached, "England hath seen her best days, and now evil days are befalling us: God is packing up His Gospel" (Thomas Hooker, *The Danger of Desertion: or a Far[e]well Sermon of Mr. Thomas Hooker* [London, 1641], 15). For an overview of the English Civil War, see Maurice Ashley, *England in the Seventeenth Century*, Pelican History of England 6 (Baltimore, MD: Penguin Books, 1975).

⁵ As one example of this Parliamentary initiative for church reformation, the Presbyterian-heavy Westminster Assembly, called by the Long Parliament, had been hard at work since 1643. For an introduction to the Assembly's work that positions it amid the debates of its time, see Robert Letham, *The Westminster Assembly: Reading its Theology in Historical Context* (Philipsburg, NJ: P&R Publishing), 2009.

⁶ Timothy George, *John Robinson and the English Separatist Tradition* (Macon, GA: Mercer University Press, 2005), 90. The phrase is from *Plymouth Church Records*, I, 44.

that now appeared poised for a glorious advance through those politically stronger and more strategically positioned than themselves?

This chapter joins Bradford in reflecting on the Pilgrims' ecclesial legacy on the quadricentennial of their arrival in Plymouth Bay. I argue, in short, that the simple presence of New Plymouth as a viable colony as well as, to a lesser extent, the particulars of their congregational practice, was an extraordinary fact that exercised a seminal influence on the ecclesial development of the Bay Puritans and the model they subsequently recommended to England. Furthermore, I argue that this forerunning role, what Michael Winship describes as erecting "a small-scale city on a hill," is precisely the role the Pilgrims understood themselves as playing from the outset of their enterprise.[7] In order to give their legacy its proper due, therefore, we should recognize the Pilgrims as those willing to hazard "the first brunt" of planting both a new colony and a new form of congregational life in the new world. Beyond this historic achievement, like a sprinter who enters the starting block intending to exhaust his own strength in arriving at the relay point, we should recognize that the Pilgrims ran their race from 1620 with the aim of enabling those who came after them to take ground they themselves would never reach.[8]

Framing the Pilgrim's legacy in these terms raises two questions that have provoked lively and enduring debate in studies of the "new Plimmouth men."[9] First, what is the support for the claim that this preparatory role—calling attention to the need for a national conversation on ecclesiastical discipline without providing the final word—was in fact the one the Pilgrims understood themselves to be playing? Second, to what degree did the development of the church, particularly in New England, bear out the Pilgrim's expectation that Plymouth would exert a formative influence on succeeding generations of colonists? These perennial questions frame the two main sections of this chapter. I will answer the question of the Pilgrim's intention by tracing the work of their most prolific and incisive spokesman, William Bradford. Then I will engage the question of Plymouth's influence by taking up their relationship with the Puritan churches of both Salem and Boston.

"Out of small beginnings greater things"
Governor Bradford's reflection led him, in 1648, to put down the colony's chronicle he had been compiling since 1630 and try his hand at a genre more

---

[7] Michael Winship, *Godly Republicanism: Puritans, Pilgrims, and a City on a Hill* (Cambridge, MA: Harvard University Press, 2012), 112.

[8] The phrase appears in the letter John Robinson sent after the Pilgrims once they had departed from Leyden and were on their way to Southampton and, from there, the new world.

[9] "John Cotton to Samuel Skelton," in Sargent Bush ed., *The Correspondence of John Cotton* (Chapel Hill, NC: The University of North Carolina Press, 2001), 144.

responsive to current events, the dialogue.¹⁰ Cast as a conversation between "some yonge-men borne in New-England; And some Ancient-men, which came out of Holland," these dialogues allowed Bradford to articulate the angst experienced in the colony at watching Cromwell repeal the reason for their withdrawal from Church and country while, at the same time, provide an answering perspective from the remaining "fore-fathers" like Bradford himself.¹¹ The substance of Bradford's message was that, far from casting the necessity of their sacrifice into doubt, current developments at home and abroad should be considered good fruit from the seed planted at Plymouth.

"The blessing of God upon our way"
Some scholars find it irresistible, examining Bradford's writing at this later point, to challenge the continuity of his message. In their view, the optimism evident in the early pages of *Plymouth Plantation*—what Robert Daly calls Bradford's "Eusebian vision" of God's special purpose for the pilgrims in the work of reformation—can be seen to dissipate across the disappointments of the 1630s and 40s.¹² To account for such a vastly altered situation, the story goes, Bradford's tale of "providential history" was reworked in a decidedly Augustinian direction, emphasizing hope deferred to a heavenly City of God that replaced any expectation of establishing its earthly instantiation.¹³ Evidence for this account is often found toward the end of *Plymouth Plantation* as the account devolved from an epic tale to a lament and, finally, into disordered lists lacking even the veneer of narratival cohesion. A similar sense of discouragement is also used to explain why Bradford's dialogues attempt to scrub the Pilgrims clean of separatism and position them in the main channel of trans-Atlantic reformation. On this reading of Bradford, the original plantation had not only failed in its own right, it

---

[10] This was, of course, *Of Plymouth Plantation*. Everett Emerson expresses broad scholarly consensus when he describes Bradford's history as an "epic" and "the greatest book from seventeenth-century America" (Everett Emerson, *Puritanism in America: 1620-1750* [Boston, MA: Twayne Publishers, 1977], 38). The best study of Bradford's work is Douglas Anderson, *William Bradford's Books: Of Plymouth Plantation and the Printed Word* (Baltimore, MD: Johns Hopkins University Press, 2003).

[11] Bradford wrote three dialogues, of which only part of the first and the third remain extant. For the first dialogue see, William Bradford, "A Dialogue or the sume of a Conference between som younge men borne in New England and sundry Ancient men that came out of holland and old England Anno domini 1648," *Publications of the Colonial Society of Massachusetts*, 22 (Boston: The Society, 1920). For the third dialogue, see William Bradford, "A Dialogue, or 3rd Conference betweene some Young-men borne in New-England, and some Ancient-men, which came out of Holland and Old England, concerning the Church, and the Gouerment thereof," *Proceedings of the Massachusetts Historical Society* 2 (1870): 426–461.

[12] Robert Daly, "Bradford's Vision," 557–561.

[13] See, for example, Alan Heimert and Andrew Delbanco eds., *The Puritans in America: A Narrative Anthology* (Cambridge, MA: Harvard University Press, 1985), 51; Andrew Delbanco, *The Puritan Ordeal* (Cambridge, MA: Harvard University Press, 1989), 194–195.

now appeared not to have been necessary in the first place.[14]

The question of continuity in Bradford's presentation of the Pilgrim's purpose is significant because it elucidates the heart of their corporate self-understanding. Were they opportunists, willing to re-conceptualize their program for a seat on the right side of history? Or, in fact, as one of the last of the "ancient" men, did Bradford perceive a meaningful continuity between their current situation and the accomplishment of their original purpose, all of the intervening disappointments notwithstanding?[15] There are compelling reasons to read him as operating consistently from this latter conviction. In terms of his historiographical model, Bradford held the perspectives of Eusebius and Augustine in constructive tension across the span of his commentary. He cited Eusebius positively, for example, not only at the beginning of his *Plantation* but also again in his *First Dialogue*.[16] This suggests that Bradford sustained his conviction that the Saints' undertaking not only achieved a goal of temporal significance but had been divinely appointed to do so. At the same time, Augustine's emphasis on the believer's heavenly destination framed the entire narrative of *Plymouth Plantation*, as Mark Sargent notes, already "in its first chapters, not just in his final disillusioned notes."[17] Seeking the city that was to come, therefore, did not serve merely as a refuge from cynicism. From the outset of their time in Holland, Bradford noted, appropriating the language of Hebrews 11, "they knew they were pilgrims."[18]

The apparent tension between *either* "laying the foundation of a Commonwealth

---

[14] Some scholars argue that Bradford's historiography was "Augustinian" from the beginning. This has the advantage of acknowledging continuity across his writings, but it misses the this-worldly good Bradford clearly understood the pilgrims to have accomplished (Perry Miller, *The New England Mind: The Seventeenth Century* Cambridge, MA: Harvard University Press, 1939], 3–34); Alan Howard, "Art and History in Bradford's *Of Plymouth Plantation*," *William and Mary Quarterly* 28 (1971): 243–244.

[15] Bradford does acknowledge both disappointments and surprises. To take one disappointment, toward the end of *Plymouth Plantation*, he laments that the "worser" part of the colony had, numerically speaking, become the "greater" (Bradford, *Plymouth Plantation*, 316). He also admits that their flight from England was precipitated by the church only "as it then was," admitting that, had current circumstances prevailed in the sixteen-teens, such costly measures would not have been necessary (Bradford, *First Dialogue*, 414–415).

[16] Bradford, *First Dialogue*, 420. It should be noted that his interest is in the purity of the apostolic church rather than with Constantine's empowering of the prelacy which, to his mind, marked the time when "Congregational discipline began to be neglected through the usurped authority of the bishops and the presbyters" (Bradford, *3rd Conference*, 426).

[17] Mark Sargent, "William Bradford's 'Dialogue' with History," *New England Quarterly* 65.3 (1992): 395. Sargent notes that "for each of his references to Deuteronomy [the Eusebian transfer of the blessings of Israel's covenant to the church], Bradford more than once invokes the *parousia* of the New Testament epistles." Augustine is discussed in Bradford, *First Dialogue*, 430, 431.

[18] This phrase has proven popular in titling books on the history of the Plymouth Colony. More often than not, however, the phrase is understood to point up the Pilgrim's willingness to hazard the perils of crossing the Atlantic in their quest after an earthly Canaan. But in its biblical context—and one the Pilgrims would have known very well—Abraham and his family demonstrate their faith by continuing to seek heavenly rest.

and ... Church" here on earth, *or* anticipating eternal rest is resolved when we recall the hold that John Foxe's (1516–1587) *Acts and Monuments* exercised on the imagination of Pilgrims and Puritans alike.[19] For Foxe, it had been the deaths of Calvinists at Queen Mary's (r. 1553–1558) pyres that incited Elizabeth I (r. 1558–1603) to further church reform. Likewise, it had been the sacrifice of Separatists like Henry Barrow (1550–1593) and John Greenwood (1556–1593) that served as the "true cause" behind Elizabeth's own decision no longer to execute dissenters.[20] The moral of these stories, which Foxe traced from the apostles through to the English reformers, was that suffering not only marked the true church but effected a favorable transformation among the political powers that be.

Their experience of a disruptive emigration in 1609, and again in 1620, invited the Pilgrims to connect their own story in this broader narrative. Bradford's embrace of Foxe's paradigm was evident not only as he built his first dialogue around a long list of Separatist martyrs—what Sargent calls a "Separatist counterpart to John Foxe's *Acts and Monuments*"—but also in his unusually animated response to John Cotton's insinuation that Pilgrim sufferings had been but "a *minori*."[21] Often deferential toward the Boston minister, Bradford recognized that this diminution of their suffering struck at the central dynamic of the Pilgrim legacy. With some energy, therefore, Bradford returned that Pilgrim sufferings "would not only equalize" but "farr exceede" the "sufferings of those reproached by the name of puritans."[22]

In Bradford's appropriation of Foxe, Pilgrim willingness to suffer persecution in England and then privation in New England exhibited the apostolic purity of their practice. More than that, for friends of non-conformity, it also catalyzed the thorough-going transformation of Church and State that was emerging across the 1640s. Reflecting on some four decades of Pilgrim suffering, therefore, Bradford claimed with sincere satisfaction that Cromwell's "great and gratious &

---

[19] The phrase comes from peripatetic Pilgrim ambassador Edward Winslow, *Hypocrisy Unmasked* (London, 1646). Four editions of Foxe's compendium were published in his lifetime: 1563, 1570, 1576, 1583. For a discussion of the impact of Foxe's schematization of history see William Haller, *The Elect Nation: The Meaning and Relevance of Foxe's Book of Martyrs* (New York, 1963), 110–139; V. Norskov Olsen, *John Foxe and the Elizabethan Church* (London, 1973), 51–70. For comments on John Robinson's appropriation of Foxe, see George, *John Robinson*, 11, 17–22, 28, 125, 134, 242; Emerson, *Puritanism in America*, 40. Emerson notes that the Separatists took Foxe's presentation of an underground church—in London—during Mary's reign as the historical inspiration for their tradition.

[20] Bradford, *First Dialogue*, 433. The necessity of uniform religious expression within a single political entity was assumed in the sixteenth and seventeenth centuries.

[21] Sargent, "Bradford's 'Dialogue,'" 412; John Cotton, *The Way of Congregational Churches Cleared from the Historical Aspersions of Mr. Robert Baylie* (London, 1648), 17.

[22] Bradford, *First Dialogue*, 2. He continued outlining the "exceeding" Separatist sufferings for another six pages. Bradford's appreciation for Cotton is apparent in his lament for New England that singles out the dimming of the Puritan, rather than the Pilgrim, light. "O New England, thou canst not boat, Thy former glory thou hast lost. When Hooker, Winthrop, Cotton died, And many precious ones besides, Thy beauty then it did decay, And still doth languish more away" (Bradford, *3rd Dialogue*, 482).

glorious victories" in these "late warres" were among the "many testimonies of the blessing of God *upon our way*."[23] For those with eyes to see, the Pilgrim seed, having fallen into the harsh New England ground and died in apparent obscurity, was now bearing much fruit.[24]

"One small candle may light a thousand"
Images that Bradford deployed throughout his writings reinforce this conclusion and open another avenue for examining the continuity of his perspective regarding the Pilgrim's purpose. For example, Bradford summarized the Pilgrim contribution toward the achievements of the Bay Puritans and English Parliament, as a single candle flickering from Cade Cod to ignite reform across the nation; "Thus out of small beginnings greater things have been produced by His hand that made all things out of nothing…and as one small candle may light a thousand, so the light kindled *here* hath shone unto many, yea in some sort of our whole nation."[25] It will not do to suggest this was simply a late attempt to claim credit for an otherwise unfortunate situation. The image of a single torch kindling a glorious conflagration echoed a dynamic similar to the one Bradford adopted toward the beginning of *Plymouth Plantation*. Before they left Leyden, the Pilgrims,

> Cherished a great hope and inward zeal of laying good foundations, or at least of making some ways towards it, for the propagation and advance of the gospel of the kingdom of Christ in the remote parts of the world, even though they should be but stepping stones to others in the performance of so great a work.[26]

This image of "good foundations" and "stepping-stones" carries twin implications that do much to elucidate the Pilgrim mindset as Bradford maintained it. First, the image acknowledges participation in a project of staggering scope and significance—the (re)building of a house upon arrival at a long-sought destination. Second, it admits a realistic understanding of the Pilgrim's preparatory or initiatory role within this much larger project. Such language echoed that

---

[23] Bradford, 3rd *Dialogue*, 462. Emphasis added.

[24] Summarising the message of Bradford's third dialogue, Bernard Bailyn writes, "However obscure they might have seemed, they, in their suffering and persecution, had ignited concern for the nature of true ecclesiastical discipline all over England" (Bernard Bailyn, *The Barbarous Years: The Peopling of British North America: The Conflict of Civilizations, 1600–1675* [New York: Alfred A. Knopf, 2012], 364).

[25] Bradford, *Plymouth Plantation*, 236. Emphasis added. Bradford conceived of the English "nation" as encompassing England and her colonies. Baylyn's comment here is apt, "England's expansionist tendencies were driven by its sense of responsibility for the survival of Protestantism abroad, by the dawning of a [uniquely] British ideology of empire" (Baylyn, *Barbarous Years*, 37).

[26] Bradford, *Plymouth Plantation*, 21.

of their spiritual leader, John Robinson (1575–1625). While in Leyden, it was Robinson who had taught his congregation to yearn for the day they could gaze upon "Sion ... on the top of every hill."[27] Further, Robinson explained, a church gathered according to congregational principles was "the only ordinary beaten way" to arrive at that glorious end. Realistically, however, providing a beaten path for others required someone to tread the as-yet-uneven ground for the first time. Likewise, laying out stepping-stones for others meant that the Pilgrims must endure being, "here and there, up and down, without sure footing is our portion in this present evil world."[28] Again, though it must quickly be covered over, construction on even the most magnificent city was required to begin with the foundation. This costly privilege, their beloved pastor encouraged the Forefathers, was theirs. By clothing their accomplishment in images of single candles and stepping-stones, therefore, Bradford deliberately drew on Robinson's original conviction and suggested that, though he had not lived to see it, their pastor's words were coming to fruition already in the second generation.

"The Pilgrim saddle was on the Bay horse"

To this point I have argued that the legacy Bradford claimed for the Pilgrims in 1648 carried significant continuity with their original self-understanding. Their endeavor was intended to advertise the viability, even in the wilderness of the new world, of non-conformists "provid[ing] for themselves without the anti-christian burden they had to endure in England."[29] The Pilgrim foundation, therefore, would be successful to the extent that it drew others after them to build upon what they had done. To that end, Bradford exulted as he took in both the Bay Puritans and developments in England, Plymouth plantation had surpassed their greatest expectations.[30] The remainder of this chapter takes up the pricklier task of historical verification. What evidence is there that the Pilgrim plantation

---

[27] The quote is found in George, *John Robinson*, 93. The implicit congregationalism of this image provides an interesting contrast with John Winthrop's more familiar, and seemingly unitive, "city on a hill."

[28] John Robinson, *A Justification of Separation from the Church of England* (Amsterdam, 1610), 62, 122. This image of the stepping/foundation stone forged a parallel, in the popular imagination, with Plymouth rock. Already in the first half of the nineteenth century, as Alexis de Tocqueville made his tour of the young nation, he wondered that, "The rock where the pilgrims disembarked is still a landmark. This rock has become an object of veneration in the United States. I have seen carefully preserved fragments of it in several towns in the Union...Here is a stone trodden by the feet of a few wretched people but for an instant, and it becomes famous; it is held in esteem by a great nation, every morsel is revered and its very dust is distributed far and wide. Yet what has become of the thresholds of palaces?" (Alexis de Tocqueville, *Democracy in America*, 45).

[29] Winship, *Godly Republicanism*, 112.

[30] As Emerson recognized, "Bradford saw the creation of this new church at Salem and the subsequent gathering of later Congregational churches on Massachusetts Bay after Salem's example as a part of the continuing action of God that began with the coming of the Pilgrims to America" (Emerson, *Puritanism in America*, 42).

bore the first-fruits Bradford claimed? To what degree did Plymouth's example induce not only the colonization of the new world but the congregational structure of the churches gathered there?[31] Perhaps most immediately, what questions could we explore to shed light on the answer?

The question of Plymouth's influence over the Puritans has generated significant debate from Bradford's own time. Already in 1646 Edward Winslow was laboring to distinguish the Puritans merely taking counsel with the Pilgrims regarding how they should "fall upon a right platform of worship," from their "taking Plymouth for their precedent" and so being seduced by avowed Separatists into political sedition.[32] Whether or not we judge Winslow's attempt at a nuanced distinction to be a success—and many in his own time did not—it is undeniable that subsequent presentations of the relationship between Plymouth and Boston have rarely attempted, much less achieved, a similar nuance. From at least the late nineteenth century, re-constructions of the interaction between these two colonies, especially on the topic of ecclesiology, have ricocheted between untenable extremes. One side asserts that Plymouth was "pathetically" irrelevant to events in Massachusetts Bay while the other asks us to imagine that the Pilgrims converted the Puritans to a previously unconsidered Separatism within weeks of their arrival.[33] As Bradford modeled in the give-and-take of his dialogues, however, history rarely unfolds along such a tidy binary. The inter-dependence expected between fledgling colonies three-thousand miles from home requires the religious dimension of the association between Plymouth and the Puritans to be framed as a matter of degrees. What is needed is a fresh way to engage overly familiar lines of argumentation and a compelling, responsible way to determine that degree.

It is not an exaggeration to say that progress on the question of the degree to which Plymouth influenced the Puritans has stalled. This stalemate is owing principally to the fact that both sides come armed not only with primary sources that can be read in support of their position but also with a commensurate readiness to dismiss contrary evidence as politically motivated or otherwise

---

[31] Winship is correct to remind us that our conception of the relationship between Plymouth and Salem/Boston carries far-reaching implications. Speaking of Salem's decision to seek advice from Plymouth, Winship comments, "Much New England and even English history flowed out of that decision" (Michael Winship, *Hot Protestants: A History of Puritanism in England and America* [New Haven, CT: Yale University Press, 2018], 85).

[32] Winslow, *Hypocrisie Unmasked*, 92. This language of "counsel" was no more than John Cotton himself had recommended. Before they departed, Cotton had encouraged Winthrop and his company "to take advise from them at Plymouth."

[33] It was T.D. Bozeman who dismissed the Pilgrims as "pathetically unimportant" (Theodore Dwight Bozeman, *To Live Ancient Lives: The Primitivist Dimension in Puritanism* [Chapel Hill, NC: University of North Carolina Press, 1988], 115). For a summary of the principal contributors to this debate see Slayden Yarbrough, "The Influence of Plymouth Colony Separatism on Salem: An Interpretation of John Cotton's Letter of 1630 to Samuel Skelton," *Church History* 51.3 (1982): 290–303; Winship, *Godly Republicanism*, 288–89.

disingenuous.³⁴ This posture itself is largely the result of a handful of key data points having been pressed too far and spread too thin for too long. The discussion needs a fresh angle of approach. The remainder of this chapter gestures toward that approach. It is important to begin by acknowledging that the majority view among senior students of American puritanism recognizes, as the seventeenth-century folk saying put it, that "the Pilgrim saddle was often on the Bay horse." In other words, despite their relative weakness as a colony, Plymouth did indeed exert a significant level of influence over the government of both the colonies and congregations to their north.³⁵

As an assessment of the relationship between Pilgrims and Puritans it enjoys ample evidence. It begins, as Marion Starkey has noted, with the simple fact that "the Pilgrims got to American first" and so "had demonstrated the viability of New England well before 1628."³⁶ Given their providentialist view of history, which privileged chronological priority, Puritan receptivity toward Plymouth's influence was inevitable.³⁷ When, therefore, governor John Endecott arrived at Salem in 1628—the vanguard of the Puritan migration which began in earnest in 1630 with the arrival of the Winthrop fleet—he requested Plymouth deacon Samuel Fuller to clarify the Pilgrim's congregational model. The deacon did so in a manner that "satisfied" Endecott "touching [their] judgments of the outward form of God's worship."³⁸ The ensuing cooperation between Plymouth and Salem was sufficiently pronounced to be apparent from England. In October of 1630, reports from Salem roused John Cotton from his sickbed to rebuke the recently installed pastor, Samuel Skelton. Cotton was surprised by the separatism, as he then perceived it, that Skelton evidenced in refusing to admit the Winthrop party to the sacraments; some of whom came from Cotton's own parish. In his letter, Cotton laid responsibility for this radical development in the praxis of his

---

³⁴ To give but two examples, George Willison speaks of the Puritans "maintain[ing] the fiction" that they did not embrace Separatism and Slayden Yarbrough accuses John Cotton of "attempting to hide his Separatist roots" (George Willison, *Saints and Strangers* [New York: Reynal & Hitchcock, 1945], 270); Yarbrough, "Influence," 300.

³⁵ Larzer Ziff's exhortation provides a useful summary: "While mindful of Plymouth's individual tradition, students of New England history would do well to return again to a recognition of Plymouth's influence in the far more prosperous ecclesiastical establishment of Massachusetts Bay" (Larzer Ziff, "The Salem Puritans in the 'Free Aire of a New World,'" *Huntington Quarterly Library* 20 [August 1957]: 383–384).

³⁶ Marion Starkey, *The Congregational Way: A Narrative of the Role the Pilgrims, the Puritans, and Their Heirs Played in Shaping American History* (Garden City, NJ: Doubleday, 1966), 4. This bare fact disguises a remarkable claim when it is remembered that the Pilgrims (as Separatists from the State church) were disparaged as both religious and civic outcasts.

³⁷ Emerson, *Puritanism in America*, 46.

³⁸ Salem was first called Naumkeag, after its native inhabitants. For a history of the settlement, beginning with its short-lived founding by the Dorchester Company in 1623, see John Turner, *They Knew They Were Pilgrims: Plymouth Colony and the Contest for American Liberty* (New Haven, CT: Yale University Press, 2020), 138–139.

former colleague at the feet of the "new-Plimouth men."[39] By the time Cotton himself arrived in 1633, however, he was prepared not only to retract his earlier rebuke but also to lead Boston's First Church in further straightening its membership requirements.[40] Owing to the considerable influence he was to wield in the Bay colony, Cotton's "conversion" meant that Boston would follow Salem and Plymouth in gathering almost exclusively congregational churches.[41] The uniformity of this polity, from a group that did not emigrate with an explicit aim to execute a specific approach to church government and, further, had not enjoyed the opportunity to experiment with independent polity before embarking, does suggest that "England's transplanted puritans were remaking themselves in Plymouth's image."[42]

These facts, if beginning to wear a bit thin from extended use, provide adequate historical warrant for the claim that Plymouth exerted an influence on New England that was disproportionate to its size. They have proven insufficient, however, either to identify the nature and degree of that influence or to persuade those who are inclined to read the evidence in a different direction.[43] In working to achieve additional clarity, therefore, I propose that the case for Plymouth's

---

[39] "John Cotton to Samuel Skelton" in Bush, *Correspondence*, 144. When Skelton refused to admit new arrivals to the sacraments because they were not members of a covenanted (rather than parish) churches, Cotton wrote, "You went hence of another judgment, and I am afraid your change hath sprung from the New Plymouth men." Ironically, Robert Baillie would accuse Cotton himself of coming under the deleterious influence of Plymouth (Robert Baillie, *A Dissuasive from the Errours Of the Time* [London, 1645], 54).

[40] Winship, *Hot Protestants*, 85–90. For Cotton's retraction, see John Cotton, *A sermon preached by the Reverend Mr. John Cotton deliver'd at Salem, 1636* (Boston, 1713), 41–43. For a discussion of the test(imony) of faith, though he reserves less of a role for Plymouth's influence, see Edmund S. Morgan, *Visible Saints: The History of a Puritan Idea* (Ithaca, NY: Cornell University Press, 1963), 33–112.

[41] As he had done in England, Cotton continued to shape the theology and polity of future pastors in his "house-hold seminary." James Cooper includes future New England ministers Richard Mather, John Eliot, John Davenport, Edward Norris, Zechariah Symmes, Thomas Allen, John Knowles "and a number of other future divines" as early members of Boston's First Church (James Cooper, *Tenacious of their Liberties: The Congregationalists in Colonial Massachusetts* [Oxford: Oxford University Press, 1999], 22). Cotton also served several terms on the Board of Governors of Harvard College, thereby extending his interest and ability to shape the education of future ministers. In terms of establishing a congregational pattern, Winship points out that the first five churches on the shore of Massachusetts Bay were congregationalist, reinforcing the pattern for those seventy ministers who would follow in the Great Migration of 1630–1640. Winship, *Godly Republicanism*, 153. See also Frederick Lewis Weis, *The Colonial Clergy and the Colonial Churches of New England* (Lancaster, MA: Society of the Descendants of Colonial Clergy, 1936), 1977.

[42] Turner, *Pilgrims*, 142. Winship records Arthur Hildersham's advice to the three Salem-bound ministers that they agree upon a form of church government before they departed. He also records William Hubbard's account that they, in fact, "were not precisely fixed upon any particular order or form of [church] government" before departing. In his view this both removes the possibility that the Puritans carried congregational convictions into their emigration and reserves a significant role for the "functioning church template" they were to discover at Plymouth (Winship, *Godly Republicanism*, 139–140).

[43] It is premature to dismiss efforts to construe the relationship in other terms as "speculative" and "evidence free." Contra Winship, *Godly Republicanism*, 154, 155.

legacy can be well served by exploring four supplementary lines of inquiry. The purpose of raising these queries is not to undercut the fact of Plymouth's influence. The aim, rather, is to situate the current consensus within previously neglected dimensions of the relationship between Plymouth and the Puritans so that the aspects of their religious association take on a more robust significance.

The Networked Wilderness

Endecott's letter to Bradford, mentioned above, often takes pride of place in denominating Plymouth's influence on Salem's ecclesiology. When the Governor's grateful admission is coupled with the fact that Salem gathered a covenanted congregation shortly thereafter, it is tempting to read between the lines—even over contemporary protestations to the contrary—to claim that Salem arrived in the new world as an ecclesiological *tabula rasa* upon which Plymouth proceeded to etch their brand of congregationalism.[44] Winship's conclusion in this regard is representative:

> In 1629, two ministers had arrived at the tiny advance settlement of Salem, keen to "gather" a church with the inhabitants. No one had decided in advance what this new church should look like, and Salem's ministers and laity took as their inspiration the only Protestant reformed church on the continent, the separatist Congregational church down Massachusetts Bay at Plymouth.[45]

However, letters soliciting or responding with satisfaction to assistance of all kinds—social, legal, financial, as well as religious—were common between colonies in New England.[46] More specifically, the correspondence between Plymouth and Salem (and later Boston) was, from the beginning, robust and reciprocal.[47] Claims regarding the specific significance of Endecott's statement, therefore, would be strengthened, and possibly chastened, by situating them within this wider context.

The place to begin is to contextualize Endecott's comments within the letter itself. The Governor's acknowledgement that Deacon Fuller's account had "satisfied" him concerning "[Plymouth's] judgments of the outward form of God's worship," was immediately followed by the confession that this satisfaction was

---

[44] Endecott's letter to Bradford came from May of 1629, with the church gathered at Salem in August of 1629. Ziff, "Salem Puritans," 381. Winship has the church gathered on July 30 (Winship, *Godly Republicanism*, 153).

[45] Winship, *Hot Protestants*, 85.

[46] Matt Cohen, *The Networked Wilderness: Communication in Early New England* (Minneapolis, MN: University of Minnesota Press, 2010).

[47] For an example of the social give and take between Plymouth Pastor John Reyner and Elder William Brewster, see Bush, *The Correspondence of John Cotton*, 291–299.

cause for relief. Endecott was glad to discover that Plymouth's actual position was "far differing from the common report that hath been spread of you." This reassured response suggests that Salem's Puritans arrived in the new world with critical ecclesial questions for their Pilgrim neighbors. Endecott's satisfaction, therefore, did not originate from the fact that he found Plymouth worshipping merely in a congregational manner but that he found their congregationalism to be, "no other than is warranted by the evidence of truth and the same which I have professed and maintained."[48] As Larzer Ziff understood, in Fuller's presentation of Plymouth's practice Endecott heard "the outward form which would appropriately clothe his inward convictions."[49] His ensuing gratitude, when set against its epistolary context, refines our appreciation of the contribution Plymouth made to the Puritan forerunners. In encountering a model that accorded well with their convictions and provided, in the disorienting wilderness of the new world, a fixed point from which they could receive "the right hand of fellowship"—the very presence of Plymouth's church did much to relieve puritan anxiety.

"Come over and help us"
The limitations endured by the Plymouth church between 1620 and 1629 represents the other side of this context coin that also should be kept in mind. After the majority vote of his Leyden congregation prevented John Robinson from participating in the voyage to America, the Pilgrims were unable to secure an "able and godly" minister until 1629. As the church's lay-elder, William Brewster's preaching was pious and "sincere." Lacking ordination, however, he was not able to administer the sacraments to the congregation.[50] Still hoping to sail from Holland himself, Robinson forbad Brewster, in December of 1623, from administering the sacraments in his stead. The turmoil caused by John Lyford in

---

[48] John Endecott to William Bradford, 11 May 1629, quoted in George D. Langdon, *A Pilgrim Colony: A History of New Plymouth, 1620–1691* (New Have, CT: Yale University Press, 1996), 108. The Governor was not alone in claiming to have "maintained" a kind of congregationalism resonant with Plymouth's approach before arriving in the new world. Preaching at Salem in 1636, John Cotton specifically identified the purportedly separatist practice of gathering a congregation by covenant as he reminded his auditors that "some of us saw the truth…in our native country, namely the necessity of a church covenant to the institution of a church." Cotton, *Sermon at Salem*, 55. Bush ascribes the continuity of Cotton's thought on both sides of the Atlantic to his "life-long commitment to work toward the achievement of a purer, more scripturally defined, Christ-centered church" (Bush, *Correspondence*, 16). Richard Mather, according to his son Increase, was "of the Congregational persuasion from his youth unto his dying day reading and seriously considering Mr Baynes' *Diocesans Trial*, and Dr. Ames' his *Divinity* and *Cases of Conscience*, caused him to be so afore he saw New England" (Increase Mather, *The Life and Death of that Reverend Man Richard Mather* [Cambridge, 1670], 10).

[49] Ziff, "The Salem Puritans," 381.

[50] This sacramental drought may be one way to account for the strange lack of comment concerning worship at Plymouth in Bradford's writings. Though he does briefly mention the concern expressed over "the want of both of the sacraments" as a run-up to the confrontation with Lyford and Oldham (Bradford, *Of Plymouth Plantation*, 338).

1624, as he undertook to end the "sacramental drought" by baptizing children and celebrating the Lord's Supper, exposed how acutely the colonist felt this lack. They had emigrated anticipating the "opportunitie of freedom and libertie to injoye the ordinances of God in puritie among His people" but, after years of risk and toil, had yet to realize this joyous freedom. Robinson's death in 1626 not only dispelled any hope of the Pilgrim church once again enjoying his ministry, it also threw the perpetual nature of their sacramental poverty into sharp relief.[51]

Timothy George argues that discipline, connected as it was to admission to the sacraments, was one of the *notae* of the church and even the "central tenet" of Robinson's ecclesiology. Further, Plymouth continued to be shaped by Robinson's theological program until his death.[52] And yet, until short months before the Puritans arrived at Salem, the Pilgrims would have been hobbled in the exercise of their own polity by the inaccessibility of the ordinances. As a community that could not celebrate the Supper, Plymouth had not yet faced a situation where they had to determine who they would, or would not, admit to the sacraments. When Samuel Skelton arrived at Salem in 1629, therefore, Plymouth was not able to serve as a model of sacramental practice adapted to the free air of the new world. While his decision to refuse access to font and table for members of the Winthrop party is sometimes described as unthinkable apart from Plymouth's influence, in point of fact it had to be made without the benefit of reference to pilgrim practice. This relative inexperience on Plymouth's part may also account for the speed at which John Cotton was able to surpass existing standards for church membership by requiring a relation of grace.[53] It certainly explains why, though acknowledging that "there is no small appearance that" the Salemites received their "way and manner of first covenanting together" from "those of New Plymouth," William Hubbard

---

[51] This section is based on the discussion in Winship, *Godly Republicanism*, 111–131; and Turner, *Pilgrims*, 105–119. Neither Winship nor Turner connect this condition in Plymouth with Skelton's decision in Salem.

[52] George, *John Robinson*, 106–107.

[53] It may also account for why Cotton, in preaching to Winthrop's party in 1630, chose to focus on "the liberty of the ordinances" in the context of Acts 16:12 as the central warrant for planting a colony. Cotton, *God's Promise*, 9. The significance of this verse is that Philippi represented not only the place the Roman empire died with Caesar in BC 42, but also the place where the first Christian church was established in Europe in AD 49. As Mark Peterson explains it: "As Philippi was the site of the first Christian church planted on a new continent, superseding the corrupt imperial remnant of the formerly virtuous Greek and Roman republics, so Boston in New England would bring the first reformed Christian commonwealth to a new continent, escaping the imperial decay and religious persecution that threatened England's government and church" (Mark Peterson, *The City-State of Boston: The Rise and Fall of an Atlantic Power, 1630-1865* [Princeton, NJ: Princeton University Press, 2019], 13). The mention of Boston as the "first" reformed church in the new world may be a condescending dismissal of Plymouth's significance. More likely, however, Cotton was aware that Plymouth's sacramental drought (and thus incomplete complement of *notae*) challenged their identity as a fully formed, fully functioning congregation. It was not only the natives, therefore, who could be understood to call out, "come over and help us." These words from Acts 16:12 were placed on the Great Seal of the charter of the Massachusetts Bay Colony in 1629, clearly forming an important aspect of their self-understanding.

could also write that these first arrivals were "by some sort of covenant moulded into a church … until Mr Cotton and Mr Hooker came over … who did clear up the order and method of church government according as they apprehended was most consonant with the word of God."[54] Enduring its decade of sacramental drought, Plymouth was unable to provide a model for navigating some of the most acute questions generated by congregational church order and discipline in the new world. In these cases, the Puritans forged their own way and Plymouth quickly found themselves learning from their lately-arrived neighbors to the north.

"All due means"
There are two further scenarios, roughly contemporary with Salem's reception of Deacon Fuller and evidencing intriguingly similar dynamics, that prove illuminating if we are willing to open the aperture of our search wide enough to admit them. First, in 1630, William Bradford wrote to the newly arrived John Winthrop, governor in Boston, regarding the execution of John Billington. Billington, disruptive since his arrival in 1620, had now ambushed his neighbor in a field and shot him to death. Pilgrim statutes, on the books since 1623, invested "a jurie" of "twelve honest men" with the authority to try "all criminal facts" and deliver a verdict.[55] Billington was duly arraigned, as Bradford recorded in *Plymouth Plantation*, and found guilty of "willfull murder by plaine & notorious evidence."[56] Nevertheless, as this was to be the first execution carried out in the colony, Bradford noted that the Pilgrims "used all due means about his trial," including taking "the advice of Mr Winthrop and other [of the] ablest gentlemen in the Bay of Massachusetts that were then lately come over."[57] With the Bay providing their assent, Billington was hung that same September.

It is noteworthy that, by the time of the trial in 1630, Plymouth's statute book contained a clear process for handling capital cases and had done so for seven years. Nevertheless, confronted with the inaugural application of their own statue, Plymouth's civic leaders consulted with their counterparts in Massachusetts Bay. Given the relative lack of "gentlemen" among them—men accustomed to navigating such momentous decisions—this is not surprising. The Pilgrims looked to Boston, then, not for instruction or ideation but for the comfort of confirmation. It is worth considering to what degree, in gathering their initial congregation, Salem consulted with Plymouth from similar motivations. In this vein, Harold Worthley's discussion of the diverse sociological backgrounds of the two groups—specifically the way this sociological difference shaped their

---

[54] William Hubbard, *A General History of New England* (Boston, 1878), 181.

[55] Quoted in Willison, *Saints and Strangers*, 285.

[56] Bradford, *Plymouth Plantation*, 329.

[57] Bradford, *Plymouth Plantation*, 157.

experience of the new world—has been under-developed.[58] In England, even non-conforming Puritans prosecuted their ecclesiology with reference to the State and the national Church. The Pilgrims, on the other hand, had a decade of experience in Holland cultivating their ecclesiology from the "outside," independent of any over-arching national structure. This experience operating as what Worthley terms a "sect" prepared the Pilgrims well, in turn, to establish and govern their congregations in the "free aire" of the new world; a familiarity the Puritans lacked when disembarking in Massachusetts Bay, their initial opportunity to execute their congregational convictions.[59] Thus it is conceivable that Puritan claims to have gained a pre-departure clarity in their ecclesial theory can be taken at face value while reserving a significant role for Plymouth's presence. The primary support Plymouth provided, in this light, was the welcomed relief of confirmation of Salem's own congregational "statutes" from men experienced in these matters.

"We commend our necessities to your Christian consideration"
A second appeal to Boston, this time from 1642, forms a more recognizable parallel. In the Fall of that year, Philip Bennett arrived with an petition from some seventy-four Puritans from "the upper new farms in Virginia."[60] As Winthrop recorded it in his *Journal*, the letter Bennett carried both "bewail[ed] their sad condition for want of the means of salvation" and "earnestly entreat[ed] a supply of faithful ministers" from Boston who the Virginia churches might call to office.[61] Three new churches were being gathered, each of which promised to maintain the pastors recommended by Winthrop as well as to "willingly receive them, subjecting ourselves to their teaching in discipline."[62] Though this request was born out of great need, Virginia's Puritans made it clear that Boston's recommendation needed to be made with care. The congregations in Upper Norfolk were acquainted both with the prerogative of the saints to call their own pastors as well as the vital importance of "pureness of doctrine and integrity of life"

---

[58] Harold Field Worthley, "Doctrinal Divisions in the Church of Christ at Plymouth, 1744–1801," in L.D. Geller ed., *They Knew They Were Pilgrims: Essays in Plymouth History* (New York: Poseidon Books, 1971), 102–103.

[59] John Robinson recognized the significance of the Pilgrim's sect-like experience at self-government. He prophesied, "there will be no difference between unconformable ministers and you when they come to the practice of the ordinances out of the Kingdom" (Quoted in Willison, *Saints and Strangers*, 272).

[60] The best history of the southern Puritans is Babette Levy, "Early Puritanism in the Southern and Island Colonies," *American Antiquarian Society Proceedings* 70 (1960): 69–348.

[61] James Kendall Hosmer, ed., *Winthrop's Journal "History of New England" 1630–1649* (New York: Charles Scribner's Sons, 1908), 2:94–95.

[62] Discovered copied into Henry Dunster's notebook, the two letters that comprise the appeal are printed in Jon Butler, "Two 1642 Letters from Virginia Puritans," *Proceedings of the Massachusetts Historical Society* 84 (1972): 99–109. The quote is found on pages 105–106.

for an effective ministry. To that end, being recommended by a Massachusetts minister was important but insufficient. While the Virginians remained "well persuaded of your sincere affection to Christ's truth, and of your holy walking in the order of the gospel," they could not "rest on man's person or doctrine further than his preaching and government shall be approved by the word of God."[63] When, as all anticipated, the ministers Boston dispatched gave satisfaction to their congregations, they would be called to office, "upon experience of their gifts and godliness."[64]

In Jon Butler's analysis of this appeal, Virginia's "request did not mean that they were dependent on New England for spiritual vitality."[65] It was true that, given circumstances beyond their control, they found themselves in need of assistance from a colony well provisioned with "spiritual necessities." But it was also true that, even as beggars, they intended to retain their rights as choosers, subjecting all assistance Boston might provide to the litmus test of God's word. Only once this biblical "tryal" had been satisfactorily passed would they joyfully submit to an authoritative ministry. Salem's solicitation of and satisfaction with conceptions of church government recommended by Plymouth thirteen years prior echoes this dynamic in Virginia's request. The echo is apparent in Edward Winslow's description of the satisfaction Plymouth was able to provide the Salem Puritans. Often accused of making a distinction without a difference, Winslow's apology takes on a more measured meaning when read against the Virginians' letter:

> Tis falsely said [the Salem Puritans] took Plymouth for their precedent as fast as they came; 'tis true, I confess, that some of the chief of them advised with us…how they should do to fall upon a right platform of worship, and desired to that end, since God had honored us to lay the foundation of a Commonwealth and to settle a church in it, to show them whereupon our practice was grounded…We accordingly showed them the primitive practice for our warrant, taken out of the Acts of the Apostles and the Epistles… Which being by them well weighed and considered, they also entered into covenant with God and one another…So that here thou mayest see they set not the church at Plymouth before them for example, but the primitive churches were and are their and our mutual patterns and examples…a pattern fit to be followed of all that fear God.[66]

---

[63] Butler, "Two Letters," 105.

[64] Hosmer, ed., *Winthrop's Journal*, 2:73.

[65] Butler, "Two Letters," 101.

[66] Winslow, *Hypocrisy Unmasked*, 92.

Conclusion

This chapter has reflected on the ecclesial legacy of the Pilgrim fathers from the perspective of the four-hundredth anniversary of their arrival in the new world. As evident from the imagery of William Bradford's writings, these men and women ventured the hazards of their trans-Atlantic voyage and the labors of planting a colony on inhospitable shores with a vision turned prayerfully toward the future. They aimed not only to create a place their children could worship in the freedom of biblical obedience, but also conceived of their role as laying a foundation—stepping-stones—for the Englishmen who would come after them. By 1640, as their countrymen did indeed arrive, developments up north in Massachusetts and back home in England had the effect of marginalizing the efforts of the Plymouth colony. But this was not before their path-breaking service had strengthened the fledgling Puritan enterprise first at Salem, then at Boston, and from there throughout New England. Locating the evidence of this influence within the framework of its broader colonial context highlights the fact that it was the remarkable fact of the presence of New Plymouth as a viable colony and, to a lesser extent, the particulars of their congregational practice, that confirmed and encouraged the ecclesial development of those very Bay Puritans whose city would rise on their foundation.

A.S. Burbank's representation of William Brewster in A.C.
Addison, *The Romantic Story of the Mayflower Pilgrims
and its Place in the Life of To-day*
(Boston: L.C, Page & Co., 1911), 45.

CHAPTER NINE

"Such Like Weighty Employments": A Vindication of Elder William Brewster's Quest for Religious Liberty

ANDREW S. BALLITCH

Late in 1607, the Pilgrims determined to flee England and seek safe haven in Holland. They were a Separatist congregation and had endured the suffering of persecution to such an extent that they were willing to leave their homes, jobs, friends, and family in order to worship God according to their consciences. It being illegal to leave the country without official permission, the Pilgrims secretly hired a ship at an exorbitant rate to take them from Boston in Lincolnshire to Amsterdam. When they had loaded all their belongings by night and boarded themselves, the captain betrayed them by notifying the authorities. Trapped on the boat, they waited until officers dragged them onto lifeboats and pilfered them. Stripping off layers of clothing in search for money and ransacking their belongings, the agents then presented them to the local magistrates and sent word to the royal authorities. After a month imprisonment, most were released. Seven remained, including William Brewster (c.1566–1644), and awaited judgment and sentencing from the higher court, after which they were dismissed. More acutely aware of persecution and the impossibility of staying in England, Brewster and the other leaders went back to their people to devise a second plan of escape, which would turn out to be an only semi-successful attempt at leaving from Hull the following Spring.[1]

Introduction
Brewster shepherded the Mayflower Pilgrims for the first ten years of the congregation's existence in the New World, the only ruling elder accompanying them from the mother church in Leiden. He faithfully preached twice each Lord's Day and cared for the people through the travails of establishing the fledgling colony, though he never officially became the pastor. Frustratingly, no sermons and few letters have survived, making a traditional biography difficult and an evaluation of his motivations from his own perspective impossible.[2] But a narrative does exist in William Bradford's *Of Plymouth Plantation* and a smattering of other details have been unearthed, both of which point to liberty of conscience as the overwhelmingly chief impulse behind Brewster's repeated emigrations.

Recent scholarship analysing Brewster's origins, education, diplomatic experiences, and wording of the Mayflower Compact suggests the picture is not quite so clear. Rather, secular ideas were also influencing Brewster and the Pilgrim project. He and his brethren fled from social ills, out of frustration with upward mobility, and out of a sense of adventurous heroism, this deemphasising the pursuit of religious freedom.[3] While surely complex and multifaceted, there are no compelling reasons to question Bradford's recounting, which focuses persistently on freedom of religion as the motivator of the Separatists and their spiritual leader. They fled England for the Netherlands as persecution intensified. Brewster's publishing of nonconformist books made him an eager candidate for the *Mayflower*. And he devoted himself to religion once in New Plymouth. In a day when religious liberty in general, and Christian liberty in particular, is under attack, the place and privilege of this human right in the story of America's founding needs to shine every bit as bright as it does in the primary source documents.

A Pilgrim in the Making
Being born to William and Mary Brewster brought with it the advantage of some means for the younger William. His father served as Bailiff and Receiver for the Archbishop of York at Scrooby in Nottinghamshire. The responsibilities of

---

[1] William Bradford, *History of Plymouth Plantation, 1620-1647* (Boston: Houghton Mifflin Company for The Massachusetts Historical Society, 1912), 1:28-31.

[2] For biographies that focus on Brewster's historical context and experience as one of the Mayflower Pilgrims, see Ashbel Steele, *Chief of the Pilgrims, or, The Life and Time of William Brewster* (Philadelphia: J.B. Lippincott, 1857); Dorothy Brewster, *William Brewster of the Mayflower: Portrait of a Pilgrim* (New York: New York University Press, 1970); Mary B. Sherwood, *Pilgrim: A Biography of William Brewster* (Falls Church, VA: Great Oak Press of Virginia, 1982); Harold Kirk-Smith, *William Brewster:The Father of New England* (Boston: Richard Kay, 1992); Sue Allan, *William Brewster: The Making of a Pilgrim* (Burgess Hill, West Sussex: Domtom Publishing Ltd, 2016).

[3] For the preeminent example of this argumentation, see Nick Bunker, *Making Haste from Babylon: The Mayflower Pilgrims and Their World* (New York: Alfred A. Knopf, 2010), 125-144.

Bailiff included occupying and tending to the manor estate and arbitrating local disputes, thus maintaining legal and social order. As Receiver, Brewster senior would have collected rents and payments in the Archbishop's stead.[4] He later added to his status the position of Master of the Queen's Post at Scrooby, which included ensuring timely and safe mail transit between Scrooby and Tuxford to the South and Scrooby and Doncaster to the North.[5] These positions afforded the young William the opportunity of an education, first at grammar school, then at Cambridge University.

Brewster matriculated to Peterhouse College, Cambridge in 1580 as a "pensioner," one able to pay his own fees and devote himself exclusively to study. Cambridge was a hotbed of Puritanism in the 1580s, even of the radical sort. Thomas Cartwright's Presbyterian ideas were fomenting and Brewster's time at Cambridge actually overlapped with Robert Browne, after which later Separatists were labeled "Brownists." His tenure also coincided with John Henry, the father of Welsh non-conformity, and John Greenwood and Francis Johnson, who were instrumental in the founding and perpetuation of the Separatist congregation known as the Ancient Church. In 1593, Greenwood would give his life at the gallows for his involvement and Johnson would lead the Ancient Church to Amsterdam, where he unknowingly awaited a reunion with Brewster, who came with the Pilgrim Church fifteen years later.[6] These ideas, acquaintances, and relationships at Cambridge are what Bradford refers to as Brewster being "first seasoned with the seeds of grace and virtue."[7] But Brewster would not finish his degree. After roughly two to three years of study, an opportunity too good not to pursue presented itself.

Brewster came into the employ of William Davison, a career diplomat, and accompanied him to represent the Queen's interests in the Netherlands.[8] The context was war between the Protestant United Provinces and Roman Catholic Spain. Davison was a non-conformist in league with the Presbyterians John Field, Walter Travers, and Thomas Cartwright, and he treated Brewster as a son, a close confidant, and friend.[9] This close relationship turned out to be reciprocal when Davison fell out of favor with Queen Elizabeth. After his service in the Low Countries, Davison, in 1586, was appointed Secretary of State, making him part of

---

[4] Allan, *William Brewster*, 35.

[5] Kirk-Smith, *William Brewster*, 51.

[6] Allan, *William Brewster*, 76–77; Kirk-Smith, *William Brewster*, 28.

[7] Bradford, *Plymouth Plantation*, 2:343.

[8] For family connections that likely afforded Brewster his position, see Bunker, *Making Haste from Babylon*, 138.

[9] Allan, *William Brewster*, 93; Bunker, *Making Haste from Babylon*, 140; Bradford, *Plymouth Plantation*, 343–344.

the Queen's Privy Council. The prestigious position did not last long. Elizabeth used him as a scapegoat, relieving pressure from herself and assuaging her own conscience after the execution of her cousin, Mary Queen of Scots in 1587. As Davison languished in the Tower of London, Brewster coordinated his personal and business affairs. Bradford tells us he "remained with him till his troubles, that he was put from his place aboute the death of the Queene of Scots; and some good time after, doeing him manie faithfull offices of servise in the time of his troubles."[10] It is beyond probable, that during his time with Davison in London, Brewster worshipped with his non-conformist master, as he had done in the Netherlands, together with other non-conformists in the capital.[11]

Davison was released in 1588, about the same time Brewster returned to Scrooby, to take over his ailing father's position as Master of the Queen's Post and settle his affairs. The transition was realized in 1590, and thus Brewster settled down in his hometown, wedding Mary and naming their children Patience, Fear, Love, and Wrestling, a clear advertisement of the family's Puritan piety. In 1598, the Brewsters, along with several other families, were reported by their parish churchwarden for attending other churches. Absenteeism, traveling elsewhere for godly preaching, was a hallmark of Puritanism. Brewster was also accused of illegally repeating sermons in the Scrooby church. The dissenters evaded severe punishment, but it was the mix of such non-nonconformist laity with several deposed ministers that created the Separatist churches that would flee England in response to religious persecution.[12]

Emigration to Holland
It was Gainsborough, Lincolnshire that saw the formation of the Separatist mother church of Brewster's Scrooby congregation, about twelve miles to the East. John Smyth, who served for a time as fellow at Christ's College, Cambridge and then as a contentious nonconformist preacher landed in Gainsborough. John Robinson, who also served as a fellow at Cambridge, but at Corpus Christi College, and later nonconformist pastor in Norwich, returned to the Nottinghamshire region where he was from. While Smyth and Robinson illegally preached, Richard Clyfton, another non-conformist pastor in Nottinghamshire lost his parish in 1605 for refusing to wear the surplice, something he had refused for fifteen years. These leaders and others, Bradford retells,

> joyned them selves (by a covenant of the Lord) into a church estate, in the felowship of the Gospell, to walke in all his wayes, made known, or to be made

---

[10] Bradford, *Plymouth Plantation*, 2:345.

[11] Allan, *William Brewster*, 107–108.

[12] John G. Turner, *They Knew They Were Pilgrims: Plymouth Colony and the Contest for American Liberty* (New Haven: Yale University Press, 2020), 20–21.

known unto them (according to their best endea[v]ours) whatsoever it should cost them, the Lord assisting them.¹³

In this covenant they declared themselves free from ecclesiastical tyranny and human corruption in worship and bound to one another.¹⁴

Bradford goes on to say, "these people became 2 distincte bodys or churches," one pastored by Smyth with the patronage of Thomas Helwys in Gainsborough and the other in Scrooby, pastored by Clyfton with Brewster as patron.¹⁵ It was Clyfton who introduced Brewster to the young Bradford, who became like an adopted son. Shortly after this second church was established, Robinson, the future pastor, came and joined as Clyfton's assistant. The Scrooby congregation ironically gathered at the manor house owned by the Archbishop of York, for whom Brewster likely served as Bailiff and Receiver as his father before him. When Tobie Matthew succeeded Matthew Hutton as Archbishop in 1606, peacefully meeting underground without notice became largely impossible and life became more difficult.¹⁶

The Archbishop successfully pressured one of the region's Separatist ministers, Richard Bernard, to recant and be restored to the Church of England. He then preached a sermon entitled "Contra Brownists" in the village of Bawtry, very near to Scrooby.¹⁷ The Pilgrims knew they were marked. From Bradford's perspective,

> They could not long continue in any peaceable condition; but were hunted and persecuted on every side, so as their former afflictions were but as flea-bitings in comparison of these which now came upon them. For some were taken and clapt up in prison, others had their houses besett and watcht night and day, and hardly escaped their hands; and the most were faine to flie and leave their howses and habitations, and the means of their livelehood.¹⁸

The ensuing persecution was both real and perceived, but Bradford was not exaggerating. The Pilgrims were on the radical fringe of Puritanism, but the

---

¹³ Bradford, *Plymouth Plantation*, 1:22.

¹⁴ Turner, *They Knew They Were Pilgrims*, 21–23. See also Kirk-Smith, *William Brewster*, 67–71.

¹⁵ Bradford, *Plymouth Plantation*, 1:22.

¹⁶ Kirk-Smith, *William Brewster*, 73–79.

¹⁷ Turner, *They Knew They Were Pilgrims*, 23.

¹⁸ Bradford, *Plymouth Plantation*, 1:24–25. "Their former afflictions," is a reference to the struggle Bradford describes during their non-conformity, before separating from the established church (Bradford, *Plymouth Plantation*, 16–18).

nonconformist community as a whole experienced the persecution together.[19]

As for Brewster, after the failed attempt at leaving the country from Boston, the experience of Archbishop Matthew's crackdown continued. Brewster failed to appear at the Court of High Commission twice, incurring a twenty-pound fine in each instance. Other members of the two congregations were fined as well, and even imprisoned.[20] With Matthew's ire showing no sign of abating, Brewster and his fellows hatched a second plot for escape. This time plans were frustrated not by betrayal, but by timing and circumstance.

The women, children, and belongings arrived at the rendezvous outside of Hull by boat, a day before the Dutch ship arrived, the men making their way by land. The sea was rough, so the boat carrying the women and children tucked up into a creek for the night, and when the tide receded, they were stuck in the mire. When the hired ship arrived, the captain assessed the situation and sent a lifeboat to start ferrying the men from shore. After one boatload made it to the ship, the captain spied, "a greate company (both horse, and foote) with bills, and gunes, and other weapons (for the countrie was raised to take them)," and pulled anchor and hoisted the sails.[21] The men on board watched helplessly as their brothers, who were in the greatest danger, fled and their families were surrounded. After a hazardous voyage, those on the ship arrived in Amsterdam, and eventually the group left behind were released and slowly made their way to Holland after them. Brewster and his fellow Pilgrims fled England for religious liberty.[22]

Emigration to the New World

The Pilgrim congregation only briefly settled in Amsterdam before removing to Leiden in an effort to avoid being drawn into the controversies surrounding the Ancient Church and the Smyth's slide to Baptist convictions and eventually the Anabaptist fold. Robinson became pastor and Brewster was elected to be a lay elder.[23] In Leiden, the church adjusted to a new culture and the challenge of providing for themselves. Brewster eventually began comfortably taking care of his family as a much-loved tutor of English at the University of Leiden. However, it was his part in the publishing collaboration that has come to be known as the

---

[19] Turner asserts that the Scrooby and Gainsborough Separatists did not suffer the persecution described by Bradford (Turner, *They Knew They Were Pilgrims*, 24). For analysis of Puritan networks and communal experience, see Tom Webster, *Godly Clergy in Early Stuart England: The Caroline Puritan Movement, c.1620–1643* (Cambridge: Cambridge University Press, 1997).

[20] Turner, *They Knew They Were Pilgrims*, 25.

[21] Bradford, *Plymouth Plantation*, 1:32.

[22] Bradford, *Plymouth Plantation*, 1:33–34.

[23] Turner, *They Knew They Were Pilgrims*, 28–31. Brewster served as Robinson's assistant before becoming an elder (Martyn J. Whittock, *Mayflower Lives: Pilgrims in a New World and the Early American Experience* [New York: Pegasus Books, 2019], 164).

Pilgrim Press that got him in trouble and served as a catalyst for his transition to America.

The Pilgrim Press operated as a joint venture for three years, from 1617 to 1619. Thomas Brewer was the financial sponsor; John Reynolds was the printer by trade, with Edward Winslow as his assistant printer, and Brewster was the apprentice. These roles had to be assumed on paper due to the regulations of the guild system in Leiden, but Brewster was the senior member of the team and unofficially served as the manager of the enterprise.[24] The press was in his house, making his home the base of operations. The Pilgrim Press existed to advance the cause of pure Christianity by printing materials that would be smuggled into England. Eighteen books are known to have been published, with three bearing Brewster's name. Two titles, especially, would turn the memories of persecution into a reality again.[25]

The two books that caused the English government to start a manhunt for Brewster were *De Regimine Ecclesiae Scotticanae* and *Perth Assembly*, both anonymously by David Calderwood. Together they were an intense and pointed attack on King James's plan to impose episcopacy on the Presbyterian Church of Scotland. In short, Calderwood heralded James as a political and ecclesiastical tyrant. *Perth Assembly* was smuggled into England, without author or publisher information, and read eagerly and widely. James, infuriated, intensified the search for Calderwood, who had already made his way to Leiden and was worshipping with the Pilgrim congregation. The English ambassador Dudley Carleton learned of the Pilgrim Press's involvement and leaned on Dutch authorities to arrest and extradite the perpetrators. Committed to a level of religious freedom, Leiden officials let Brewster get away, while seizing the type, books, and papers from the press to appease England. Brewster existed as a fugitive for his remaining days in Europe.[26]

During all of this, the Pilgrim church explored the colony of Virginia as a second option to Leiden. Brewster had his personal reasons for putting the Atlantic Ocean between he and James, but many of the other church members were eager to leave as well. There were a number of reasons for this. For one thing, the Synod of Dordt and the following stern measures against the Remonstrants made it clear that religious liberty in the Netherlands was no guarantee. For another, the twelve-year truce negotiated between Spain and the United Provinces was expiring, so peace was not certain. But even more significant was the fact that their

---

[24] Rendel Harris, Stephen K. Jones, and Daniel Plooij, *The Pilgrim Press: A Bibliographical & Historical Memorial of the Books Printed at Leyden by the Pilgrim Fathers* (Cambridge: W. Heffer and Sons, 1922), 6–9.

[25] Harris, Jones, and Plooij, *The Pilgrim Press*, 32. While only three works explicitly identify Brewster as the publisher, the other fifteen are virtually undisputed because of the painstaking work done by Harris, Jones, and Plooij.

[26] Kirk-Smith, *William Brewster*, 127–30; Turner, *They Knew They Were Pilgrims*, 42–43.

children were becoming more Dutch than English. So, while their immediate religious liberty may not have been in question, the Pilgrims were confronted with the specter of losing their freedom to perpetuate their religion.[27]

In order to emigrate, two intermingled things were necessary: sponsorship and permission. Brewster and Robinson, as elders of the church, lead the charge for both. If the Virginia Company was going to accommodate their settlement, it had to be convinced that the Pilgrims were not the Separatists that they were. The pastoral team put together a list of seven articles intended to show that the Leiden congregation were Reformed Christians and loyal to the crown, while at the same time obscuring their conviction that the Church of England was not a true church. The first article affirmed the thirty-nine articles, the confession that made the Church of England officially Reformed in doctrine. The second affirmed that both conformists and non-conformists in England were true Christians and that the desire was to keep spiritual communion with them. It would take an astute and informed reader to identify the fact that this did not mean that the Separatists would worship together at church with such sincere Christians. Loyalty to the king in all things not contrary to God's word was the commitment in article three. Articles four, five, and six was where the real work of obfuscation needed to be done. Here the authors affirmed the king's prerogative of appointing bishops and the legitimacy of the office, however, they failed to recognize that bishops have any spiritual authority. The final article simply voiced the Separatists' peaceful intentions.[28]

The seven articles appeased the Virginia Company, but the King's Privy Council, which had to sign off on the whole deal, had some questions. The desired clarifications centered on obedience to the king and, understandably, the Pilgrims' understanding of the ministry. Robinson and Brewster responded by stating their willingness to take the Oath of Supremacy and asserting their conformity with the French Reformed churches, with a few slight differences, which they enumerated. Their identification with the doctrine and practice of the Reformed Churches in France was an effort at legitimatization. The response never would have passed muster, so the Virginia Company buried it, as by then James had already agreed neither to help nor hinder the new settlement in Virginia.[29] This whole episode of seeking permission to go to the New World highlights the fact that the Separatist congregation enjoyed little freedom to express their religious beliefs. When articulating their doctrine and worship practice they had to censor and speak with deliberate lack of clarity. Elder Brewster and his fellow

---

[27] Kirk-Smith, *William Brewster*, 133–135; Michael P. Winship, *Godly Republicanism: Puritans, Pilgrims, and a City on a Hill* (Cambridge, MA: Harvard University Press, 2012), 112; George D. Langdon, *Pilgrim Colony: A History of New Plymouth, 1620–1691* (New Haven: Yale University Press, 1966), 7–8.

[28] Bradford, *Plymouth Plantation*, 1:72. For discussion of the covert nature of the seven articles, see Winship, *Godly Republicanism*, 113–115.

[29] Bradford, *Plymouth Plantation*, 1:78–82; Winship, *Godly Republicanism*, 114–116.

Pilgrims painfully made their way across the Atlantic in pursuit of religious liberty.

The Spiritual Shepherd

The Pilgrims who set sail on the *Mayflower* were not the whole of the Leiden church. In fact, the majority stayed back with pastor Robinson, with the minority who would found New Plymouth sent out under the spiritual leadership of Elder Brewster.[30] The ensuing events are familiar and well documented, events such as the circumstances surrounding the Mayflower Compact, the brutal first winter, early meetings with the natives, and the struggle for survival that marked the early years of the colony. Brewster was in the thick of all of it. He likely wrote the Mayflower Compact, and was one of a handful that physically took care of the rest of the sick colonists that first winter, was part of the leadership who first interacted with the indigenous peoples, and he farmed and labored alongside everyone else in order to cling to survival.[31] Bradford's account transitions from a history of the Pilgrim church to a history of the Pilgrim colony after 1620, yet the church remains central and the spiritual leadership of Brewster is highlighted again and again.

Brewster and his fellow Pilgrims left Leiden as "an absolute church of themselves," by "mutuall consente and covenante."[32] Because the journey was treacherous and settlement no guarantee, they divided fully aware that they may not be reunited. The hope was that Robinson and the others would join as soon as possible (a hope that never materialized) at which point the two congregations would automatically be reunited as one church. Sunday and Thursday services, regulating worship, maintaining Separatist theological fidelity, and enforcing discipline all fell to Brewster as his primary responsibilities, and ended up remaining his for almost ten years.

Brewster was a gifted preacher and teacher. His sermons were full of content and well-delivered. He devoted himself to study, on top of doing his part in stabilizing the struggling colony, which, coupled with his long experience, produced

---

[30] Brewster sailed with his wife Mary, children Love and Wrestling, and two other children in their custody, Richard and Mary Moore. Their children Patience, Fear, and Jonathan would join them later (Caleb H. Johnson, *The Mayflower and Her Passengers* [Philadelphia: Xlibris, 2006], 91).

[31] Brewster was the only one on the *Mayflower* to have received university training. This coupled with his diplomatic experience makes it almost certain that he largely formulated and wrote the Mayflower Compact. Bunker assumes this and uses it to advance his thesis downplaying the role of religious liberty as a reason for Brewster and the Pilgrims to emigrate. He notes that it is a republican document, with government at the consent of the governed. Also, that it did not insist on a religious creed or require sectarian faith. He asserts that "it contained not a single phrase with a specifically Puritan meaning or source" (Bunker, *Making Haste*, 286). To whatever extent the Mayflower Compact is a republican document, something debated by scholars, the Separatist, congregational ecclesiology of Brewster should be included in discussions of its development. For the full discussion, see Bunker, *Making Haste*, 283–286. For a more compelling exposition, see Turner, *They Knew They Were Pilgrims*, 57–60.

[32] Bradford, *Plymouth Plantation*, 1:98.

powerful and profitable preaching, such that there were many converts from his ministry. He was known as a man of prayer, gifted in prayer in fact. He thought it better to pray more frequently in worship and keep the prayers short, a practice apparently appreciated by congregants used to characteristically long and dense Puritan prayers. His character, personality, and pastoral wisdom were such that he was loved by both those inside and outside the church, and people responded well to his attempts to maintain discipline. When a member of the church caused disunity or strayed theologically or morally, it would have been Brewster who did the initial interviewing. It would only be in cases of failure to reach resolution at this initial step that the matter would be considered by the whole church. One significant disadvantage, however, to Brewster not being an ordained minister, was that the congregation was deprived of the sacraments.[33]

Until an ordained minister came to Plymouth, the Pilgrims were unable to baptize their children or celebrate communion, problems both acutely felt and urgent. Brewster wrote and asked Robinson whether he could go ahead and administer the sacraments as a ruling elder. Robinson's letter of reply, dated 1623, said:

> I judg it not lawfull for you, being a ruling Elder, as Rom. 12. 7. 8. and I. Tim. 5.17. opposed to the Elders that teach and exhorte and labore in the word and doctrine, to which the sacraments are annexed, to administer them, nor convenient if it were lawfull. Whether any larned man will come unto you or not, I know not; if any doe, you must *Consilium capere in arena*.[34]

It would seem that the issue barring Brewster from becoming the minister of the Pilgrim church was a lack of learning, perhaps a reference to his incomplete degree from Cambridge. This would make sense of why he "would never be perswaded to take higher office upon him," as there was certainly no deficiency in either his ability or character.[35] Robinson's Latin exhortation for when a qualified pastor arrived was to, like gladiators, "make their plans in the arena."[36] That is precisely what Brewster led the church to do when John Lyford was sent.

Lyford arrived as a potential pastor in 1624. He was a Puritan, not a Separatist, but was met with a warm welcome. He joined the church and became a lay preacher alongside Brewster as a kind of trial period. During this period Governor Bradford intercepted a number of letters from Lyford back to England, slandering the Pilgrims as wanting to take over the colony for themselves with no place for non-church members and advising that Robinson and the rest of the

---

[33] Bradford, *Plymouth Plantation*, 2:348–351; Kirk-Smith, *William Brewster*, 217–218.

[34] Bradford, *Plymouth Plantation*, 1:371.

[35] Bradford, *Plymouth Plantation*, 1:403.

[36] Winship, *Godly Republicanism*, 286 n. 27.

Leiden church be barred from coming, advising instead that likeminded immigrants seeking reform of church and commonwealth be sent. Bradford kept the correspondence close to the chest until Lyford and his faction met by themselves for worship and celebrated the sacraments. The whole colony was summoned as a tribunal and Lyford banished. What he had done was in direct contradiction to Brewster's Separatist convictions and teaching.[37]

And so Brewster continued in his role of primary spiritual leadership until finally, in 1629, Ralph Smith arrived and became pastor, reinstituting the sacraments among the Pilgrims until his departure in 1636. Roger Williams came as his associate for three years starting in 1631. He was dismissed because of his more extreme separatism. Brewster warned of his critical spirit, in his vocal condemnation of the practice of Separatists attending a Church of England service.[38] Brewster stood in the gap between Smith and John Rayner, who became pastor in 1637 and brought stability with a tenure of eighteen years. During all of the turnover, Brewster served faithfully as an elder until his death in 1644.

Bradford recounts Brewster dying peacefully in his bed, surrounded by those he loved, after a very short sickness. He remained conscious and able to speak almost to the very end, offering comfort to others. In discussing Brewster's passing, Bradford describes him as

> My dear and loving friend … a man that had done and suffered much for the Lord Jesus and the gospells sake, and had bore his parte in well and woe with this poore persecuted church above 36 years in England, Holand, and in this wilderness, and done the Lord and them faithful service in his place and calling.[39]

After arrival in America, the faithful Elder devoted himself to helping his fellow Pilgrims properly exercise the religious freedom for which they had traveled so far.

Conclusion

William Brewster's journey to Plymouth was motivated by a pursuit for religious liberty. William Bradford, his close friend and confidant, like an adopted son to him, is clear in his account. Brewster and the Scrooby church experienced increased persecution for their religious convictions and practices. It became untenable for him to worship according to his conscience and remain in England. Therefore, he made his way with the others, in great danger and at great cost, to

---

[37] Bradford, *Plymouth Plantation*, 1:380–396. For an exposition and interpretation of the whole affair, see Winship, *Godly Republicanism*, 123–133.

[38] Turner, *They Knew They Were Pilgrims*, 149.

[39] Bradford, *Plymouth Plantation*, 2:342.

the Netherlands. In Leiden he officially became an elder in the Separatist congregation led by Robinson and during the last few years there operated a clandestine printing press to make some of their religious sympathies public in England. This brought the fury of King James, and with a warrant out for his arrest and English authorities actively searching for him, he again, in great danger and at great cost, fled, this time permanently to the New World. Despite the struggle for survival and all of the work to be done in stabilizing the colony, Brewster from the start devoted himself to the spiritual care of the Pilgrims. He was the solo leader for almost ten years and the spiritual patriarch of the church until his death, aiding the congregation in the exercise of their religion in freedom.

These considerations are hard to reconcile with claims that his motivation for his repeated emigrations was a "blended ideology, an amalgam between religious beliefs and secular concepts of virtue, gentility, and heroism."[40] That is not the portrait painted by Bradford. Human motivations are complex to be sure, and it would be historically naïve to argue that Brewster's reason for leaving his home in England and then in Holland was purely religious liberty. But the idea that the impetus for Brewster's coming to America was that "life in Nottinghamshire was unheroic, and unholy" and "contained barriers to advancement," is an inference, whereas Bradford's account highlighting a continued search for religious freedom in response to persecution is explicit.[41]

Transposing a twenty-first century American concept of religious liberty into the minds and desires of Brewster and the Pilgrims would be anachronistic. This is clear from the systems they put into place. Magistrates did not force individuals to attend worship, join churches, or have their children baptized. At the same time, public airing of dissenting opinions and gathering for alternative religious practices was not allowed. Plymouth colony taxed all of its inhabitants to build churches and pay ministers. It was later in the colony's history that Quakers and Baptists received toleration, but they were not exempt from the tax supporting the established church.[42] There was no separation of church and state and the Pilgrims essentially fled persecution to turn around and persecute others for their alternative religious convictions. So what kind of freedom were these Separatists after?

Perhaps a more helpful category is Christian liberty. The Pilgrims saw ecclesiastical republicanism as the New Testament order, which led to the total rejection of the Church of England. They rejected the Church of England in order to have the freedom to form their own church and select their own officers. The Pilgrim Separatists came to America to preserve this freedom to worship God according to their understanding of Scripture. Christian liberty mandated

---

[40] Bunker, *Making Haste from Babylon*, 126.

[41] Bunker, *Making Haste from Babylon*, 127.

[42] Turner, *They Knew They Were Pilgrims*, 4.

ecclesiastical polity and precise forms of worship. It demanded religious uniformity at a minimum, if not compelled religion and even religious persecution.[43] The Pilgrim project was not to impose the colony's will on others, but those who wished to share in its privileges were expected to submit to certain restrictions.[44] However, the desire for freedom for religious uniformity planted seeds for a society of religious pluralism, true religious liberty.

The freedom to worship according to conscience, and to express religious convictions outside of the church, through vocation and in the public square, was precisely why Elder Brewster and his fellow Pilgrims came to America. The freedom that Americans enjoy today to do the same is precious and must be preserved if America is going to continue as America. Americans cherish religious liberty, yet public discourse reveals some of the same tension observed in the Pilgrim colonial experiment: Who is entitled to constitutional rights? Is religious liberty simply license to discriminate?[45] The free exercise of religion has been restricted in recent years, and the walls are closing in at an accelerating pace. The new orthodoxy of identity politics is a powerful agent of shame and the judicial branch of government defies the separation of powers enshrined in the constitution by legislating. Neither bode well for true religious freedom, together they are lethal. Americans should appreciate the founding fathers and mothers in Plymouth colony, but they ought to value above all the religious liberty accomplished since and refuse to return to a secular aberration of the Christian liberty that once was.

---

[43] Turner, *They Knew They Were Pilgrims*, 4–5.

[44] Kirk-Smith, *William Brewster*, 241–242.

[45] Turner, *They Knew They Were Pilgrims*, 6.

"The March of Miles Standish"
by George Henry Boughton.
(New York Public Library Digital Collections)

CHAPTER TEN

The Pilgrim Fathers: The First Critical Years

ROLAND BURROWS

After more than sixty days at sea after leaving Southampton, and four months after leaving Delfshaven, Holland the Pilgrims caught their first sight of land, the Highlands of Cape Cod. The Pilgrims' first intention appears to have been to settle near the mouth of the Hudson River, and Captain Christopher Jones turned his vessel southwards to run down the two hundred and fifty miles or so to their intended destination. After sailing for about seven hours they suddenly fell among dangerous shoals and roaring breakers and the captain rightly perceive the ship to be in great danger. Conscious that he was not only without a chart of these waters, and his passengers were now exhausted and in a sickly state, he put the helm of the ship hard over onto the starboard tack and sailed East North-east out again into the open Atlantic, where they spent the night. The next day the *Mayflower* continued northbound passing the curved tip of Cape Cod and entering into Providence Town Harbour; the date November 11, 1620, ended their sixty-five-day passage.[1]

The Pilgrims had in fact no charter for this piece of land and as far as they were concerned no charter had been drawn up for it. Some of the 58 non-pilgrim

---

[1] For many years an idea has circulated that Captain Jones had secretly, prior to the voyage, made an agreement with the Dutch who had set their sights on a settlement at the Hudson River, to keep the Pilgrims clear of this place, see Alexander Young, *Chronicles of the Pilgrim Fathers* (London: Dent & Sons, 1920), 20. This accusation however can be doubted, as Sir Dudley Carleton's report to the Privy Council on February 5, 1622 specifically denies any such plot and it would seem hardly likely that, as England's ambassador in the Hague, he was not in a position to make the necessary enquiries. See Vernon Heaton, *The Mayflower* (Exeter: Webb & Bower, 1980), 95.

passengers on the *Mayflower* expressed the belief that when they landed they would be free to do as they liked, as in this place there was no recurrence to English law. The Pilgrim leaders aware of this therefore drew up what came to be known as, the Mayflower Compact and before the ship landed all were required to sign it.

What is of special note in regard to this contract is that it established government by consent at a time when England's liberties were still conditioned by the remnants of feudalism. Some have gone so far as to describe it as the cornerstone of American democracy, though it was the case that equal votes and rights for all were still some way off. The Compact certainly laid down a solid foundation for local self-government, and the words of John Quincy Adams, who rediscovered the Compact in 1802, are most certainly valid. "It was," he remarked, "the first example in modern times of a social compact system of government instituted by voluntary agreement conformably to the laws of nature, by men of equal rights and about to establish their community in a new country."[2]

After the signing of the document, they elected John Carver to be their first Governor, and this too was highly significant—John Carver held no church office. This meant that they had separated Church and State. It became the norm from that time onward that no church officer hold a political post and no political officer, for example the Governor, was an officer of the church.

Although the Pilgrims had no legal right to occupy this stretch of land in New England, Brewster would have been aware of a resolution or order by the Virginia Company to the effect that the leaders of any plantation could form an association to make orders and ordinances, etc., until a form of government had been settled. Unknown to the Pilgrims, the Plymouth Council for New England had drawn up a charter during the time of the *Mayflower's* voyage. Though the Pilgrims began their settlement without a charter they were nevertheless within their rights of association to make orders and ordinances, etc., "until a form of government had been settled."[3] When the merchant adventurers at home heard about this they accepted the situation quite blandly.[4] An official charter for the colony of New Plymouth was granted to William Bradford and his associates in 1629.

Conditions on Landing

The *New England Chronicle* makes this comment on the condition of the territory they were about to occupy:

> Many attempts have been made to settle this rough and northern country;

---

[2] Francis Dillon, *A Place for Habitation* (London: Hutchinson, 1973), 142.

[3] Dillon, *A Place for Habitation*, 141,

[4] Dillon, *A Place for Habitation*, 135.

first by the French, who would fain account it part of Canada, and then by the English, and both from mere secular views. But such a train of crosses accompanied the designs of both these nations, that they seemed to give it over as not worth the planting, till a pious people of England, not allowed to worship their Maker according to his institutions only, without the mixture of human ceremonies are spirited to attempt the settlement, that here they might enjoy a worship purely scriptural and leave the same to their posterity.[5]

Their first impression of Cape Cod Harbour was that it could easily hold "1000 ships" and that it was protected on every side except in the North. Not only did it provide much needed protection from the open sea but there was also a plentiful supply of fresh food in the form of shellfish; moreover, ducks, geese, and other foul were available in abundance. To the amazement of the passengers they could see countless whales frolicking in the seas in and around the Cape.

The *Mayflower* arrived at what would become Providence Town Harbour on Saturday, November 11, 1620. As the next day was the Sabbath, the Pilgrims remained on board ship and worshiped God under the direction of their elder, William Brewster.

The following day the ship's shallop (small boat) was taken ashore and reassembled. While this was taking place, some passengers were able to leave the ship. There was what they termed "a great need" for washing, and the women found a small pond suitable for this near to the present site of Providence Town. Here they continued what had been in England and what was to become in the United States of America, a tradition of Monday washing.

As the tide went out, it revealed many barnacles and mussels on the rocks along the shore and ready for eating. This was their first fresh food since the beginning of the voyage; sadly, later many of them fell victim from the vomiting and diarrhea associated with shellfish poisoning.

The First Reconnaissance Expedition
On the Wednesday of the first week, a party of sixteen men was formed to carry out their first reconnaissance of the area. This group was under the direction of Captain Miles Standish, and included William Bradford, Stephen Hopkins (whose previous experience in Virginia it was felt might help them should they encounter any Indians), and Edward Tilley. They set out on foot, each of them equipped with a musket, sword and a light form of body armor that included a metal breastplate.

They made their way southward and not much more than a mile or so down the beach encountered a group of about six native Indians plus a dog. These however, on seeing the Pilgrims, ran for the woods, and although the group were

---

[5] As quoted in Young, *Chronicles of the Pilgrim Fathers*, 22.

anxious to make contact with them they were not seen again.

The next day they discovered what was one of the chief aims of their exploration, that being a spring of fresh water. There they recorded, we "drunk our first New England water with as much delight as ever we drunk drink in all our lives."[6] At this point, from the shore they could see the *Mayflower* anchored just four miles to the north-west across the bay. Here they made camp and lit a fire, partly as a prearranged signal to let their friends on the ship know that all was well.

The next morning, they discovered stubbled fields which they discerned had been planted with corn within the last few years. They also found several native grave mounds. Further on they found some sawn planks and an old iron ship's kettle, which they assumed had come from the French shipwreck of 1615. Moreover, after this, they discovered the mouth of the river that they had seen from the *Mayflower*, after arriving in the bay. This was actually a two-pronged saltwater creek, known today as the Pamet River. Further on they came upon other mounds, which further investigation revealed to be stashes of Indian corn. These they were loath to touch, but the situation of these people was extremely precarious. They were in a survival situation. Their food supplies were dangerously low, they were in the midst of a severe and bitter winter, and many of them were at the point of total exhaustion. Hardly knowing if they could survive for much longer, they took the corn, resolving to make reparation for it at a later date.

That night it rained, and they spent a long-wet night under a hastily constructed barricade of tree trunks and branches. The next morning, they made their way back through the woods, at one point becoming lost, and later William Bradford found himself temporarily snagged by the leg in an Indian deer trap. Eventually they got back to the ship, again in the words William Bradford, "we came weary and welcome home."[7]

The Second Reconnaissance Expedition

Ten days later the carpenters finished putting together the shallop which had been partly dismantled for storage purposes during the voyage and had also suffered damage in the various storms encountered during the crossing. On completion of this work, on Monday, November 27, another expeditionary party set out, this time by sea, under the leadership of Christopher Jones, the master of the *Mayflower*.

This group was made up of thirty-four men including Miles Standish, Carver the Governor, Bradford, Winslow, John and Edward Tilley (the first a silk worker, the second a cloth worker), and John Howland, the goodhearted Christian servant to Carver. Alongside these were the two mariners hired by the

---

[6] H.G. Wood, *Venturers for the Kingdom* (London: Hodder & Stoughton, 1919), 128.

[7] Nathaniel Philbrick, *Mayflower* (New York: Penguin Books, 2006), 65.

Pilgrims, from among the London contingent or "strangers." There was Warren, a merchant, the experienced Hopkins and his quarrelsome servant, Edward Doty. From among the *Mayflower* crew there were two who had been in the New World before, Clark the first mate and Coppin the pilot. The Master Gunner and several more completed the party.[8]

After a night in the boat, the temperature dipping well below freezing, their wet shoes and stockings began to freeze. The sea spray falling on their coats and hats froze immediately and caused them to look as if they had been glazed. "Some of our people that are dead," Bradford later wrote, "took the origin of their death here."[9] It has been pointed out that in 1620, North America was in the midst of what climatologists have called "a little ice age."[10] At this time, they were more than a month away from finding a settled place to live. One of the reasons why they encountered so few Native Americans up until now was that the tribes in this part of the country spent their winters inland and their summers on the seacoast.

The next morning, there was six inches of snow on the ground. They were exploring the region of Pamet Harbour, which is near to the modern town of Truro. At this time, they were so frostbitten that they had no choice but to name the inlet *Cold Harbour*. The river itself turned out to be not so much a river as a swampy tidal estuary and not a suitable place to settle. Again, Indian stashes of corn were found. After several hours marching up and down the steep hills and deep valleys of this region, which were by this time a foot thick with snow, Captain Jones, being fifty years old, returned to the *Mayflower* with the plundered corn and those who were too ill to continue the exploration.

The party was now under the leadership of Miles Standish. Again aboriginal graves were found and though the first expeditionary party had wisely refrained from touching them, one of these was dug up revealing the skull of a man with fine yellow hair still on it, alongside which lay a sailor's knife and sewing needles. It was concluded that these were the remains of a crew member of a French ship that had been wrecked on these shores some years before. When the party eventually returned to the *Mayflower*, it was debated whether or not this location was suitable in which to settle. Some were in favour of settling in this location because there was good fishing opportunity in that area, and they argued if further expeditions were carried out it would mean the possibility of more loss of men through the appalling conditions they were experiencing. Others argued that since the Pamet was not flowing river, and that fresh water would have to come from the nearby pond, therefore this was not a suitable place to settle. It was decided to send out a further expedition party.

---

[8] Dillon, *A Place for Habitation*, 149.

[9] Philbrick, *Mayflower*, 65.

[10] Philbrick, *Mayflower*, 66.

The Third Expedition

At this point Robert Coppin, who had been in New England before, spoke of the navigable river and a good harbour he believed to be at the other side of the Cape. It was decided to send the shallop out once again, with ten of their principal men and some seamen, to investigate the place. The temperature was so low, that two of the men in the shallop fainted with cold.

This party was led by the two ships officers, Robert Coppin and John Clark. These were accompanied by the Master Gunner and three sailors. The Pilgrims were represented by Bradford, Carver, Standish, Winslow, John Tilley and his brother, Edward, John Howland, Richard Warren, Stephen Hopkins, and Hopkin's servant, Edward Doty. This was less than half the number of the previous expedition. Illness and freezing temperatures, now in their low twenties, if not colder was already taking its toll.

On their way they encountered a group of aboriginal people clustered around a black object on the beach, which turned out to be the carcass of a pilot whale, the blubber of which they were cutting up into long strips for food. Again, catching sight of the Pilgrims they melted away into the nearby forests. Later on, this party experienced their first hostile reaction from a group of Indians. Suddenly feathered arrows over a yard long began to descend upon their encampment. The group responded with musket shot, and again their attackers disappeared into the woods. The Pilgrims realised by the strength of this attack that they could not fight or kill their way to a permanent settlement in New England, and it was clear to them that goodwill was to be the difficult but only way to achieve this.

With the wind from the southeast they continued on their journey sailing along the southern edge of Cape Cod Bay. Soon the weather deteriorated. The wind picked up, and with the temperature hovering above freezing, horizontal sleet, and freezing salt spray drenched them to the skin. The waves were running high and it became increasingly difficult to steer the shallop. The strain on the rudder proved unequal to its strength and the pressure wrenched it from its transom. They were in extreme danger, but the two men standing in the stern thrust two long oaken oars into the water and they were able to keep the ship on course and move along the coast. However, this was only a temporal alleviation of their conditions and the tide ran so strongly against them that Coppin cried out, "Lord be merciful unto us, for my eyes never saw this place before!"[11] When all seemed lost, the sailor steering with the oar shouted, "be of good cheer," and exhorted them to row with all their might; for he had spotted a shallow cove into which they could run ashore.[12] This they did and the light of morning, which was a Saturday, revealed that they were on a heavily wooded island. Here, safe from attacks, they could dry out and get some respite. The island was from then

---

[11] Philbrick, *Mayflower*, 74.

[12] Philbrick, *Mayflower*, 74.

known as *Clark's Island*, as John Clark, one of the *Mayflower* pilots, had been the first of their company to set his foot on its shore.

The following day was the Lord's Day and they kept it for rest and worship, as was their practice. On the following Monday morning, they circled the harbour in the shallop and were convinced that it was a safe haven for the ships. In fact, the harbour was large enough to hold a substantial number of moderately sized ships but as they were to discover later there was not enough depth of water to allow a ship drawing as much water as the *Mayflower*, to come within a mile of the shore. However, Plymouth Harbour, as well as being a safe haven had many other advantages. Here again they found various cornfields and little running brooks.

Rising up from the shore was a 165-foot hill that provided a spectacular view of the surrounding coastline. They quickly came to realize that a strong cannon-equipped fort on this hill would provide all the security they could ever hope for.

There was also the presence of the rock, to serve as a landing place. This rock has become known as the famous Plymouth Rock onto which the Pilgrims are believed to have first stepped ashore. Also meeting the bay at this point was a larger brook, a perfect haven for smaller craft. This has since come to be known as *Town Brook*.

The expeditionary party was also surprised to find again no indication of recent aboriginal settlement. Just three years before, even as the Pilgrims were beginning their preparations to settle in America, there had been between one thousand and two thousand people living along these shores. As a map drawn by Samuel Chaplin in 1605 showed, the banks of the harbor had been dotted with wigwams, each with a curling plume of smoke rising from the hole in its roof and with fields of corn, beans, and squash growing nearby. Dugout canoes made from hollowed out pine trees plied the waters, which in summer were choked with bluefish and striped bass. The lobsters were so numerous that the Indians plucked them from the shallows of the harbour. The mud flats were so thick with buried clams that it was impossible to walk across the shore without being drenched by squirting bivalves.

Then from 1616 to 1619, disease brought this centuries-old community to an end. No native dwellings remained in Plymouth in the winter 1620, but gruesome evidence of the epidemic was scattered all around the area. "Their skulls and bones were found in many places lying still above the ground," Bradford wrote, "a very sad spectacle to behold."[13] It was here, on the bone-whitened hills of Plymouth, that the Pilgrims hoped to begin a new life.[14]

After having thoroughly explored the area, the party prepared to return to the

---

[13] Philbrick, *Mayflower*, 80.

[14] Philbrick, *Mayflower*, 79.

Mayflower. They spent the Saturday of that week repairing the boat. The next day being the Lord's Day they rested, and on December 11, being thoroughly convinced of the suitability of the place, they set off towards the *Mayflower*, which was lying at anchor some twenty-five miles across the bay. Those on board the ship were waiting anxiously for the party's return, and one can imagine many anxious thoughts crossed their minds as to whether or not those who had gone out from them were safe, or even still alive.

Great joy was expressed upon their return, but the joy was mixed with sadness, for William Bradford learned, to his deep sorrow, that his wife Dorothy May of Wisbech, Cambridgeshire, whom he had married in Amsterdam seven years before, had fallen overboard and was drowned. Once again, we might observe that their pathway was chequered at every step by deep trials of faith. Though in popular books and films, this tragic accident is sometimes portrayed as a suicide, there is no evidence whatsoever that this was the case. This is not to say that Dorothy Brewster had no cause to despair, as she had to leave her own three-year old son in the care of others on the other side of the Atlantic, it being too dangerous to take an infant child on such a tortuous and dangerous journey. Moreover, her husband had been away for some considerable time, and just prior to this point was almost given up as lost. Let this be coupled with the exhaustion of the transatlantic journey in winter, the bitter cold, the lack of food, and before them an uncertain future and we are made aware of some of the enormous mental and psychological pressures these people must have experienced at this time.

We think of the Pilgrims as resilient adventurers upheld by unwavering religious faith but they were also human beings in the midst of what was, and continues to be, one of the most difficult emotional challenges a person can face—immigration and exile. Less than a year later another group of English settlers arrived at Providence Town Harbour and were so overwhelmed by this "naked and barren place" that they convinced themselves that the Pilgrims must all be dead.[15] In fear of being forsaken by the ship's captain, the panicked settlers began to strip the sails from the yards "lest the ship should get away and leave them."[16] If Dorothy should have the terror and sense of abandonment that gripped the settlers, she may have felt that suicide was her only choice.[17]

We can only imagine how William Bradford felt on arriving back at the ship, cold hungry and exhausted, to be greeted with such news. He found solace however, in the sovereignty of God and his good providence. He has left behind this short verse revealing his grief and at the same time his unfailing confidence in God.

---

[15] Philbrick, *Mayflower*, 76.

[16] Philbrick, *Mayflower*, 77.

[17] Philbrick, *Mayflower*, 76.

> Faint not, poor soul, in God still trust,
> Fear not the things thou suffer must;
> For, whom he loves he doth chastise,
> And then all tears wipes from their eyes.[18]

On Friday, December 15, the Pilgrim Fathers and the ship's crew hurriedly prepared the *Mayflower* for twenty-four-mile crossing, to Plymouth Harbour, desperately eager to see the site chosen for the settlement. The shallop that had done such sterling work for the expeditionary parties now lead the way. There was a strong wind blowing from the north-east, which prevented them from entering Plymouth Harbour until December 17. That day being a Sabbath, no attempt was made to land. After a preliminary party had gone ashore to make sure all was safe, debate was then given as to where exactly in the vicinity they would plant their settlement. It was not until Wednesday, December 20 that the decision was made that the settlement should be built on high ground overlooking the bay and where there was an extensive stretch of land on the north bank of the Town Brook. Many however, remained on the ship. On the Thursday and into the Friday of that week a gale persisted throughout the day and through the night. At the height of the gale on board the ship, Mary Allerton gave birth to a child, but it was stillborn, probably because of the conditions aboard the relentlessly pitching vessel.

By Saturday, the storm had eased, and every man who could be spared, who was fit enough to work was taken ashore in the shallop to start felling and cutting timber. Once more the Sabbath was observed. The following week was wet and it was Wednesday before the weather let up sufficiently to allow for further cutting of timber. The first objective was to build a common house so that the Pilgrims could transfer their stores and tools ashore and save themselves the often-difficult passage to and from the *Mayflower*. Exhausted and deprived of proper shelter or food, many of the Pilgrims worn out at this time, slipped away into death. This was an extremely difficult period but by January 9, the common house, some twenty foot square, had reached the stage where it needed little more than roofing. It was decided that, when the thatching and mortaring were complete, each family would work better and faster if they were then free to start on their own houses, rather than continue building the village as a communal effort. Lots were then drawn for the sites along both sides of the street. Dogged by incessant rain, sickness, fear of aboriginal attack, and death, they continue until on January 20, when using both the shallop and the longboat, the Pilgrims began to ferry ashore the food stocks and the general stores, to be stacked into the now completed common house. By the following day Captain Jones was relieved to know that his holds had been cleared of all but a few of the men and the women and children. During those busy days, occasional distant parties of aboriginal people

---

[18] Philbrick, *Mayflower*, 77.

were seen, but they never attempted to approach the settlement or the Planters.

As the year 1620 rolled around into the year 1621 despite the care of surgeon Fuller, sickness continued to spread amongst the Pilgrims and the crew of the *Mayflower*. At one point, it reached such proportions that only seven out of the whole company were left fit enough to care for the others. William Bradford wrote of those who cared for the sick at this time. "They spared no pains night or day … dressed them meat, made their beds, washed their loathsome clothes—in a word did all the homely and necessary offices for them which dainty and queasy stomachs cannot endure to hear named."[19] Amongst these Bradford particularly mentioned the loving service of elder William Brewster and Captain Miles Standish towards their suffering brethren—himself included. He remarked "The Lord so held these persons as in this general calamity they were not at all infected either with sickness or any other disability."[20] "Four whole families were wiped out. Only five out of eighteen wives survived; the servants and single men were reduced from twenty-nine to nineteen. No girl children died and only three of the thirteen sons. Either the children had the best food and the most care, or the hard unremitting toil of the men and women was more than many of them should have undertaken in their weakened state."[21] The dead were buried at night in the burial ground later to become known as Cole's Hill, the graves were generally concealed for they did not want the Indians to know how their numbers were so drastically diminished. As it came to be learned later the aboriginal people knew every aspect and detail of the Pilgrims' activities and had them under surveillance at all times.

Samoset and Squanto
On Friday, March 16, after there had been another meeting of the Pilgrims regarding safety and military matters, there appeared on what came to be known as Watson's Hill, an aboriginal who seemed to be making his way very purposefully towards the settlement. An alarm was sounded as he came near to the row of houses, but on he walked until some of the men stepped out into his path and tried to prevent him coming any further. To their surprise he greeted them in English and spoke words which have now entered the annals of history, "Welcome Englishmen!"

He was armed with a bow and just two arrows, "the one headed, the other unheaded."[22] The Pilgrims do not seem to have attached any special significance to these arrows, but they may have represented the alternatives of war and peace.

---

[19] Ian Cooper, *The Pilgrim Fathers* (Leominster, Herefordshire: Day One, 2015), 35.

[20] Cooper, *Pilgrim Fathers*, 156.

[21] Dillon, *A Place for Habitation*, 196

[22] John Brown, *The Pilgrim Fathers of New England* (London: The Religious Tract Society, 1897), 205.

Statue of Massasoit by Cyrus Edwin Dallin
in Plymouth, MA. Dallin was one of the first American
sculptors to depict the dignity
of the American Indian.

It was not long before the Pilgrim guards began to warm to this very forward guest and offered him something to eat. It is said that he asked for beer but the Pilgrims only at that time had strong water (perhaps the Aqua vitae they had drunk during their first days after landing at Cape Cod). He feasted however upon biscuits, butter, cheese, pudding, and a slice of roast duck all of which he said, "he liked well."[23] He introduced himself as Samoset[24] and he wore only a deerskin leather belt about his waist "*with* a fringe about a span long or a little more;" they gave him a soldier's overcoat as a present. Samoset explained that he was sachem or chief from the land north of Massachusetts Bay. He had come to visit his friend Massasoit, sachem of the Wampanoags, who lived some forty miles away on Narragansett Bay. He informed them that the Patuxet Indians who had formerly lived around Plymouth, had all died in a great plague a few years previously. There was one survivor known to him, who spoke English better than himself, whom he would soon introduce to them. His name was Tisquantum, whom the Pilgrims eventually came to call Squanto. Samoset informed the Pilgrims of the surrounding tribes which might be hostile towards them, but assured them that the powerful Massasoit was nearby and was willing to meet with them.

Soon after this, Massasoit appeared on a little hill looking very much a chief, imposing and dignified, with an army of sixty ferocious-looking braves around him. Edward Winslow was chosen to meet him as the Pilgrims' ambassador, a role in which he proved, not only on this occasion but on many others, to be most effective. A very good relationship developed between the two men; Winslow later paying the following tribute to the chief's character. "He was no liar, he was not bloody and cruel like other Indians; in anger and passion he was soon reclaimed; easy to be reconciled towards such as had offended him, ruled by reason in such measure as he would not scorn the advice of mean men; and that he governed his men better with few strokes than others did with many."[25]

This ceremonious first meeting concluded with the Pilgrims entering into a treaty of mutual assistance and protection with Massasoit, which assured the survival of the colony and indeed gave peace to Massachusetts Bay for forty years. The hand of God was clearly on this meeting, and set against the background of the violent and cruel events that had marked the arrival of previous settlers, it was a remarkable providence. After Massasoit departed, Squanto stayed with the Pilgrims, for they now occupied his homeland. He had formally helped to clear the aboriginal fields around Patuxet (Plymouth) Bay which the Pilgrims had now inherited. He showed them how and when to plant native corn and where to find

---

[23] Philbrick, *Mayflower*, 93.

[24] Some have conjectured that he may have been telling them his English name, Somerset, given to him by English fishermen who had reached the shores of Maine in the course of their trade.

[25] Dillon, *A Place for Habitation*, 160.

the best fishing places. Until his death in 1622 Squanto gave invaluable service. Some have questioned his motives, suggesting that he did this to gain power for himself. Of these things we cannot enter into, but he was certainly a God-given friend and guide to the Pilgrims. Bradford called him "a special instrument sent by God for their good beyond their expectations."[26]

In October 1621, a special Thanksgiving Day marked the gathering in of the first harvest from some twenty acres of corn fields. The fifty-one Pilgrims, with two new babies in their mother's arms, entertained Massasoit and his warriors to a feast of venison, roast duck and turkey, possibly with cranberries gathered, as today, in the lower boggy fields where they grow in abundance. It was said that so much was eaten that they ran short of food for weeks to come. It was not until 1863 that President Abraham Lincoln appointed the last Thursday in November as national Thanksgiving Day. Although they were not perhaps aware of it at the time the Pilgrims had even more cause for thanksgiving on that autumn day. They had established the first real Puritan bridgehead in the New World. Those that followed them in the great migration of the 1630s would look upon the Pilgrims as God's pathfinders. As William Bradford reflected in his *Journal*, "As one candle may light a thousand, so the light here kindled has shone into many, yea in some sort to our whole nation. Let the glorious name of Jehovah have all the praise."[27]

Conclusion

The question may be asked as to whether the exiles put into practice the high ideals of liberty and toleration which they professed and claimed for themselves. The answer must be emphatically "Yes," and this we would maintain in the face of a great deal of criticism of the Pilgrims emanating from some quarters today. There is often confusion in the minds of some between the Pilgrim Fathers and the Puritan settlers who began to arrive at Salem and Boston, Massachusetts from 1628 and into the 1630s. These were made up of members of the Church of England who had been harried out of the Church and out of the country by Archbishop William Laud. The tiny colony at Plymouth in 1620 was the work of a small band of battered believers who had no resources but their faith, dedication and industry. The Massachusetts Bay Company was the work of a determined group of powerful Puritans, financially well backed, equipped with a Royal Charter that gave them the right to exercise the prerogatives of the Crown. The company sent an advance guard to Salem in 1628, ahead of the great migration beginning in 1630. Soon were formed the communities of Boston, Charleston, Dorchester, Roxbury, and Watertown, under the governorship of John Winthrop. The magistrates here were men of substance and the ministers already

---

[26] John Adair, *Founding Fathers* (London: J.M. Dent & Sons Ltd. 1982), 125.

[27] Adair, *Founding Fathers*, 126.

famous scholars and preachers. In the following ten years it is estimated that over 20,000 persons settled in this region and under this authority.

Roger Williams, and others such as the Quakers received scant consideration at the hands of this group. Roger Williams, in contrast to the treatment he had received by the Massachusetts settlement, spoke of the loving advice given to him by Edward Winslow of Plymouth. He spoke of Winslow as saying to him, "I might be as free as themselves, and we should be loving neighbors together."[28] When Anne Hutchinson and her adherents were banished from Massachusetts, they applied to the colony of Plymouth for permission to settle on Aquidnick or Rhode Island. Though her tenets were no more approved by Plymouth than Massachusetts, permission was granted. Some of the early Quakers also fled to Plymouth, and probably thereby saved their lives. The suggestion that the men who went over in the *Mayflower* ever persecuted Quakers is without a shred of satisfactory proof. In fact, according to John Fox, it was not until 1656 that the Quakers made their appearance in America, by which time most of the original Pilgrims were dead. "At the accession of James I of England thirty-one crimes were made capital. This number gradually increased to two hundred and twenty-three. The Massachusetts Bay Colony made thirteen crimes capital. The Plymouth Bay settlers had only five classes of capital crime; and of these she actually punished only two."[29]

Though there were differences between the Pilgrims of the Plymouth Plantation, and the Puritans of Massachusetts, there were cordial ties between the two parties. John Endecott of Salem on his arrival in 1629 wrote to William Bradford a warm letter of greeting. After this, Deacon Samuel Fuller was sent over from Plymouth to help the newcomers in time of sickness. Though the Massachusetts settlers were officially members of the Church of England, perhaps, in some way one might say through the influence of the Plymouth settlers they quickly adapted their form of church government to that of Congregationalism.

It is well-known that in 1643 there came about the union of the colonies of Massachusetts, New Plymouth, Connecticut and New Haven. The aim seems to have been for protection and mutual support, though as John Brown comments, what was lost in this union was a loss of latitude of speech and opinion and what was gained in security and industrial progress was lost in the way of freedom and self-reliance.

The last of the *Mayflower* passengers, Mary Cushman *nee* Allerton, died in 1699, aged 83. Peregrine White, the first child born in New England and on board the *Mayflower*, lived until 1703. After 1691 there was no Plymouth colony as such, it had been absorbed by Massachusetts. In the intervening years there had been the dark period of King Philip's War. In spite of the efforts of

---

[28] Goodwin's "Pilgrims Republic" 2, quoted by Thomas W. Mason and B. Nightingale, *New Light on the Pilgrim Story* (London: Congregational Union of England & Wales, 1920), 37.

[29] Thomas W. Mason and B. Nightingale, *New Light on the Pilgrim*, 37.

noble missionaries, like John Eliot (1604–90), a spiritual weakening amongst the descendants of the first settlers, and a growing mistrust amongst the Indian population led to this bitter war, lasting from 1675–1678.

However, with all these things taken into consideration, the Pilgrim Fathers have left behind a noble and worthy testimony. Their legacy to succeeding generations is rich, theirs it has been said was a creed that did not breed either poverty, ignorance or frivolity, but was the nurse of heroes, and the mother of freedom, universal education, representative government and liberty safeguarded by law. They showed how men of various nationalities, different minds, social grades and temperaments could work together for the common good. It is sometimes forgotten that on the *Mayflower*, the *Speedwell* and four later Pilgrim ships there were people of eight differing nationalities. Their vision was for a free church in a free country, the church in Leiden had welcomed one and all adherents to, or members of any Reformed Churches to their communion. Roger Williams, the Baptist, was held by them in brotherhood. There were no witchcraft persecutions in Plymouth. This was not because there were few possible victims of this cruel delusion, but mainly because in Holland, where the Pilgrims were trained, there already had been published and widely read the first scientific attacks against this superstition, moreover tolerance had taught them charity, patience and justice.

> There was in these makers of New England a grand and masterful sincerity, a noble courage of conviction, an overwhelming sense of the authority of righteousness in human life, and an ever present consciousness of God's personal rule over the world, in spite of all its confusions. These men felt, as few men have ever felt, the greatness of that human soul for the redemption of which Christ has died; which has to work out its earthly history before the background of eternity, while passing thither to its mysterious destiny; and there was ever before their thought the glorious ideal of a kingdom of the heavens yet to be realized on the earth.[30]

---

[30] John Brown, *The Pilgrim Fathers of New England* (London: The Religious Tract Society, 1897), 341.

Memorial bas relief of the signing
of the Mayflower Compact
by Cyrus Edwin Dallin in Provincetown, MA,
below the Pilgrim Monument
(Wikimedia Commons).

CHAPTER ELEVEN

The Mayflower Compact and its Long-Term Impact on American Values

JASON EDWIN DEES

Introduction
When the fall storms of 1620 blew the *Mayflower* more than 300 miles north of their intended destination the passengers had a very difficult decision to make: should they sail south trying to reach the Virginia colony or with winter quickly approaching should they drop anchor and settle in Cape Cod? They knew that their choice would greatly impact who they would become as a company and as we now know it has impacted what America became as a country. For more than 10 days they wrestled with this decision before finally dropping anchor at Plymouth on November 21, 1620. In choosing this path, their patent from King James I (1566–1625) was null and void, and they were, as one passenger pointed out, "under no one's jurisdiction."[1] Some members of the colony even rose up with "discontented and mutinous speeches"[2] according to William Bradford (1590–1657).

Eventually the group decided to huddle together amongst themselves to draw up an agreement, a "sacred covenant" making them a "civil body politic" and

---

[1] Benjamin Hart, *Faith & Freedom: The Christian Roots of American liberty* (Springfield, VA: Christian Defense Fund, 1997), 77.

[2] William Bradford, *Of Plymouth Plantation: Bradford's History of the Plymouth Settlement, 1608–1650*, ed. Harold Paget (San Antonio, TX: Vision Forum, 2002), 84.

promising "just and equal laws."[3] As Benjamin Hart wrote, "an additional covenant was needed to form a legitimate government, necessary for their individual protection, as well as to make possible the emergence on virgin territory of civilized society."[4] After 41 male members of the Mayflower Company, as well as two indentured servants, signed the Mayflower Compact[5] they elected John Carver (a man godly and well approved amongst them) as their governor for that year. Through Carver's "wisdom, patience, and just and equal carrage of things"[6] a sense of peace and unity returned to the colony. It gave them a foundation to grow a thriving company of mutually responsible citizens.

This "sacred covenant" became known as The Mayflower Compact, and in so many ways this document laid the foundation for the kind of democratic constitutional government that America enjoys today. Its principles are clear in both the Declaration of Independence and Constitution of the United States. What follows is a short look at how The Mayflower Compact began to shape the American ideals of submission to and limits of earthly powers, democratic government and its roles, and submission to God.

The Mayflower Compact

> In the name of God, Amen. We whose names are underwritten, the loyal subjects of our dread Sovereign Lord King James, by the Grace of God of Great Britain, France, and Ireland King, Defender of the Faith, etc.
>
> Having undertaken for the Glory of God and advancement of the Christian Faith and Honour of our King and Country, a Voyage to plant the First Colony in the Northern Parts of Virginia, do by these presents solemnly and mutually in the presence of God and one of another, Covenant and Combine ourselves together in a Civil Body Politic, for our better ordering and preservation and furtherance of the ends aforesaid; and by virtue hereof to enact, constitute and frame such just and equal Laws, Ordinances, Acts, Constitutions and Offices from time to time, as shall be thought most meet and convenient for the general good of the Colony, unto which we promise all due submission and obedience. In witness whereof we have hereunder subscribed our names at Cape Cod, the 11th of November, in the year of the reign of our Sovereign Lord King James, of England, France

---

[3] Hart, *Faith & Freedom*, 77.

[4] Hart, *Faith & Freedom*, 77.

[5] Bradford, *Plymouth Plantation*, 84.

[6] Bradford, *Plymouth Plantation*, 84.

and Ireland the eighteenth, and of Scotland the fifty-fourth. Anno Domini 1620.[7]

Submission to and Limits of Earthly Powers

The Mayflower Compact was not a declaration of independence; it begins with a very clear statement of loyalty to King James (1567–1625). They recognized his authority over them as his subjects, as citizens of his reign, but they know that he had not established his jurisdiction outside of Virginia. It is interesting that they recognized the geographic limits of King James, even though they were still faithfully submitting themselves to his reign. Therefore, this compact was neither a declaration of independence from England, nor was this a seizure of new land; rather it was a document that gave the Pilgrims some sense of common order that was the result of their journey leading them to an unknown place. Incredibly, the Mayflower Compact served the Pilgrims, and the many that came after them, for 71 years—until Plymouth eventually became a part of the Massachusetts Bay Colony.

It is also interesting that the Pilgrims called King James the defender of the faith, even though they were fleeing the religious persecution that they had faced in England in order to seek the religious freedom of a new colony. Despite this, they still recognized the authority that they believed that God had given to their King, and that God had put him in this seat of power to ultimately defend the Christian faith and gospel message. Even though they disagreed with him, they respected his God-ordained position as the defender of Christianity as the sovereign King. Thus, these Puritans both understood the limits of earthly power, but they respected positions of power and the Mayflower Compact captures this tension very well.

The United States is a country that was founded in and has thrived in this tension between the respect of authority and the limits of authority. The Constitution of the United States would later call for the authority of elected officials, while limiting that authority. The Declaration of Independence is in large part a statement against the King, stating that he had overstepped the limits of his power. The colonists felt that it was necessary to dissolve the union because the King had gone beyond the limit of power that they supposed God had given him. As Thomas Jefferson wrote, and the founders signed:

> Prudence, indeed, will dictate that Governments long established should not be changed for light and transient causes; and accordingly all experience hath shewn, that mankind are more disposed to suffer, while evils are sufferable, than to right themselves by abolishing the forms to which they

---

[7] The *Mayflower Compact* at *Plimouth Patuxet: Commemorating 400 Years 1620–2020* (https://www.plimoth.org/learn/just-kids/homework-help/mayflower-and-mayflower-compact; accessed August 23, 2020).

are accustomed. But when a long train of abuses and usurpations, pursuing invariably the same Object evinces a design to reduce them under absolute Despotism, it is their right, it is their duty, to throw off such Government, and to provide new Guards for their future security.—Such has been the patient sufferance of these Colonies; and such is now the necessity which constrains them to alter their former Systems of Government. The history of the present King of Great Britain is a history of repeated injuries and usurpations, all having in direct object the establishment of an absolute Tyranny over these States.[8]

So, like the Mayflower Compact, there was a recognition of necessity of governments and their rulers but also the limitations of those rulers.

Similarly, the Constitution establishes the power of the Presidency, Congress, and Courts but it is also very intentional to limit that power creating terms, a process of removal, and, of course, a balance of power between branches. Further, both the Declaration of Independence and Constitution of the United States were people's documents. The authority that any particular leader would have would be established by the people, as Lincoln later described the Government as being, "of the people, by the people, and for the people."[9] The Constitution begins with a statement from the people:

We the People of the United States, in Order to form a more perfect Union, establish Justice, insure domestic Tranquility, provide for the common defense, promote the general Welfare, and secure the Blessings of Liberty to ourselves and our Posterity, do ordain and establish this Constitution for the United States of America.[10]

These framers of the Constitution understood the United States to be the people's government and the people both entrusted the government and the leaders of that government with any authority that they had but also had the authority to take it away.

Democratic Government
Fundamentally, the Mayflower Compact was a democratic document. As mentioned, it was, like the Constitution that followed, a document of the people.

---

[8] "Declaration of Independence: A Transcription," *National Archives: America's Founding Documents* (https://www.archives.gov/founding-docs/declaration-transcript; accessed August 23, 2020).

[9] Abraham Lincoln, *Selected Speeches and Writings*, ed. Gore Vidal (New York, NY: Library of America, 2009), 405.

[10] *The Constitution of the United States: A Transcription* at *National Archives: America's Founding Documents* (https://www.archives.gov/founding-docs/constitution-transcript; accessed August 23, 2020).

It is rightly understood as a Compact or a Covenant between the people. Its authority came from the people and as they wrote, they, "solemnly and mutually in the presence of God and one of another, covenant and combine ourselves together into a civil body politic."[11] They entered into this covenant for the sake of their own well-being and for the sake of one another's well-being. They entered into the covenant,

> for our better ordering, and preservation and furtherance of the ends aforesaid; and by virtue hereof to enact, constitute, and frame, such just and equal laws, ordinances, acts, constitutions, and offices, from time to time, as shall be thought most meet and convenient for the general good of the colony.[12]

They then pledged themselves to this union that they had formed, "unto which we promise all due submission and obedience."[13] This pattern that we see in the Mayflower Compact is the same pattern of both the Declaration of Independence and the Constitution. All of these documents represent the hope a more perfect union and mutual commitment toward that goal and to one another as the Declaration of Independence ends, "And for the support of this Declaration, with a firm reliance on the protection of divine Providence, we mutually pledge to each other our Lives, our Fortunes and our sacred Honor."[14]

At its worst the United States has been a fragmented set of individuals each existing for their own goals and purposes using one another to gain individual success, but at its best America is a covenanted democracy of individuals united together for the common goal of liberty and justice for all. This ideal of a covenanted democracy, or a "one another" democracy certainly goes all the way back to this compact that secured the rights of every company member because it was the member of the company that formed and secured this "civil body politic." Their purpose in joining together as a democratic union was to "enact, constitute, and frame" an order of governance or as they said, "laws, ordinances, acts, constitutions, and offices."[15] The Mayflower Compact thus was able to assuage the fear of William Bradford and others that some of the settlers were planning to "use their owne libertie," to ignore common rules and to take ownership of the

---

[11] *Mayflower Compact* (https://www.plimoth.org/learn/just-kids/homework-help/mayflower-and-mayflower-compact; accessed August 23, 2020).

[12] *Mayflower Compact* (https://www.plimoth.org/learn/just-kids/homework-help/mayflower-and-mayflower-compact; accessed August 23, 2020).

[13] *Mayflower Compact* (https://www.plimoth.org/learn/just-kids/homework-help/mayflower-and-mayflower-compact; accessed August 23, 2020).

[14] From "Declaration of Independence: A Transcription," *National Archives: America's Founding Documents*.

[15] *Mayflower Compact* (https://www.plimoth.org/learn/just-kids/homework-help/mayflower-and-mayflower-compact; accessed August 23, 2020).

care of their new settlement.[16]

This was very different from the parliament system from which they had come. While England had an unwritten constitution that embodied the principle of parliamentary sovereignty, this Compact established the idea of covenant, anchored in the biblical idea of a covenant between God and man. Later, more thinkers like John Locke (1632–1704) gave voice to such a covenant as a social compact among individuals themselves. Locke heavily influenced the framers of the Constitution, which does not mention God, although the Declaration of Independence does mention a "firm reliance on the protection of divine providence."[17] This idea of covenant, or social contract, or idea of mutual responsibility for the preservation of a society is what has given American a sense of self-determination that has framed the American psyche throughout its history.

Submission to God
As has been noted, this was a Democratic Compact formed by mutual agreement, but it was formed, "in the presence of God, and one another."[18] In fact, the Mayflower Compact begins with submission to God, "In the name of God, Amen" and the undersigning pilgrims also set out to establish their settlement "for the glory of God," and "for the advancement of the Christian faith."[19] Their faith in God's protection and hope in God's glory is weaved throughout the document and was an integral part of their lives. William Bradford's landmark work, *Of Plymouth Plantation*, mentions the name of God some 329 times and is full of prayers, praise, and dependence on the living God.

This dependence on God has continued to be present in American life. A reliance on God that was very present in America throughout the seventeenth century and was fueled by the Great Awakening of the eighteenth century. It has been widely noted that the Great Awakening and the American understanding of free faith in God contributed to the American Revolution in ideological, sociological, and in religious ways. As Daniel N. Gullota writes, "The revivals shattered the social order of church hierarchy, rejecting the existing power structures of the day and focusing instead on the individual."[20] Similarly,

---

[16] Eric Foner and John A. Garraty, *The Reader's Encyclopedia to American History* (Boston, MA: Houghton-Mifflin, 1991), 708.

[17] From "Declaration of Independence: A Transcription," *National Archives: America's Founding Documents*.

[18] *Mayflower Compact* (https://www.plimoth.org/learn/just-kids/homework-help/mayflower-and-mayflower-compact; accessed August 23, 2020).

[19] *Mayflower Compact* (https://www.plimoth.org/learn/just-kids/homework-help/mayflower-and-mayflower-compact; accessed August 23, 2020).

[20] Daniel Gullotta, "The Great Awakening and the American Revolution," *Journal of the American Revolution*, August 10, 2016 (https://allthingsliberty.com/2016/08/great-awakening-american-revolution/; accessed August 23, 2020).

John Adams wrote after the Awakening, reflecting on its effects, "The Revolution was effected before the war commenced. The Revolution was in the minds and hearts of the people; a change in their religious sentiments of their duties and obligations."[21] Even as late as 1956 the official motto of the United States was changed by congress from *E Pluribus Unum* (Out of many, One) to *In God We Trust*.

Through all of this reliance on the care and protection of God, the American idea has always been committed to a religious liberty dating all the way back to the Mayflower Compact. This document was established with reliance on God, but it did not itself establish an official church or belief system. These Pilgrims were fleeing such an order, and the American ideal of the "freedom of conscience" has long been a part of the American psyche. Their fellow nonconformist, Thomas Helwys (1575–1616) had written, just about a decade before their departure, that "men's religion to God is between God and themselves. The king shall not answer for it. Neither may the king be judge between God and man."[22] His work certainly influenced the Pilgrims, the broader understanding of the freedom of religion and the broader idea of freedom of conscience. Helwys went on, "Let them be heretics, Turks, Jews, or whatsoever, it appertains not to the earthly power to punish them in the least measure. This is made evident to our lord the king by the scriptures."[23]

America's ability to rely on the care of God and to anchor its understanding of morality and truth in the Christian revelation of God, while giving religious freedom to all sorts of religions even irreligion has been one of great values of its long history and certainly dates back to the Mayflower Compact. The first amendment is a great example of this American balance, "Congress shall make no law respecting an establishment of religion, or prohibiting the free exercise thereof."[24] It both prohibits a state forced or mandated religion, while recognising the freedom of the people to worship God or not worship however they should choose. The wisdom of the Pilgrims to both honour the providence of God and the freedom of man attempted to create in American culture, a God honouring liberty.

---

[21] John Adams, "Letter to Hezekiah Niles, February 13, 1818," in *The Works of John Adams*, ed. Charles Francis (Boston, MA: Little, Brown, and Company, 1850–1856), 10:282.

[22] Thomas Helwys, *A Short Declaration of the Mystery of Iniquity (1611/1612)* (Macon, GA: Mercer University Press, 1998), 53.

[23] Thomas Helwys, *A Short Declaration of the Mystery of Iniquity (1611/1612)* (Macon, GA: Mercer University Press, 1998), 53.

[24] "1st Amendment to the Constitution of the United States" at *Constitution Annotated: Constitution of the United States* (https://constitution.congress.gov/constitution/amendment-1/; accessed August 23, 2020).

Conclusion

This short chapter does not adequately praise the wisdom and courage of these early American Settlers. Their understanding of the afore-mentioned ideals; submission to and limits of earthly powers, democratic government and its roles, and submission to God, have given shape to American structure and thought for 400 years. Sadly, within 2 to 3 months of the Pilgrims signing the Mayflower Compact nearly half of the company was dead.[25] None of them could have imagined what they began, but we honour them now and we join countless others who have faithfully remembered their legacy. These include Calvin Coolidge (1872–1933) who on the 300th anniversary of the Mayflower Compact, gave these words honoring its signers:

> The compact which they signed was an event of the greatest importance. It was the foundation of liberty based on law and order, and that tradition has been steadily upheld. They drew up a form of government which has been designated as the first real constitution of modern times. It was democratic, an acknowledgment of liberty under law and order and the giving to each person the right to participate in the government, while they promised to be obedient to the laws. But the really wonderful thing was that they had the power and strength of character to abide by it and live by it from that day to this. Some governments are better than others. But any form of government is better than anarchy, and any attempt to tear down government is an attempt to wreck civilization.[26]

---

[25] Bradford, *Plymouth Plantation*, 84.

[26] Calvin Coolidge, "Speech on the 300th Anniversary of the Mayflower Compact," *The New York Herald* (November 23, 1920) (https://www.loc.gov/item/sn83045774/1920-11-23/ed-1/; accessed August 23, 2020).

The First Thanksgiving depicted in 1914
by Jennie Augusta Brownscombe (1850–1936)
(Public Domain).

CHAPTER TWELVE

Spiritual Lessons from the First Thanksgiving

DAVID ROACH

Studying all extant eyewitness accounts of the first Thanksgiving is not difficult. It requires reading just 152 words, written in late 1621 by Plymouth colony statesman Edward Winslow:

> Our harvest being gotten in, our governor sent four men on fowling, that so we might after have a special manner rejoice together after we had gathered the fruit of our labors; they four in one day killed as much fowl, as with a little help beside, served the company almost a week, at which time amongst other recreations, we exercised our arms, many of the Indians coming amongst us, and among the rest their greatest King Massasoit, with some ninety men, whom for three days we entertained and feasted, and they went out and killed five deer, which they brought to the plantation and bestowed on our governor, and upon the captain, and others. And although it be not always so plentiful as it was at this time with us, yet by the goodness of God, we are so far from want that we often wish you partakers of our plenty.[1]

---

[1] Edward Winslow and John Bradford, *Mourt's Relation: A Journal of the Pilgrims at Plymouth, 1622, Part VI*, The Plymouth Colony Archive Project (http://www.histarch.illinois.edu/plymouth/mourt6.html accessed March 17, 2020). Some regard William Bradford's classic work *Plymouth Plantation* as a second eyewitness account. While Bradford recounted gathering in the 1621 harvest, he made no specific reference to the first Thanksgiving. He did, however, mention a "great store of wild Turkeys" consumed at harvest time, perhaps a reference to the first Thanksgiving turkeys. See William Bradford, *Bradford's History of "Plimoth Plantation,"* Book 2, "Anno 1621," 127, Project Gutenberg e-book (http://www.gutenberg.org/files/24950/24950-h/24950-h.htm#a1621 accessed March 17, 2020).

The celebration bore marked differences from some traditional portrayals. The ninety Wamponoags present were nearly double the fifty Englishmen still alive after their first grueling winter in Plymouth, down from 102 who arrived on the *Mayflower*. Since few buildings had been constructed in Plymouth by that time, the celebration probably took place outdoors, with celebrants sitting on the ground or any makeshift seat available rather than at tables. They ate more venison and seafood than turkey. It was September or October rather than November. Pumpkin pies hadn't been invented, so berries were the dessert of choice.[2]

In some quarters, it has become popular to suggest even deeper differences between traditional American Thanksgiving celebrations and what occurred at Plymouth in 1621. Contrary to the traditional portrayal of families gathered around their tables with heads bowed in prayer, revisionist historians question whether Christian spirituality should be associated with the first Thanksgiving. James Deetz and Patricia Scott Deetz claimed, for example, that "Thanksgiving as we think of it today is largely a myth."[3] The original celebration was a "secular event," which "transformed over time," because America "needed a myth of epic proportion on which to found its history."[4] Indeed, of the surviving Englishmen at the first Thanksgiving, only about half were Separatists, those who came to the New World in search of freedom to live out their Christian faith. The rest were "strangers," individuals who made the journey out of nonreligious motives. Between the aboriginal people and Englishmen, fewer than 20 percent of participants in the first Thanksgiving had declared themselves committed followers of Christ.[5] New England historian Joseph Conforti described the first Thanksgiving feast as "disorderly, even raucous" and not the mythologized "placid feast dominated by pious settlers."[6] Even Sydney Ahlstrom's classic work on American religious history insinuated the first Thanksgiving may not have been a God-centred assembly. Ahlstrom described the Pilgrim Fathers as "not theologically minded, nor ... aggressive or self-conscious in their churchmanship."[7]

Yet Americans long have assumed a spiritual heritage in their Thanksgiving celebrations. In 1789, President George Washington proclaimed a Thanksgiving

---

[2] James Deetz, and Patricia Scott Deetz, *Times of their Lives: Life, Love, and Death in Plymouth Colony* (New York, NY: Freeman, 2000), 5–9.

[3] Deetz and Deetz, *Times of their Lives*, 9.

[4] Deetz and Deetz, *Times of their Lives*, 9, 10.

[5] This percentage is calculated by comparing the roster of 102 new arrivals on the Mayflower with the list of 53 English settlers present at the first Thanksgiving and noting survivors who were members of the Separatist congregation in Leiden.

[6] Joseph Conforti, *Saints and Strangers: New England in British North America* (Baltimore, MD: Johns Hopkins University Press, 2006), 39.

[7] Sydney E. Ahlstrom, *A Religious History of the American People*, 2nd ed. (New Haven, CT: Yale University Press, 2004), 138.

Day devoted "to the service of that great and glorious Being, who is the beneficent Author of all the good that was, that is, or that will be—That we may then all unite in rendering unto him our sincere and humble thanks."[8] Annual Thanksgiving celebrations continued largely as a New England holiday until 1863, when President Abraham Lincoln set aside the last Thursday in November as a national holiday. Lincoln proclaimed "a day of Thanksgiving and praise to our beneficent Father who dwelleth in the heavens."[9] Lincoln's precedent of declaring a day of Thanksgiving by executive fiat was followed by every U.S. president until 1941, when Franklin Roosevelt signed legislation making Thanksgiving an official national holiday each year. That legislation remains in force, and the spiritual nature of Thanksgiving continues to be assumed. Donald Trump proclaimed in 2019 that "on Thanksgiving Day, we remember with reverence and gratitude the bountiful blessings afforded to us by our Creator."[10] He harkened back to the Pilgrims as a historical foundation for his proclamation.[11]

Such conflicting interpretations of the 1621 Thanksgiving celebration may make us wonder whether it is reasonable to draw spiritual lessons from the first Thanksgiving. Was it merely a secular harvest festival, or did the Pilgrim Fathers celebrate in deep gratitude for God's providential care? Even the most cursory reading of Pilgrim literature strongly favors the latter option. Despite the relative scarcity of primary sources and the wave of historical revisionism, a wealth of spiritual instruction may be gleaned from the first Thanksgiving. The lessons to be examined here relate to providence, gratitude, and the priesthood of all believers.

Lesson One: Thankfulness Flows From a High View of Providence
The Pilgrim Fathers' assessment of themselves as "partakers" of "plenty" on the first Thanksgiving comes into sharper focus when we consider the mediocrity of their first harvest. As Winslow put it, "Our corn did prove well" but "our barley indifferent good" and "our peas not worth gathering."[12] With three centuries of hindsight, historian George Willison put matters more bluntly: "All in all, their first harvest was a disappointment."[13] Though they brought in twenty acres of

---

[8] George Washington, "Thanksgiving Proclamation," October 3, 1789, *National Archives* (https://founders.archives.gov/documents/Washington/05-04-02-0091; accessed March 17, 2020).

[9] Abraham Lincoln, "Proclamation of Thanksgiving," October 3, 1863, *Abraham Lincoln Online* (http://www.abrahamlincolnonline.org/lincoln/speeches/thanks.htm; accessed March 17, 2020).

[10] Donald Trump, "Presidential Proclamation on Thanksgiving Day, 2019," November 27, 2019, *WhiteHouse.gov* (https://www.whitehouse.gov/presidential-actions/presidential-proclamation-thanksgiving-day-2019/; accessed March 17, 2020).

[11] Trump, "Presidential Proclamation on Thanksgiving Day, 2019."

[12] Winslow and Bradford, *Mourt's Relation*, Part VI.

[13] George F. Willison, *Saints and Strangers* (New York, NY: Reynal and Hitchcock, 1945), 188.

corn thanks to the help of their native friend Squanto (who showed them how to grow the strange North American crop), all the Pilgrims' English crops failed. Six or seven acres of wheat, barley, and peas amounted to nothing. Bradford believed the problem may have been bad seed, late planting, or both.[14] Yet amid that failure, the Separatists still deemed their first harvest "plentiful" by "the goodness of God" and worthy of a thanksgiving celebration.

Such a celebration is best understood in light of their doctrine of providence. The Pilgrim Fathers could be thankful for mixed success and even isolated pockets of success because they viewed every good thing in life—no matter how small—as the provision of a sovereign God. Their view of providence was detailed in the 1596 Separatist confession of faith *A True Confession*. Issued in part to assure Elizabeth I of the Separatists' loyalty to the English crown, the confession articulated doctrines of God and providence in line with the Church of England's Reformed teaching on these points. *A True Confession* remained the creed of Separatists when they fled to the Netherlands in 1607 and when a group of them set sail on the *Mayflower* in 1620. After articulating a doctrine of the Trinity in line with the creeds of Nicaea (325 AD) and Constantinople (381 AD), *A True Confession* states regarding providence,

> God hath decreed in himself from everlasting touching all things, and the very least circumstances of every thing, effectually to work and dispose them according to the counsell of his own will, to the prayse and glorie of his great name. And touching his cheefest Creatures that God hath in Christ before the foundation of the world, according to the good pleasure of his will, ordeyned som men and Angells, to eternall lyfe to bee accomplished through Iesus Christ, to the prayse of the glorie of his grace. And on thother hand hath likewise before of old according to his just purpose ordeined other both Angels and men, toe etrnall condemnation, to bee accomplished through their *own* corruption to the prayse of his iustice.[15]

The key point for our purposes is the claim God made an eternal decree to administer "all things" according to his will, including "the very least circumstances of every thing."[16] This was the same doctrine of meticulous providence articulated by the Reformers and upheld in the Reformed tradition up to the present. As John Calvin put it, "God's providence governs all" such that "nothing takes place without his deliberation" and "he governs all events."[17] Those who claim God's

---

[14] Willison, *Saints and Strangers*, 188.

[15] *A True Confession*, Article 3, The Reformed Reader (http://www.reformedreader.org/ccc/atf.htm; accessed June 14, 2020).

[16] *A True Confession*, Article 3.

[17] John Calvin, *Institutes of the Christian Religion*, ed. John T. McNeill, trans. Ford Leis Battles

providence is limited to "bare foreknowledge" rather than detailed guidance of humankind's affairs, Calvin stated, "babble too ignorantly."[18] A quarter century after the Pilgrims landed at Plymouth, the Westminster divines expressed the same doctrine: God "doth uphold, direct, dispose, and govern all creatures, actions, and things, from the greatest even to the least."[19] Again two centuries later, Princeton theologian Charles Hodge wrote that God "must control the sequence of all events, so as to render certain the accomplishment of all his purposes."[20] The Pilgrim Fathers, like others before and after them in the Reformed tradition, maintained a deep sense of human responsibility. But they went further than the Arminian notion that "God's governing providence is comprehensive and active without being all-controlling or omnicausal."[21]

Some may wonder whether the English Separatists' high view of God's providence could be lived out consistently and joyfully. For the Pilgrims, it could. From their journey on the Mayflower to their business dealings with the aboriginal people, they saw God's guiding hand in every detail of life.

The Pilgrim Fathers regarded their journey to the New World as under God's providence. When they decided to leave the Netherlands for America—seeking better economic prospects, continued religious freedom, and a removal from the influence of poor Dutch morals on their children—they knew their journey would be difficult. Yet they believed many potential difficulties "by providente care and the use of good means might in a great measure be prevented."[22] In hindsight, "endured" might have been a more appropriate word than "prevented." In October 1620, the *Mayflower* encountered serious storms in the mid-Atlantic for days on end. Frigid water pounded the ship, leaking in through ever-widening seams. At one point, John Howland came on deck and was immediately swept overboard. He was saved only by grabbing some rope dragging behind the ship and being pulled in with a hook. Eventually, the Mayflower grew so leaky that there was discussion of turning back. However, the captain declared his vessel seaworthy, and the Pilgrim Fathers "committed themselves to ye will of God."[23]

No less than their transatlantic journey, the Pilgrim Fathers attributed their survival in the New World to God's providence. On one of their initial explorations of the land, they encountered mounds of sand, which they excavated and

---

(Louisville, KY: Westminster John Knox, 1960), 1:200–202. *Institutes* 1.16.3–4 in other editions.

[18] Calvin, *Institutes* 1.16.4.

[19] Chapter 5 "Of Providence," *Westminster Confession of Faith*.

[20] Charles Hodge, *Systematic Theology* (1872, Peabody, MA: Hendrickson, 2008), 1:581–582.

[21] Roger E. Olson, *Arminian Theology* (Downers Grove, IL: IVP Academic, 2006), 121.

[22] George D. Langdon Jr., *Pilgrim Colony: A History of New Plymouth, 1620–1691* (New Haven, CT: Yale University Press, 1966), 8.

[23] Willison, *Saints and Strangers*, 137.

found to be covering stores of Native American corn. They took a good share of the corn and used it as seed the following spring. It proved to be the crop that preserved their lives in 1621. Though Willison regarded their removal of the corn as "just plain larceny," the Separatists regarded it as "God's good providence."[24]

Even when tragedy struck, they saw it as providential—no less when ill befell the aboriginal people than when it hit them.[25] During their first winter in Plymouth, disease struck the Pilgrims' hard. Over a span of three months, half the English settlers died. Of all the married couples among them, both husband and wife survived in just three instances. At the height of the plague, only six or seven English persons were well enough to care for their sick neighbors. Still, the Separatists saw God's providential care. "The Lord so upheld these persons," Pilgrim statesman William Bradford wrote, "as in this generall calamity they were not all infected."[26] The aboriginal people fell victim to illness too. In 1617, a plague (likely smallpox from the Europeans) wiped out the Patuxets of Plymouth. When the Pilgrims learned about the plague, they regarded it as "another special providence of God" to clear a safe place for them in the New World.[27] The surviving aboriginal tribes caused the Pilgrims no harm, which they also attributed to providence: "It has pleased God so to possess the Indians with a fear of us, and love unto us."[28]

Business success or failure likewise fell under God's providence for the Pilgrims. Winslow attributed profit in "the fishing business" and "other trading" to "the blessing of God."[29] The Pilgrims found Boston a more desirable location than Plymouth for establishing a settlement, but Bradford said God "appointed it for another use."[30] Their native friend Squanto, who proved useful in business and communication with local tribes, was regarded as "a special instrument sent of God."[31] When reinforcements arrived from England in 1621, they came "by the blessing of God."[32]

Such a high view of providence led naturally to thanksgiving. The smallest

---

[24] Willison, *Saints and Strangers*, 150, 151.

[25] It bears mentioning that the Pilgrims seemed to possess an unfortunate degree of cultural imperialism and an apparent sense of superiority when it came to the aboriginal people.

[26] William Bradford, *Bradford's History of "Plimoth Plantation,"* Book 2, "The Remainder of Anno 1620," 111, (http://www.gutenberg.org/files/24950/24950-h/24950-h.htm#a1620; accessed June 14, 2020).

[27] Willison, *Saints and Strangers*, 172.

[28] Winslow and Bradford, *Mourt's Relation*, Part VI.

[29] Winslow and Bradford, *Mourt's Relation*, Part VI.

[30] Bradford, *Bradford's History of "Plimoth Plantation,"* Book 2, "Anno. 1621," 127.

[31] Willison, *Saints and Strangers*, 185.

[32] Winslow and Bradford, *Mourt's Relation*, Part VI.

positive occurrence in life could not be overlooked because it was a gift of God no less than the major victories. That's why the Pilgrim Fathers could pause for a thanksgiving holiday following their mediocre harvest and abominable first winter in Plymouth, which leads to the second lesson of Thanksgiving.

Lesson Two: Occasional Thanksgiving Celebrations Stem From a Life of Thankfulness
One of the Pilgrim Fathers' most striking moments of thankfulness occurred the first Sunday after they reached North America. A scouting party of sixteen men returned to the *Mayflower* with a good report about the land, along with a load of juniper wood that smelled sweet as it burned—a welcome change from the stench of the ship's hold after eleven weeks at sea. Despite the voyage's difficulty, it had witnessed only one death (some transatlantic treks lost half their passengers or more).[33] In 1619, for instance, 130 of the 180 colonists on a ship died *en route* to Jamestown.[34] The collective sense of relief spurred an impromptu worship service. As Bradford put it,

> They fell upon their knees and blessed ye God of heaven, who had brought them over ye vast and ferocious ocean, and delivered them from all ye periles and miseries thereof, againe to set their feete on ye firme and stable earth, their proper elemente. And no marvell if they were joyefull.[35]

This striking scene was not an isolated incident. Bradford's history of Plymouth references the giving of thanks no less than thirty times. Being attuned to God's providence spawned a pattern of thanksgiving for the Pilgrims. Acknowledgements of the Lord's hand often were accompanied by expressions of thanks. The first Thanksgiving, rather than being an anomaly amid the drudgery of forging a new colony, fell within a rhythm of gratitude in the Pilgrims' life. Indeed, the first Thanksgiving may have been the 1621 observance of an annual English harvest festival known as Harvest Home. Some have noted this fact in attempt to deny the first Thanksgiving's spiritual character.[36] In actuality, it underscores the cyclical nature of thanksgiving in Plymouth colony.

The Pilgrim Fathers' daily and weekly patterns of worship were early indications of the cycle. Bradford's recounting of Plymouth history is peppered with references to morning prayers before daybreak "as usual" and prayer preceding

---

[33] Deetz and Deetz, *Times of their Lives*, 4.

[34] Langdon, *Pilgrim Colony*, 1.

[35] Bradford, *Pilmouth Plantation*, 94.

[36] Deetz and Deetz, *Times of their Lives*, 5. The lyrics of a traditional Harvest Home hymn suggest thankfulness to God was part of the celebration, "Come, ye thankful people, come. Raise the song of Harvest Home."

breakfast. Before the Pilgrims faced each day, they first turned to God in gratitude and intercession. The pattern persisted as half their company died that first winter and as crops failed the next year. Weekly, they took seriously observance of the Sabbath, making preparations each Saturday so Sunday could be spent in uninterrupted worship and rest. The worship included thanksgiving. Their commitment to a day of preparation and a day of Godward focus weekly was peculiarly rigorous even in the seventeenth century, with the cyclical interruption of life testing the patience of some strangers at Plymouth.[37]

Serendipitous acts of deliverance—large and small—also provoked Pilgrim expressions of thankful worship. Reflecting on their initial discovery of native corns, Bradford declared that "the Lord is never wanting unto his in their greatest needs; let his holy name have all ye praise."[38] When a scouting party survived a surprise attack by Indians armed with bows and arrows, "they gave God all sollamne thanks and praise for their deliverance."[39] Following that narrow escape, the scouting party set out to sea in a small boat. As nightfall approached, the sea became rough and they nearly capsized. They managed to dock the boat on a wooded shore none of them recognised. Yet, when the sun rose the next morning, they happily realized they had stumbled onto an island in Plymouth harbor. So they gave "God thanks for his mercies, in their manifold deliverances."[40]

The pattern of acknowledging providence and responding with thanks continued. By the time their first harvest was gathered, the Pilgrim Fathers' response was predictable. Despite a winter of widespread death and a fall of crop failure, they gave thanks, confident of God's providential care. Leaders of the colony doubled the weekly corn ration, and a holiday was declared so all could "after a more special manner, rejoyce together."[41] Winslow summarised the harvest with an exclamation of worship—"God be praised."[42]

Lesson Three: Collective Thanksgiving Celebrations Are Enhanced by Each Believer's Ability to Think Theologically
When quarreling threatened Plymouth colony's productivity and therefore its aid from England, the Pilgrims turned to a layman, Robert Cushman, to preach a sermon on the danger of selfishness. Cushman was a deacon, recently arrived from the Separatist congregation in the Netherlands from which the Pilgrim Fathers originated. His exposition of 1 Corinthians 10:24 claimed

---

[37] Willison, *Saints and Strangers*, 157.

[38] Bradford, *Plimouth Plantation*, 101.

[39] Bradford, *Plimouth Plantation*, 104.

[40] Willison, *Saints and Strangers*, 156.

[41] Willison, *Saints and Strangers*, 189.

[42] Winslow and Bradford, *Mourt's Relation, Part VI*.

grateful hearts were part of the remedy for Plymouth's trouble. Humans act selfishly, Cushman said, when they lack "heavenly conversation" and a "spiritual eye to behold the glory, greatness, and majesty, and goodness of God."[43] He continued:

> If men were conversant courtiers in Heaven, they would cry out with Paul, Rom. 11.33, *Oh the depth of the riches, wisdom, and knowledge of God* ... If men in serious contemplation, by the eye of faith, would behold the glory of God, and what great riches, beauty, fulness, perfection, power, dignity, and greatness is in God, they would leave admiring of themselves, and seeking of themselves, and would say with David, *What am I? And what is my father's house that thou shouldest bless me?*[44]

That the exposition came from a layman was not incidental. For the Pilgrim Fathers, every believer was responsible before God to apprehend biblical teaching and live it out. Neither theology nor ecclesiastical authority was limited to clergymen. Historically, this doctrine is known as the priesthood of all believers. For the Pilgrims, it enabled broad acceptance and appropriation of the first two lessons noted in this chapter.

The Pilgrims at Plymouth didn't depend on clergy to feed them Christian doctrine. For the first nine years of Plymouth's existence, the colony did not include a single ordained minister. After that, Pilgrim congregations still frequently found themselves without ministers. In the first twenty years of Plymouth's existence, only three ministers lived there. John Robinson, pastor of the English congregation from which the Pilgrims originated, died in 1625 in the Netherlands before he could join his church in the New World.[45] In the short-lived existence of the Pilgrim empire, Willison wrote, "the voice of God thundering from the pulpit never succeeded in drowning out the voice of the people."[46] The Saints "stuck to first principles, acting upon the belief that the church consisted primarily of the great body of communicants."[47] When the Pilgrims landed at Plymouth, however, it remained to be seen whether a society of Christians so independent from clergy could sustain their theological vision.

A basis for the priesthood of all believers—though they did not employ that phrase—was articulated in the Separatists' 1596 confession of faith. The church,

---

[43] Robert Cushman, *Sin and the Danger of Self-Love Described, in a Sermon Preached at Plymouth, in New England, 1621* (Boston, MA: Charles Ewer, 1846), 20.

[44] Cushman, *Sin and the Danger of Self-Love Described*, 20–21.

[45] Ahlstrom, *A Religious History of the American People*, 138.

[46] Willison, *Saints and Strangers*, 183.

[47] Willison, *Saints and Strangers*, 183.

they said, is Christ's "spirituall kingdome" on earth, which has been separated "from emongst unbelievers" as "a royall Priesthood."[48] Each local church "hath powre and commandment to elect and ordeine their own ministerie" and "to depose them from the ministerie they exercised" in the event of egregious wrongdoing.[49] The congregation likewise possesses the power "to receive or to cut off anie member."[50] The notion that hierarchical levels of clergy may exercise authority over believers in local congregations is "strange and Anti-christian" as well as not "instituted in Christs Testament."[51] Every believer in the congregation possesses equal worth and responsibility before God.

The concept of the priesthood of all believers predated the Pilgrim Fathers. Martin Luther articulated the notion in his 1520 treatise *To the Christian Nobility of the German Nation*. An assembly of believers, not a pope or bishop, has authority to ordain clergy, Luther wrote, "for whoever comes out of the water of baptism can boast that he is already consecrated a priest ... we are all priests of equal standing."[52] Calvin articulated the same doctrine, though he mentioned it less frequently than Luther. He wrote in the *Institutes* that "Christ plays the priestly role" in order to "receive us as his companions in this great office. For we who are defiled in ourselves, yet are priests in him."[53] Both the Puritan and Separatist streams of the Reformed traditions continued this doctrinal emphasis. The Puritan *Westminster Confession of Faith* and the Separatist *Savoy Declaration* alike stated that "God alone is lord of the conscience," with each believer bearing individual responsibility before God for his beliefs and practice.[54]

Yet Separatists—especially the Pilgrim Fathers—lived out the doctrine with unique consistency. A comparison of Plymouth colony with its Puritan neighbors to the north in Massachusetts Bay Colony proves helpful in this regard. While both groups believed the church should comprise only "visible saints" and that each believer bore individual responsibility before God, a Puritan could not "pursue the implications of his principles the way the Separatists did."[55] That was because Puritans never separated from the Church of England and its practice

---

[48] *A True Confession*, Article 17.

[49] *A True Confession*, Article 23.

[50] *A True Confession*, Article 24.

[51] *A True Confession*, Article 29.

[52] Martin Luther, *To the Christian Nobility of the German Nation*, trans. Charles M. Jacobs, rev. James Atkinson, in *Three Treatises from the American Edition of Luther's Works* (Philadelphia, PA: Fortress, 1970), 14.

[53] Calvin, *Institutes* 2.15.6.

[54] *Westminster Confession of Faith*, chapter 20; *Savoy Declaration*, chapter 21.

[55] Edmund S. Morgan, *Visible Saints: The History of a Puritan Idea* (Ithaca, NY: Cornell University Press, 1963), 20.

of regarding every Englishman as a church member. Only Separatists demanded a confession of faith as a prerequisite for church membership.[56] That Separatist distinctive supported the quest to make every church member a student and practitioner of God's Word. In light of that distinction between Pilgrims and Puritans, it is interesting that Plymouth became famous for its community-wide Thanksgiving celebration while Massachusetts Bay attained notoriety largely for the theological contributions of its individual ministers and the universities it founded to train them.

The Pilgrims' discernment of God's providence in sea travel, agriculture, warfare, and diplomacy was the work of theologically-minded laypeople some 3,500 miles removed from their pastor in Leiden. Their daily, weekly, and occasional expressions of thankful worship were communal, not decreed by clergy. Their two most notable literary works—both evincing an underlying grasp of Christian doctrine—likewise were the products of laymen. Bradford's *History of Plimouth Plantation* recounts God's dealings with the Pilgrims in detail, and the *Mayflower Compact* puts forth the "glorie of God" and "advancement of ye Christian faith" as two of Plymouth's aims.[57] Deacon Cushman's 1621 sermon was typical in its exhibition of lay theological acumen. In closing, he appealed—based on a catena of biblical references—for hearts of gratitude:

> Lay away all thought of former things and forget them, and think upon the things that are; look not gapingly one upon another, pleading your goodness, your birth, your life you lived, your means you had and might have had; here you are by God's providence under difficulties; be thankful to God it is no worse, and take it in good part that which is.[58]

Indeed, theology fell within the purview of every Pilgrim believer. Perhaps rigorous adherence to the priesthood of all believers is why the Pilgrims could, at the first Thanksgiving, "rejoice *together*" that "by the goodness of God, we are so far from want."

"Their Trust in Heaven"

Historians who characterize the first Thanksgiving as more legend than fact, more revelry than spirituality, have cited New England statesman Daniel Webster's 1820 speech at Plymouth Rock as a key step in formulating the Pilgrim "myth." Deetz and Deetz, for example, argued that Webster made "the Pilgrim myth accessible for the first time to an audience far beyond the confines of the

---

[56] Morgan, *Visible Saints*, 40.

[57] Bradford, *Plimouth Plantation*, 110.

[58] Cushman, *Sin and the Danger of Self-Love Described*, 32.

town of Plymouth itself."⁵⁹ Such critiques go too far. While Webster took poetic license with some details (like the importance of Plymouth Rock itself), his characterisation of the Pilgrim Fathers as thankful people of faith is borne out by the historical record. Commemorating the 200th anniversary of Plymouth colony's founding, he stated,

> The imagination irresistibly and rapidly draws around us the principal features and the leading characters in the original scene. We cast our eyes abroad on the ocean, and we see where the little bark, with the interesting group upon its deck, made its slow progress to the shore. We look around us, and behold the hills and promontories where the anxious eyes of our fathers first saw the places of habitation and of rest. We feel the cold which benumbed, and listen to the winds which pierced them. Beneath us is the Rock, on which New England received the feet of the Pilgrims. We seem even to behold them, as they struggle with the elements, and, with toilsome efforts, gain the shore. We listen to the chiefs in council; we see the unexampled exhibition of female fortitude and resignation; we hear the whisperings of youthful impatience, and we see, what a painter of our own has also represented by his pencil, chilled and shivering childhood, houseless, but for a mother's arms, couchless, but for a mother's breast, till our own blood almost freezes. The mild dignity of Carver and of Bradford; the decisive and soldierlike air and manner of Standish; the devout Brewster; the enterprising Allerton; the general firmness and thoughtfulness of the whole band; their conscious joy for dangers escaped; their deep solicitude about danger to come; their trust in Heaven; their high religious faith, full of confidence and anticipation; all of these seem to belong to this place, and to be present upon this occasion, to fill us with reverence and admiration.⁶⁰

With the passing of 200 more years, we still have reason to celebrate the Pilgrim Fathers' "high religious faith, full of confidence and anticipation," and look to them for enduring lessons on providence and gratitude.⁶¹

---

⁵⁹ Deetz and Deetz, *Times of their Lives*, 14.

⁶⁰ Daniel Webster, "Plymouth Oration, December 22, 1820," *Dartmouth University Website*, (https:/www.dartmouth.edu/~dwebster/speeches/plymouth-oration.html; accessed June 25, 2020).

⁶¹ Webster, "Plymouth Oration."

The meeting of Samoset with the Pilgrims
(Public Domain).

CHAPTER THIRTEEN

Encounter with the Indians

ROY M. PAUL

Introduction

The Pilgrims, having been in exile in Holland for a number of years, decided it was time to move. There were several deciding factors, according to William Bradford. In his account, Bradford records that many of the Pilgrims were getting older and were finding the living conditions intolerable. There was also a grave concern regarding the premature aging of their children, due to overwork. Bradford states:

> For many of their children, that were of best dispositions and gracious inclinations, haveing lernde to bear ye yoake in their youth, and willing to bear parte of their parents burden, were, often times, so oppressed with their hevie labours, that though their minds were free and willing, yet their bodies bowed under ye weight of ye same, and became decrepit in their early youth; the vigour of nature being consumed in ye very budd as it were.[1]

Additionally, many of their children were being led astray, ultimately leaving their homes and their faith, and signing up as soldiers or sailors. One of the

---

[1] William Bradford, *Bradford's History of Plimouth Plantation* (Okitoks Press, 2017), 40. To be true to the record and since the narrative is easily understood, all wording and spelling are as documented in the original.

biggest concerns was that the children were losing their English identity and becoming Dutch. Finally, Bradford says that many of the Pilgrims had missionary hearts and desired "for ye propagating & advancing of ye gospell of ye kingdom of Christ in those remote parts of ye world."[2]

And so, with the decision made to depart the Netherlands, the question of venturing to America was put forth. There were many objections raised against this destination: the long voyage by sea with its perils; the change in climate, diet and water with resulting diseases, and the high financial cost of such a trip. The one unknown, of which they were most fearful, was the prospect of what they might experience at the hands of the vicious and unpredictable natives in America. Bradford expounds:

> And also those which should escape or overcome these difficulties, should yet be in continuall danger of ye salvage people, who are cruell, barbarous, & most treacherous, being most furious in their rage, and merciles wher they overcome; not being contente only to kill, & take away life, but delight to tormente men in ye most bloodie maner that may be; fleaing some alive with ye shells of fishes, cutting of ye members and joints of others by peasmeale, and broiling on ye coles, eate ye collops of their flesh in their sight whilst they live; with other cruelties horrible to be related.[3]

These accounts had come from those who had previously voyaged to Virginia, where not only had the earlier English settlers suffered untold hardship due to sickness and starvation, but also from the relentless Indian attacks on the Jamestown settlement. Regardless, the group consensus was that great things are accomplished often in the face of great peril, and besides God had called them to this mission, and he would go before them and bless their endeavours, as was his will.

The Voyage

Having procured what appeared to be a suitable vessel called the *Speedwell*, the Leyden congregation gathered for one last time at the port in Delfshaven, with their beloved pastor, John Robinson. Interestingly, in Bradford's journal, neither the *Speedwell* nor the *Mayflower* is cited by name. Robinson preached to them from Ezra 8:21: "There, by the Ahava Canal, I proclaimed a fast, so that we might humble ourselves before our God and ask him for a safe journey for us and our children, with all our possessions" (NIV). Their last day together was spent in fellowship and prayer. The following day with many tears, the group departed,

---

[2] Bradford, *Bradford's History*, 41.

[3] Bradford, *Bradford's History*, 41.

realizing that many of their friends they would never see on earth again. Bradford recorded, "So they lefte y‍ᵗ goodly and pleasante citie which had been ther resting place for near 12 years; but they knew they were pilgrims."[4]

On July 26, 1620, at Southampton, England, the *Speedwell* joined the *Mayflower*, the second ship planning to make the voyage. The voyage of the Pilgrims, however, was fraught with difficulty from the outset. There had been difficulty getting a charter. After this had been obtained, they were confronted with an outstanding debt that would cost up to £100 per passenger. The necessary funds had to be procured by selling some of their provisions for the voyage. The *Mayflower* finally hoisted anchor and set sail on August 5, 1620 carrying 102 passengers, 50 of whom were Pilgrims. The wind was not very favourable and after three or four days of slow progress, Reynolds, captain of the *Speedwell*, announced his ship had a serious leak, and called for a stop in Durham for repairs.[5] The ship was repaired and after another delay they once more put out to sea. As Brown tells us, "The voyagers had only gone some three hundred miles beyond the Land's End when Reynolds again proclaimed the *Speedwell* to be unseaworthy."[6] The ships returned to Plymouth and it was decided that the *Speedwell*, unable to make the transatlantic voyage, would return to London. Of her passengers, eighteen became dismayed and returned with the ship, to London, while twelve were added to the already cramped *Mayflower*. The sailing season was getting late, and the *Mayflower* finally put out to sea on September 6. After a few days of favourable winds and fair sailing, the seasonal gales came on them with a vengeance. At one point a main beam was displaced and a repair only achieved by the fact that one of the passengers had brought a powerful screw, which, after considerable effort, righted the beam. They continued through a series of violent storms and the first of their casualties, William Butten, a servant to Samuel Fuller, died and was buried at sea on November 7. In one storm, young John Howland ventured up to the main deck when he was suddenly pitched overboard. In the providence of God, he managed to grab a rope dragging behind the ship, and was safely pulled back on board. Finally, on November 9, after sixty-five days at sea, the weary travelers sighted land. The anchorage appeared suitable, however Captain Jones realized they were considerably north of their intended destination at the Hudson River. He was concerned, because many of the passengers were suffering illness. He attempted to sail south to the Hudson, only to encounter severe and unfavourable seas and decided to return to the calm of Cape Cod, and get the passengers to shore.

---

[4] Bradford, *Bradford's History*, 58.

[5] John Brown, *The Pilgrim Fathers of New England* (London: The Religious Tract Society, 1906), 191.

[6] Brown, *The Pilgrim Fathers*, 191.

Plymouth Rock, Plymouth, MA
(Photo: Michael A.G. Haykin)

The Landing

With the awareness that their charter did not include the lands where they were now anchored, they realized that they had no governing authorities. Before going ashore to scope out the suitability of the location, the men prepared a rudimentary constitutional document, known as the Mayflower Compact, signed by forty-one of the men. They had brought along a shallop in which to go ashore, but it had been dismantled for the voyage and had sustained damage during the storms, which necessitated major repairs. Sixteen men were chosen to go ashore on the ship's smaller boat. They were armed with muskets, and Captain Miles Standish, a seasoned military man, was put in charge. On Wednesday, November 15, the party headed for shore. The challenge before them was that for a place suitable for a settlement, it must have a harbor into which to sail the ship close enough to shore to be readily accessible. Bradford records the relief and joy of the Pilgrims having, at long last, the ability to set foot on dry ground once more:

> Being thus arrived in a good harbor and brought safe to land, they fell upon their knees & blessed ye God of heaven, who had brought them over ye vast & furious ocean, and delivered them from all ye periles and miseries thereof, again to set their feete on ye firm and stable earth, their proper element.[7]

They ventured a mile or so, northeast, along the beach when suddenly they came upon five or six aboriginal people, with a dog, walking toward them. The two groups stood for a moment, in shock, scrutinizing each other. The natives appeared to converse, and suddenly turned and retreated into the woods. Standish and the men followed, hoping to speak with them and establish contact; however, after a chase of several miles and with darkness setting in, they had to abandon the effort. The next morning they continued their pursuit, following tracks up a tidal creek until they disappeared into the woods. They ventured into the thickets but it was so dense they found it was tearing their clothes and catching on the cumbersome armor. They arrived at a clearing with a spring of fresh water. The only drink they had with them was aqua vitae, a strong alcohol, so their thirst for water was insatiable. Bradford states that they were so thirsty that this first taste of fresh New England water was as pleasant to them as beer and wine had been to them before. To this day it is still known as Pilgrim Spring. They ventured back to the shore, where the *Mayflower* was within sight, and as had been arranged, they built a signal fire. Afterwards, they camped for the night. The next day they continued to search the area and discovered a clearing where corn had been planted. They found remnants of a building, along with several small mounds. As they began to dig, they uncovered an Indian bow and some badly decomposed arrows. Not wanting to disturb what was probably a grave, they covered the area back up. As they continued to explore the mounds, they

---

[7] Bradford, *Bradford's History*, 66.

discovered, "in them diverce faire Indian baskets filled with corne, and some in eares, faire and good, of diverce collours."[8] They took some with them back to the ship; for while they had brought peas, barley and wheat with them on the voyage, for planting in the spring, it was unknown if these would be suitable to the seasonal climate of the New World. This brazen act was not without risks, for they were stealing something of value from those with whom they had not yet established a relationship. This act could possibly serve as a further barrier to the Indians wanting to connect with them, deeming them thieves. But the Pilgrims were desperate. The winter was upon them and their provisions were beginning to dwindle. They purposed to compensate the Indians if and when they established a connection with them.

The Search
On Monday, November 27, the shallop was ready to sail and under the command of Captain Jones, thirty-four men: twenty-four passengers and ten sailors headed for land, hoping to find a suitable spot to settle. They were met with a vicious northeast wind and driving snow. With great difficulty they reached land, chilled to the bone with cold. The cold was so extreme and their suffering so severe that some of those who died later, Bradford says, "took the original of their death here."[9] By morning there was six inches of snow on the ground and after exploring the territory, it was determined that the area was unsuitable for them to establish a settlement. The next day they went in search of the original cache of corn they had found previously. Due to the frozen ground and fresh snow the search was difficult; however, they happened upon the cache and found an additional ten bushels of corn. Captain Jones decided it was time to return to the *Mayflower* with this fresh store of corn and the men who were too sick to continue the search. Standish was again in charge of those who remained on shore.

The following morning, Standish and his men once again took up the search for the Indians, without success. Unknown to them at the time, the natives tended to over-winter in the bush, where there was some protection against the elements, returning to the water when the fair weather arrived. On their return to the shore at the end of the day they came upon a larger grave than they had seen before. Edward Winslow recorded in detail what they found when they dug open the grave:

> [W]e found first a mat, and under that a fair bow, and there another mat, and under that a board about three-quarters of a yard long finely carved and painted, with three tines or broaches on the top like a crown. ... At length we came to a fair new mat, and under that two bundles, the one bigger, the

---

[8] Bradford, *Bradford's History*, 68.

[9] Brown, *The Pilgrim Fathers*, 199.

other less. We opened the greater and found in it a great quantity of fine and perfect red powder, and in it the bones and skull of a man. The skull had fine yellow hair on it, and some of the flesh unconsumed. ... We opened the less bundle likewise and found of the same powder in it, and the bones and head of a little child. About the legs and other parts of it were bound strings and bracelets of fine white beads. There was also by it a little bow about three-quarters of a yard long, and some other odd knacks.[10]

It was obvious to them this was likely the body of a French sailor that had been on the ship, whose remnants they had seen in previous searches. But what of the child? Had the soldier been taken in by the natives and fathered a child? While the mystery would remain unsettled, one thing was clear to them. Their desire in escaping the persecution in England was to re-establish a separatist colony in the New World, it was now obvious that others had already been there. As they continued their search they found intact Indian wigwams, complete with dishes, pots, baskets, and remnants of game and fish; some fairly fresh. As with the previous cache of corn they had discovered, they took some of the goods they found, again with the intention of compensating the natives once they had established contact. Once more they returned to the *Mayflower* hoping that another day would bring them better opportunities of a location for a settlement.

On Wednesday, December 6, they again ventured to shore to scout the coastline. It was so piercingly cold that Bradford said the spray from the waves froze on their coats making them look, "as if they had been glased."[11] They worked their way along the coast and toward evening they spotted about a dozen Indians on the shore, busily cutting up the remains of a stranded pilot whale, also called a blackfish. When the natives saw them, they hastily grabbed what they had cut and retreated into the bushes. The shallop landed at a safe distance and they built a roughly secured camp for the night. In the distance they could see the glow of the natives' fire. In the morning the party divided in two: one group continuing down the coast in the shallop, the other searching the shoreline. The land party found the remains of the whale, more graves and wigwams, but no Indians or suitable place to settle. At the end of the day they rendezvoused with their compatriots from the shallop and set up another fortified camp for the night. About midnight, they were awakened by a wild howling and the camp sentinel calling them to arms. After they fired a couple of shots, the howling ceased and it was speculated that the wailing had probably been wolves. The party was up at 5 a.m. to catch the tide back to the ship. As they were preparing breakfast it was decided they should prepare by taking some things to the shallop. This turned out to be a potentially serious tactical error, as some had

---

[10] Kate Caffrey, *The Mayflower* (New York: Stein and Day, 1974), 120–121.

[11] Bradford, *Bradford's History*, 69.

taken their muskets and left them at the shoreline. Suddenly, there was the same sound of shrieking and howling they had heard the previous night. One of the men came running in screaming, "Men, Indians! Indians!" Out of the woods came a flurry of arrows, and the men began to fire back. Standish ordered them to hold fire until they could take proper aim. Those who had taken their guns to the beach, dashed to retrieve them and were almost trapped with no retreat. Bradford tells of one large Indian:

> Yet ther was a lustie man, and no less valiante, stood behind a tree within halfe a musket shot, and let his arrows flie at them. He was seen shoot 3. arrows, which were all avoided. He stood 3. shot of a musket, till one taking aime at him, and made ye bark or splinters of ye tree fly about his ears, after which he gave an extraordinary shrike, and away they wente, all of them.[12]

In a show of courage, some of the men chased the Indians for about a quarter of a mile, firing a couple of shots after them. Returning to camp, they assessed the damage, and found that, except for a few arrow holes in the coats that had been hanging, everything and everyone was unscathed. Bradford records, "Afterwards they gave God sollame thanks & praise for their deliverance, & gathered up a bundle of their arrows & sente them into England afterward by ye m^r. of ye ship, and called that place ye first encounter."[13] Today this area is called First Encounter Beach, and is found in Eastham, Massachusetts.

They boarded the shallop and set out to find a more suitable location around the bay. Later in the day the wind rose, freezing rain poured down and the waves grew. In the midst of the stormy conditions, in the rough seas, the rudder broke. It took the full effort of two sailors, using oars to steer and keep them from disaster. To add to their peril, the mast broke into three pieces and the sail went overboard. Only with maximum effort, the fear of being lost, and the fact that the tide was with them were they saved. They rounded the tip of what was Saquish, and finally found calmer water in the lee of an island. Discussion ensued as to their course of action. Should they venture to shore or should they remain on the shallop, safe from potential native attack? The group was divided. Some went to shore and started a fire. When the wind turned to the northeast and froze hard, the remaining men came to shore to get warm. The next morning, Saturday, December 9, dawned clear and sunny and they discovered they were on an island, which they named Clarke's Island after John Clarke, the *Mayflower*'s mate. Since they were under no threat from the aboriginals, they took the day to dry everything, clean their weapons and prepare for the Sabbath. After resting

---

[12] Bradford, *Bradford's History*, 69.

[13] Bradford, *Bradford's History*, 70.

Sunday, they continued on Monday to explore the area and take depth soundings. They found that it was quite suitable for the *Mayflower* to come and anchor. Caffrey tells us, "Eventually they landed, somewhere between what is now called Captain's Hill and the spot named Plymouth Rock."[14] This event has been heavily romanticised in the ensuing four hundred years, with much folklore added to the occasion. In reality, it would have been a very ordinary and uneventful occasion. Neither William Bradford in his, *Of Plimouth Plantation*, nor Edward Winslow in his account entitled, *Mourt's Relation*[15] make mention of landing at a rock. Once more we look to Bradford for a first-hand account of the event. "On *Munday* they sounded ye harbor, and founde it fitt for shipping, and marched into ye land, & found diverse cornfields, & little running brooks, a place (as they supposed) fitt for situation; at least it was ye best they could find, and ye season, and their presente necessitie, made them glad to accepte of it."[16] While not the most ideal location, their present circumstances determined that this was where they would settle. They sailed back to the *Mayflower* and informed the others that a suitable site had been found. The relief and any excitement felt by Bradford was short lived as he was informed that five days previously, his beloved wife of seven years, Dorothy May Bradford had slipped over the side of the *Mayflower*, and drowned.

The Settlement

On Friday December 15, Jones headed the ship toward their landing spot when a storm blew in. After riding it out all night they came to anchor on Saturday in Plymouth harbour. In the days ahead, they searched the area for a suitable location to build their common dwelling. They found evidence of previously cultivated corn fields, and to their horror, skeletal remains scattered throughout the area. The natives had been decimated by a plague. They chose a location called Cole's Hill and erected their new home. Plans were laid out for a town, with defensive installations. Some construction was begun; however, the conditions were beginning to take their toll. Within a few short weeks, their number had dwindled to half. The remaining settlers, always fearful of native attack, did their best to hide their true conditions. They buried the dead at night and covered the ground, lest it be discovered how weak and vulnerable they had become. They encountered the Indians, from time to time, but always from a distance. On one occasion, one of the men out duck hunting was concealed in the reeds, when a number of Indians passed by. He ran back

---

[14] Caffrey, *The Mayflower*, 127.

[15] Caleb Johnson, "The Plymouth Colony Archive Project," *Mourt's Relation: A Journal of the Pilgrims at Plymouth, 1622* (http://www.histarch.illinois.edu/plymouth/mourt1.html; accessed August 24, 2020).

[16] Bradford, *Bradford's History*, 70.

to where some men were working at the edge of the forest; dropping their tools, they ran back to retrieve their weapons. When they returned, there was no sign of the Indians, and their tools were gone. The settlers laboured, as best they could, through the winter and tended to the sick. Jones, who had intended to return to England with the *Mayflower*, once the Pilgrims were settled on shore, had to await the recovery of some of his sailors before he could set sail for home. Casual sightings of the Indians continued to occur but each time the settlers attempted to approach, the Indians would hasten away. On Friday, March 16, while the settlement was holding a meeting, a lone Indian appeared on the hill and confidently strode down into the encampment. The alarm was raised, but he continued, confidently walking up to the men. He hailed them and said, "Welcome, Englishmen!" He told them his name was Samoset, which he may have taken as an English variant of Somerset. He explained that he was not from that area, but was an Algonquin sachem or chief from the Pemaquid Point in Maine, near Mohegan Island. He had learned English from the fishing vessels that had frequented his area. The Pilgrims provided him with some gin and various samplings of their food, which he recognized as English fare. He provided them with invaluable information about the area and its inhabitants. He said the area where they were settled was called Patuxet, and the local tribe had been decimated some years earlier by a plague that had swept through the area. The tribe, numbering about one hundred, who had stolen their tools, were called the Nausets. They were friendly; however they had previously been deceived by the English Captain Thomas Hunt. After establishing a trading relationship with them, Hunt's men kidnapped twenty-seven of them and sold them as slaves to Spain. He informed them that the supreme leader of the local Indian confederacy known as the Wampanoags, was named Massasoit. He resided about forty miles away at a place called Pokanoket, and with Massasoit resided another Indian, named Squanto, who was even more fluent in English than he was. Samoset made it clear he planned to stay the night and so with some reticence regarding the uncertainty surrounding this new "friend," it was decided he would stay the night with the Stephen Hawkins family.

The following morning, Samoset left them with the promise to return with some of Massasoit's men. Samoset returned with five natives, with black-painted faces and a deer skin across their shoulders. As a sign of goodwill, they left their bows and arrows outside the town and brought with them the previously stolen tools. It was clear they wished to enter into trade but being the Sabbath, the Pilgrims graciously declined and plied them with some token gifts. The Indians accepted them gladly and departed, promising to come back. On March 22, Samoset returned, and accompanying him was Tisquantum, or Squanto, who as it turned out was the only Patuxet survivor of the plague in that area. Squanto had been one of Hunt's captives that had been sold into slavery. He had managed to escape his captivity in Spain and made his way to England where ultimately, he became a servant to Captain John Dermer who was exploring the New England coast. Squanto made it back to his homeland, only to find his tribe was all dead. He connected with Massasoit, and would prove to be his powerful ally in negotiating with the English. But Squanto would prove even more crucial to the survival of the Pilgrims. Caffrey explains, "He told the Pilgrims where to find the best fish and how to catch them; where to plant corn and how to fertilize it; he guided and piloted many of their first expeditions, and in fact stayed with them for the rest of his life."[17] While the Indians had brought some fresh fish and a few furs to trade, the real reason for the visit was to inform them that Massasoit and his brother, Quadequina were in the area and wished to meet with them. A short time later, Massasoit, Quadequina and about sixty armed warriors appeared on the hill before the settlement. As the groups eyed each other warily, Squanto went out to meet the chief and returned with the message that Massasoit wished to meet with their leader. Edward Winslow, clad in armor and sword, acting as the representative of their Governor John Carver, accompanied Squanto out to meet with the chief. He presented Massasoit and his brother with gifts of knives, copper chains, a pot of alcohol and some biscuits and butter. Winslow told the chief, "King James saluted him with words of love and peace, and did accept of him as his friend and ally, and that our governor desired to see him and to truck [trade] with him, and to confirm a peace with him, as his next neighbor."[18] After Massasoit had eaten some biscuits and had a drink, he left Winslow in the custody of his brother, while he took twenty of his men, unarmed, to meet with Governor Carver. The meeting was friendly and cordial, and after partaking of some meat and drink, they proceeded to establish a six-point treaty which Bradford recorded as follows:

1. That neither he nor any of his, should injurie or doe hurt to any of their people.
2. That if any of his did any hurt to any of theirs, he should send ye offender, that they might punish him.
3. That if any thing were taken away from any of theirs, he should cause it to be restored; and they should doe ye like to his.
4. If any did unjustly warr against him, they would aide him; if any did war against them, he should aide them.
5. He should send to his neighbours confederats, to certifie them of this, that they might not wrong them, but might be likewise comprised in ye conditions of peace.
6. That when ther men came to them, they should leave their bows &

---

[17] Caffrey, *The Mayflower*, 140.

[18] Johnson, "The Plymouth Colony Archive Project."

arrows behind them.[19]

A treaty was now established with the most powerful chief of the area. This treaty was mutually beneficial, in that in the ensuing years the Indians would help keep the Pilgrims from starvation and the settlers would provide protective assistance to the Wampanoags in their conflicts with the Narragansetts. While the future would include some incidences of strained relations with the natives, this treaty would remain relatively intact for almost fifty years. After the death of Massasoit, his son, Metacom, who dubbed himself King Philip, would ultimately go to war against the colonists in 1675.[20] Philip led his tribe, along with the Nipmuck, Pocumtuck and Narraganset tribes against the English settlers, in a failed attempt to drive them out. The war ended in 1676 with Philip's defeat.

Satisfied that the Pilgrims were settled and his remaining men were well enough to sail, on April 5, 1621, Captain Jones headed the *Mayflower* out to sea and back to England. Philbrick gives this summary, "Like the Pilgrims, the sailors had been decimated by disease. Jones had lost his boatswain, his gunner, three quartermasters, the cook and more than a dozen sailors. He had also lost a cooper but not to illness. John Alden had decided to stay in Plymouth."[21] The *Mayflower* arrived safely back in Rotherhithe on the Thames, on May 6, 1621. The return voyage took them less than half the time it had taken to voyage to America.

---

[19] Bradford, *Bradford's History*, 73–74.

[20] For a detailed discussion on King Philip's War, consult Philbrick, *Mayflower*.

[21] Philbrick, *Mayflower*, 100.

George Henry Boughton, "Priscilla and John Alden"
(New York Public Library Digital Collections)—
depicting John Alden (c.1599–1687) and
his wife Priscilla (c.1602–c.1685).
Among their descendants were
US Presidents John Adams and John Quincy Adams
and Henry Wadsworth Longfellow.

CHAPTER FOURTEEN

The Pilgrim Mothers

PRISCILLA WONG

In celebrating the 400-year anniversary of the voyage of the Mayflower, we can certainly appreciate the plethora of literature now available. The history hunter need not look far to learn about the complex economic, political, and religious situation of early seventeenth-century England that sent the Pilgrims onto that hazardous trek across the Atlantic and into that uncertain New World. The level of detail in these accounts is remarkable, with narratives that graphically depict the conditions of the time, from a giant beam on the *Mayflower* ship that splintered in the midst of a raging storm halfway through that sixty-six day ocean voyage to the strawberry and sassafras root broth prepared by a Pilgrim that revived a dying aboriginal chief. William Bradford, who governed Plymouth colony for thirty years, had undertaken the momentous task of recording an in-depth account of the migration to and settlement in New England. Titled *Of Plymouth Plantation* and lauded by one historian as "the greatest book written in seventeenth-century America," the manuscript was written over a period of two decades and numbers 270 pages.[1] This primary resource, along with letters, historical printed works, and material valuables of the Pilgrims, brings the modern reader incredibly close to a revered but remote history. Yet, for all the evidence, the constructed picture of the Pilgrim experience leaves us wanting without an understanding of the woman's narrative. In telling the story of Susanna White,

---

[1] Nathaniel Philbrick, *Mayflower: A Story of Courage, Community, and War* (New York, NY: Penguin, 2007), 7.

one of the *Mayflower* matrons, one writer describes the meagre evidence as a trail of breadcrumbs.[2] Of course, the problem with the largely unaccounted stories of women is not unique to this group or period. The dearth of historical records over the centuries capturing the personal experiences of women is a widespread reality. The question is how we are to satiate our hunger for the stories of these Pilgrim women when what we have are breadcrumbs.

Let us consider the situation by imagining that a film is to be made about the Pilgrims. It begins with a bird's eye view of the actors and actions below. On the Atlantic, it captures the approximately 100 x 25 feet, 180-ton *Mayflower* ship sailing against the violent winds, even the rare figure emerging onto the upper deck to take in some fresh air. In New England, it captures the Pilgrim men armed with their muskets exploring the new territory, them cutting down the trees and assembling houses in freezing temperatures, and their guarded encounters with the natives. Chilling cries of mysterious creatures—possibly cougars or wolves—are heard in the distance. Taking refuge from that wilderness, the women remain inside the ship while the men launch into the immense work of rendering the land habitable. Bradford depicts the wintry scene weeks after the Pilgrims' arrival:

> The weather was very cold, and it froze so hard that the spray of the sea froze on their coats like glass. Early that night they got to the lower end of [Cape Cod] bay, and as [the men and sailors] drew near the shore they saw ten or twelve Indians very busy about something. They landed about a league or two from them … It was late when they landed, so they made themselves a barricade of logs and boughs as well as they could in the time, and set a sentinel and betook them to rest, and saw the smoke of the fire the [natives] made that night.[3]

Here we are presented with an intimate view of the experience of this Pilgrim leader at a precise time and place. It is intensely vivid: we can sense the unforgiving elements lashing out at the men's exposed bodies, their movements across the water, their uneasy spotting of the Natives, and their apprehension and exhaustion as they collapsed onto the ground, smoke from a distant blaze still lingering in the frigid night air.

Upon viewing this close-up scene, we begin to develop a craving for such views of the Pilgrim women. On the periphery, without access to and freedom of the pen, the women's innermost thoughts and feelings go unheard, the full and precise nature of their activity unseen, and hence the significance of their role

---

[2] Martyn Whittock, *Mayflower Lives: Pilgrims in a New World and the Early American Experience* (New York, NY: Pegasus Books, 2019), 43.

[3] William Bradford, *Of Plymouth Plantation*, ed. Harold Paget (Mineola, NY: Dover, 2006), 46.

in the formation of the colony minimized. One writer in 1879 lamented: "Unnumbered thousands have passed beautiful, strenuous and brave lives far from the scenes of civilization, and gone down to their graves leaving only local, feeble voices, if any, to celebrate their praises."[4] He further observed that the missing female perspective meant the loss of the "impressible" since women

> are more susceptible to pain and pleasure; enjoying and sorrowing more keenly than her sterner and rougher mate, she possesses often a peculiarly graphic power in expressing her own thoughts and feelings, and also in delineating the scenes through which she passes.[5]

What other emotive or striking scenes might have accompanied the ones already depicted by notable leaders of Plymouth Colony? Deprived of a direct channel into the private lives of these women, we must consider much more weightily the principal factors that ruled and stirred their hearts as they plunged into the dangers of that ocean crossing and bore the hardships of an unknown land. For the Pilgrim women, faith and theological conviction were the fire and force that guided and informed their daily activities. To look intimately into their lives, the camera must pan to the places where their spiritual life was most manifest. We may not be privy to their specific reflections, but observing their endurance in times of trial, self-sacrifice in times of need, and steadfast service in times of weariness bear witness to their deeply felt and lived beliefs. To ponder earnestly the spiritual context of these Pilgrim women is therefore to appreciate more fully how their faith permeated their outward activities.

Pilgrim Women as Partakers in a Community of Faith

We begin with William Bradford's church in Scrooby from 1606 to 1608, twelve years before the Pilgrims boarded the *Mayflower*. The camera must first capture the heart of this Scrooby congregation in which biblical convictions about what constituted the "true church" were deeply rooted, hence its decisive step to "purify" itself by breaking free from the state church, which was vehemently believed to possess too many unscriptural elements, or in the words of Bradford, "men's inventions" which hindered the "right worship of God."[6] This group of Puritans, or Separatists (they were "separating" Puritans), refused to conform and were willing to put themselves at risk of being caught by agents under King James who was determined to be rid of such citizens who were a

---

[4] William W. Fowler, *Woman on the American Frontier. A Valuable and Authentic History of the Heroism, Adventures, Privations, Captivities, Trials, and Noble Lives and Deaths of the "Pioneer Mothers of the Republic"* (Hartford, CT: S.S. Scranton & Company, 1879), 195–196.

[5] Fowler, *Woman on the American Frontier*, 195–196.

[6] Bradford, *Plymouth Plantation*, ed. Paget, 2.

threat to his monarchial rule. Under the preaching of Separatists John Robinson and William Brewster, secretly meeting in Brewster's home, the men and women of this congregation gathered together in worship every Sabbath with a unified vision of forming a community that was uncorrupted by the impositions of the state. Convicted by Paul's words in 2 Corinthians 6:17, "be ye separate, saith the Lord, and touch not the unclean thing," these devout individuals yearned to be a fellowship of believers like the first Christians in the New Testament. To capture the heart of the members of this congregation is to capture the spiritual intimacy of their bonds and sincere commitment to one another as a body of Christ. Their separation from the Church of England cannot merely be seen as an event, a point on a timeline, but the result of a prayerful process of deliberation, a burden carried by all members of this congregation, the men and women.[7] Their religious and geographical act of separation would have far-reaching effects and every member as part of this community bound themselves to the outcome of this decision. They were "touched with heavenly zeal for his truth" and "joined themselves together by covenant as a church, in the fellowship of the gospel to walk in all His ways, made known, or to be made known to them, according to their best endeavours, whatever it should cost them, the Lord assisting them," and as Bradford's history would reveal, it most certainly did "cost them something."[8] The camera zooms in to capture "fiercely united and determined men and women [putting] their faith firmly in the will of God."[9] The decision to separate was a collective one made in faith by men and women who were mindful of the consequences. Persecution, alienation, and loss of personal comfort and security would be the price for the freedom to practice their religion and form a community of faith.

Pilgrim Women Transcending Traditional Female Roles
Once the camera is rightfully directed at places of worship like Scrooby, with the spotlight shining on the genuineness and vigour of the Pilgrims' faith, we come closer to developing a richer and more meaningful view of the Pilgrim women. No longer are they mere shadows. Indeed, women of the past occupied more limited roles. Addressing the insufficient historical accounts of women, however, one source pointed out: "All human beings are subject to some degree of social forces that limit freedom, but within those limits people

---

[7] See Sandra Goodall, "Chapter Six: A Theology of Separation," in "Beyond Bradford's Journal: The Scrooby Puritans in Context" (PhD dissertation, Arizona State University, 2015), 178.

[8] Bradford, *Plymouth Plantation*, ed. Paget, 5.

[9] Jay Parini, *Promised Land: Thirteen Books That Changed America* (New York, NY: Anchor Books, 2008), 7–28, *passim*.

are able to exercise greater or lesser degrees of control over their own lives."[10] In the case of the Pilgrim women, their Puritan faith within a closely-knitted Separatist community enlarged their roles:

> [T]he spiritualized household elevated the importance of motherhood, fostered affectionate companionate marriages, and enhanced the moral authority of women in the family ... In its attempt to integrate godliness into daily practice, its emphasis on a type of sainthood within ordinary life, and its creation of a godly community of lay figures, Puritanism offered women new opportunities to redefine traditional relationships and roles.[11]

Standing alongside the men were Pilgrim women holding to the same faith and theological convictions, their actions carried out in service to a grander vision. For, as Bradford described it, their hearts were "set on the ways of God" and they desired "to enjoy his ordinances;" in the face of adversity, the Pilgrims "rested on His providence, and knew Whom they had believed."[12] From this camera angle, the minutiae of the Pilgrim women's activities on the ship and in the new settlement becomes infused with spiritual significance. In an era when a woman's role was limited, a Pilgrim woman's role—be it as wife, mother, church member, caretaker, cook, gardener, or farmer—was vital to upholding the values of her Puritan community. In boarding the *Mayflower* ship, the Pilgrim women not only carried with them food, clothing, and furniture for the making of a future home but also the making of a godly one. The camera must therefore enter the Puritan home.

Pilgrim Women as Godly Wives and Mothers

When the oppressive atmosphere in England made it increasingly difficult for this group of Separatists to faithfully live out their vision of being a godly community, they willfully became exiles in the Netherlands, eventually settling in Leiden in 1609. The Pilgrims had secured religious freedom, but as foreigners

---

[10] Paul Halsall, *Internet History Sourcebooks Project* (http://sourcebooks.fordham.edu/women/womensbook.asp; accessed August 24, 2020).

[11] Diane Willen, "Godly Women in Early Modern England: Puritanism and Gender," *The Journal of Ecclesiastical History* 43 (1992), 565, 578. In her discussion, Willen explains: "If intense spirituality dominated the Puritan's existence, it ought also to provide the framework for an examination of the interaction between Puritanism and gender. The Puritan practised experiential religion sought the assurance of salvation, and practised godly behaviour—activities accessible to women" (Willen, "Godly Women in Early Modern England: Puritanism and Gender," 563). She continues: "The rewards of piety had always included a sense of self-worth and the opportunity for spiritual self-expression; religion also offered the means to cope with the perils of childbirth, and through Christian humanism, enhanced esteem for motherhood. These rewards crossed denominational boundaries. Puritanism, however, now offered women additional advantages and opportunities" (Willen, "Godly Women in Early Modern England: Puritanism and Gender," 566).

[12] Bradford, *Plymouth Plantation*, ed. Paget, 6.

they faced hard labour (even the children), marginal economic opportunity, and grim living conditions. The worldly culture in Holland was also of grave concern, for there "greed and competition transformed the Sabbath into a working day."[13] There was also cause for alarm regarding the spiritual upbringing of the children in such surroundings: "But still more lamentable, and of all sorrows most heavy to be borne, was that many of the children, influenced by these conditions, and the great licentiousness of the young people of the country, and the many temptations of the city, were led by evil example into dangerous courses, getting the reins off their necks and leaving their parents," Bradford wrote, fearing for "the danger of their souls, to the great grief of the parents and the dishonour of God."[14]

The spiritual fate of the children was among the reasons that the Separatist community resolved to settle in America. In examining the first marriage taking place in the new colony in May 1621 between Susanna White and Edward Winslow (both Pilgrims had lost their spouses during that first winter, the former William White and the latter Elizabeth Winslow, widow Susanna having been left to care for five-year-old Resolved and six-month-old Peregrine), it was stressed by one writer that the new bond was a godly one and great spiritual emphasis was placed on their marriage and family as it was for the others in the faith community: these "saints ... regarded the family as a small world, a community in miniature, that mirrored wider society. It was a little commonwealth. And like the bigger commonwealth, it assisted its members to understand and worship God."[15]

The camera thus moves to capture some of the families aboard the *Mayflower*: Leiden church elder William Brewster with his wife Mary and two youngest sons Love and Wrestling; deacon John Carver, a "godly man and highly approved" by those who elected him the first governor of Plymouth colony, whose wife Katherine was a "gracious woman" and "one of the more prominent women in the English separatist church at Leiden" (the Carvers brought with them the fatherless youth Desire Minter); Isaac Allerton, another leading member in the Leiden congregation, with his pregnant wife Mary and his young son Bartholomew and two daughters Remember and Mary; Miles Standish, military leader and friend of the Separatist community, with his wife Rose; and James Chilton with his wife and 13-year-old daughter Mary—whose parents would die that first winter of infection yet she would live until old age and in her will was written: "I commend my soul into the hands of Almighty

---

[13] Nick Bunker, *Making Haste from Babylon: The Mayflower Pilgrims and Their World: A New History* (New York: Vintage Books, 2010), 219–220.

[14] Bradford, *Plymouth Plantation*, ed. Paget, 13.

[15] Whittock, *Mayflower Lives*, 53–54, as quoted. in F.J. Bremer, *The Puritan Experiment: New England Society from Bradford to Edwards* (Hanover, NH; London: University Press of New England, 1995), 113.

God my Creator hoping to receive full pardon and remission of all my sins; and salvation through the alone merits of Jesus Christ my redeemer."[16]

Hence, the role of the Pilgrim women in the family unit cannot be viewed in the strictly traditional or conventional sense, for both men and women had their respective duties to practice and nurture godliness in the household.[17] In a God-ordained marriage, Puritan women submitted to the authority of their husbands, their respect rooted in their biblical understanding of such a union. The husband's duties included leading the household in Bible reading and prayer while the wife's duties, in addition to the daily household tasks, was to serve as helper to her husband in ministering the gospel to the family. Christian ministry within the family was especially intensified for this Separatist community because of the spiritual inadequacy of their environment. Of course, in a fallen world, this biblical model was not always upheld, but the Pilgrims would have been held accountable by the Word of God and the example of Christ.[18]

The camera must present a view of the Pilgrim women under this spotlight, especially to the modern audience who might otherwise blunder by defining the contribution or character of these women solely by their external position and activities and erroneously applying a reductionist lens (a Feminist lens would therefore fail to recognise the authentic experiences of these women).[19] We must see, even without their personal accounts, Pilgrim women reading their Bible, instructing their children in it, and clinging to its promises as they tended to their household responsibilities. Their commitment to their appointed tasks was an outworking of their relationship with God: "If a Christian's calling comes from God, there is inherent in that belief a strategy for accepting one's tasks," even in times of trial.[20] The Pilgrim women who embodied these biblical family values can be commended for their obedience in shouldering this "self-denying work," which calls for virtues of piety, humility, patience, submission, often silence, as they resigned reason and will to their husbands, and alongside their husbands, became heirs together of the grace of life.[21]

Pilgrim Women Pressing Forward in the Face of Uncertainty and Danger
The purpose of beginning with the spiritual context from which the Pilgrim

---

[16] Caleb H. Johnson, *The Mayflower and Her Passengers* (n.p.: Xlibris, 2006), 107, 118.

[17] Willen, "Godly Women in Early Modern England: Puritanism and Gender," 567.

[18] Whittock, *Mayflower Lives*, 57.

[19] See Leora Hall, "Understanding Puritan Womanhood in Feminist America" (https://www.coursehero.com/file/24374392/10-Hall-Historypdf/; accessed August 25, 2020).

[20] Leland Ryken, *Worldly Saints: Puritans as They Really Were* (Grand Rapids, MI: Zondervan, 1986), 215.

[21] Willen, "Godly Women in Early Modern England: Puritanism and Gender," 564.

women came is essential to understanding their very act of stepping onto the *Mayflower*. There were 102 passengers—about half were Separatists from Leiden (the "Saints") and the other half comprised the crew, merchants, craftsmen, and servants (the "Strangers")—about 47 were men and the rest women and children.[22] Eighteen wives were onboard while three of them were pregnant.

The Pilgrims were aware of some of the perils of the sea voyage and colony settlement from reports of past expeditions to America.[23] They knew about the deadly winters and the hostile exchanges between the Europeans and the aboriginals. In fact, when the plan was announced to the community, they began to express their fears and doubts: "The hopeful ones tried to encourage the rest to undertake it; others more timid, objected to it," and with good reason, for the hesitant among them insisted that the perils of the lengthy sea voyage would be too much for the women, elderly, and infirm, what with the scarcity of food, insufficient clothing, and questionable air and water.[24] The members had already experienced privations as foreigners in the Netherlands, and these would only be crueller in America.

Upon hearing of the conceivable obstacles, the "weak" began to "quake and tremble," wrote Bradford, but, once again, the spiritual leaders among them sought to embolden the members to move forward with "the gospel of the kingdom of Christ in the remote parts of the world," even if they were merely "stepping stones" for others.[25] They reminded the members that

> all great and honourable actions are accompanied with great difficulties, and must be both met and overcome with answerable courage … For, many of the things feared might never befall; others by provident care and the use of good means might in a great measure be prevented; and all of them, through the help of God, by fortitude and patience, might either be borne or overcome."[26]

The implorers moved the members to determine the merit of the decision by considering that "their ends were good and honourable; their calling, lawful and urgent; therefore they might expect the blessing of God on their proceedings," yet also conceded in faith that, "Yea, though they should lose their lives in this action, yet might they have the comfort of knowing that their endeavour was

---

[22] Bunker, *Mayflower Pilgrims and Their World*, 31.

[23] Philbrick, *Mayflower*, 19.

[24] Bradford, *Plymouth Plantation*, ed. Paget, 13.

[25] Bradford, *Plymouth Plantation*, ed. Paget, 13.

[26] Bradford, *Plymouth Plantation*, ed. Paget, 14.

worthy."[27]

Ultimately a third of the Leiden congregation agreed to go on the first voyage to America under the interim religious leadership of Brewster, with Pastor Robinson as well as the more vulnerable and wary to follow once the early foundations had been laid (that number would drop by over a quarter on their actual departure date when further complications ensued).[28] Even so, the ones who were willing, or compliant, while reasonably apprehensive or hesitant, were certainly not the faint of heart.

Pilgrim Women and Trials Amid the Sea Voyage

Even prior to their actual voyage at sea, the women experienced the first agonies of their decision upon leaving Leiden: bidding farewell to those nearest and dearest to them. They knew that this would likely be a permanent separation: "with such a dangerous voyage before them, and removal to such a distance," Bradford wrote, "it might happen that they should never meet again, as a body, in this world."[29] Few scenes are recorded in Bradford's history of the Pilgrim women's interactions, but the future governor could say of that painful departure:

> They went aboard and their friends with them, where truly doleful was the sight of that sad and mournful parting, to see what sighs and sobs and prayers did sound amongst them, what tears did gush from every eye, and pithy speeches pierced each heart ... Yet comfortable and sweet it was to see such lively and true expressions of dear and unfeigned love ... And then with mutual embraces and many tears they took their leaves one of another, which proved to be the last leave to many of them.[30]

The most heartrending separation would have been between parents and their children, most notably between William and Dorothy Bradford and their three-year-old son John, whom they deemed best to unite with them once the colony was settled.

Joining the other *Mayflower* passengers in England, the Pilgrims caught a final glimpse of their home. For the women, leaving England meant parting with all that was comfortable and familiar: the mild climate, the assuring sight of a cultivated and civilized land, neighbours and friends, and even the most commonplace tools that made a home "home." Recording the experience of spotting land after the long voyage, Bradford wrote:

---

[27] Bradford, *Plymouth Plantation*, ed. Paget, 14.

[28] Philbrick, *Mayflower*, 21, 29.

[29] Bradford, *Plymouth Plantation*, ed. Paget, 23.

[30] William Bradford, *Of Plymouth Plantation, 1620–1647*, ed. Samuel Eliot Morison (New York, NY: Alfred A. Knopf, 1952), 48.

But here I cannot but make a pause, and stand half amazed at this poor people's present condition ... they now had no friends to welcome them, nor inns to entertain and refresh their weather-beaten bodies, nor houses—much less towns—to repair to ... Let it be remembered, too, what small hope of further assistance from England they had left behind them, to support their courage in this sad condition and the trials they were under.

In uprooting themselves completely, the women would be cut off from the very support they needed for strength and encouragement.

During the sea voyage and before lodgings could be erected in the new land, their "home" was a dark, damp, and malodourous space of about five feet high and seventy-five feet long between the cargo hold and upper deck. A male might have freely emerged to take in the air amid calmer seas, but the women, due to the danger of falling overboard or being spotted by unidentified ships, were stuck below.[31] Thin wood dividers formed cramped compartments that granted the women a measure of privacy. Susanna White, Mary Allerton, and Elizabeth Hopkins, all well into their pregnancies, must have endured the worst of seasickness as the ship shook violently amid the fiercest winds and storms (Elizabeth gave birth to a baby boy aptly named Oceanus in these rough conditions). Children had to be fastened to fixtures to be protected from harm.[32] Though the passengers would be elated to finally step foot on sturdy land, the women would be confined to the stifling space between the ship's decks for much longer as they waited on the men to explore and work the land. In fact, half of the passengers did not survive that first ruthless winter, but much fewer women survived. In addition to malnourishment, the women had much less exposure to fresh air from inside the ship where disease spread more easily, so they were much more susceptible to falling fatally ill.

The Pilgrim women also had to bear the cursing and crassness of some of the haughtier males among the ship's crew.[33] As emigrants and Puritans—they were targets of contempt.[34] This set of passengers comprised a mixture of individuals that were unlike those of past expeditions and the women joining incited additional occasions for scorn.[35] Moreover, the women had to adapt to sharing their limited living space with Strangers, some who clashed sharply with

---

[31] Johnson, *Mayflower*, 39.

[32] Carole Chandler Waldrup, *Colonial Women: 23 Europeans Who Helped Build a Nation* (Jefferson, NC: McFarland Publishers, 1999), 4.

[33] Bradford, *Plymouth Plantation*, ed. Morison, 78. Also Bunker, *Mayflower Pilgrims and Their World*, 55–56.

[34] Bradford, *Plymouth Plantation*, ed. Paget, 39–40.

[35] Noyes, *Women of the Mayflower*, 114, 116.

them in morality and conduct: "Indeed it is our calamity that we are, beyond expectation, yoked with some ill-disposed people, who, while they do no good themselves, corrupt and abuse others."[36] Accustomed to the shared values of the Separatist community, the women, if disturbed or distressed by the behaviour of such worldly company, would have had to take to heart the counsel of their Leiden Pastor Robinson, who, foreseeing the challenges that lay ahead of them in relating with the Strangers, advised the Pilgrims in his farewell letter "to do everything they could to avoid conflict" with them.[37] Though there would be continual occasion for offense, Robinson exhorted them to quench grievances with "forbearance" and "patience."[38] This must have been valuable counsel for the women who had to thicken their skins and adopt a more open spirit.

Pilgrim Women and Trials in The New World
One writer recognized the painful nature of the woman's position in the colony: she must "both work and weep."[39] If Bradford could describe the New World as that "hideous and desolate wilderness, full of wild beasts and wild men,"[40] how much more terrifying it would have been for the women. After arriving at the threshold of winter in November 1620, a party of the stoutest men went off on a series of expeditions to scour the land for food and habitable terrain. Meanwhile, the women were waiting—the healthier among them keeping watch of the children, tending to the sick, mending and washing clothes, preparing food from scanty provisions—anxious to hear news of the men's return. It would be almost two long months before the men found a place to settle and finally begin to build the first houses, which was stalled due to the bitter weather. So, the women waited—shuddering as beastly noises were heard in the wilderness, trembling as the Indians belted out their war cries. Plodding along in their work, separated from their men by a vast expanse of the unknown, many of them in their loneliness and helplessness must have desperately repeated prayers for protection.

While no women and children died on the sea voyage—one by one—death became a harrowing reality once on land. Less than a month after their arrival into the New World, Dorothy Bradford would be among the first to die; tragically William Bradford had been away on exploration and only received the news upon his return—that his wife had fallen over the side of the anchored *Mayflower* and drowned in the freezing waters of Cape Cod.[41] How demoralizing

---

[36] Bradford, *Plymouth Plantation*, ed. Paget, 61.

[37] Philbrick, *Mayflower*, 29–30.

[38] Bradford, *Plymouth Plantation*, ed. Paget, 36–37.

[39] Fowler, *Woman on the American Frontier*, 27.

[40] Bradford, *Plymouth Plantation*, ed. Paget, 43.

[41] Many have speculated whether Dorothy Bradford had committed suicide given her bleak

it would have been for the Pilgrim women to have lost one of their own so early on. The losses would continue. Within the same period, Mary Allerton gave birth aboard the ship to a stillborn son and she herself would pass later that February. Rose Standish died at the end of January. Seventeen-year-old Priscilla Mullins' family, William and Alice Mullins and her fifteen-year-old brother Joseph, would all perish that first winter, leaving her an orphan.[42] Thirteen-year-old Elizabeth Tilley not only lost her parents, John and Joan Tilley, but also her uncle and aunt, Edward Tilley and Ann Cooper Tilley, the latter leaving behind their one-year-old niece, Humility Cooper, the youngest *Mayflower* passenger.[43] After tearfully sending off the *Mayflower* ship back to England in April 1621, the Pilgrim women would lose Katherine Carver, who died so soon after her husband's passing (the governor died only weeks prior) that many believed she had died of a broken heart. By the time the first crushing hurdle of adapting to New World conditions was over, the only Pilgrim women remaining were Susanna White and Mary Brewster, who not only had to care for their own children but the children who lost their mothers.[44]

In the thick of that period, Bradford noted that there were points when they had lost two to three people a day. How vital the Pilgrims' faith would have been as they faced tragedy at every turn: "What, then, could now sustain them but the spirit of God, and his grace?"[45]

The Sacrifices of the Pilgrim Women

Yet upon recording the stark number of fatalities, in the same stroke Bradford could commend the six to seven faithful individuals who took care of the weakest among them—and while he only mentions William Brewster and Miles Standish by name—the Pilgrim women can certainly be counted among them:

> In the time of worst distress, there were but six or seven sound persons, who, to their great commendation be it spoken, spared no pains night or day, but with great toil and at the risk of their own health, fetched wood, made fires, prepared food for the sick, made their beds, washed their infected clothes, dressed and undressed them; in a word did all the homely

surroundings and dismal circumstances (being separated from her son John); however, there is no evidence to substantiate this.

[42] Orphaned, Priscilla Mullins moved into the household of William and Mary Brewster (Waldrup, *Colonial Women*, 8). Priscilla would marry John Alden and have 10 children.

[43] Elizabeth Tilley would marry Mayflower passenger John Howland and live until 1687. She and John would have 10 children who all lived until adulthood. In her will, she passed on to her daughter Lydia one of her treasured books, *Observations Divine and Moral* written by Leiden Pastor John Robinson, a popular book that circulated in the colony. Johnson, *Mayflower*, 237.

[44] Whittock, *Mayflower Lives*, 51–52.

[45] Bradford, *Plymouth Plantation*, ed. Paget, 44.

and necessary services for them which dainty and queasy stomachs cannot endure to hear mentioned; and all this they did willingly and cheerfully, without the least grudging, showing their love to the friends and brethren; a rare example, and worthy to be remembered.[46]

Indeed, the tasks of the Pilgrim women were great, especially considering how few of them remained. Not only did they have to cook, they had to be sparing in their rations and even give up their own portions for the sake of the children. Hunger was a persistent reality: many had died of starvation, and the women's sacrifices were likely the reason more children survived in the colony than women: "Who can doubt that these women often went hungry that others might have more?"[47] Cooking, housekeeping, nursing, assisting in childbirth and childcare—these acts monotonous and wearisome in and of themselves—but regarded as a whole made all the difference.

The Pilgrim Women Worshipping Amid Trials
The camera must not neglect vital shots of the Pilgrims worshipping—which make sense of how a colony could cope with such defeating losses. Grappling with the hardships suffered by the Pilgrims, we must not forget all the religious events that breathed spiritual vigour into their sagging spirits. It is not sufficient to simply be informed of the religious community from which they came: we must bear in mind that this community gathered and expressed their faith regularly *as* they dealt with the turmoil in the New World. Acts of worship were interwoven in their experiences. The film has captured a shot of the Pilgrims' emotional departure from Holland, but it must also focus on Pastor Robinson falling on his knees and commending them with the most fervent prayers.[48] The film has captured a shot of the *Mayflower* at last docking on land, but it must also focus on elder Brewster praying over them and the Pilgrim women singing hymns of thankfulness alongside their brothers and sisters in Christ.[49] The camera has captured the Pilgrim women suffering from hunger, but it must also focus on the leaders initiating a day of prayer in their hour of desperate need. The film has captured the women fulfilling their daily duties, but it must also

---

[46] Bradford, *Plymouth Plantation*, ed. Paget, 50.

[47] Ethel J.R.C. Noyes, *The Women of the Mayflower and Women of Plymouth Colony* (Plymouth, MA: Memorial Press, 1921), 94.

[48] Like Bradford, Pilgrim Edward Winslow also recorded the heartfelt scene that day: "And when the ship was ready to carry us away, the brethren that stayed having again solemnly sought the Lord with us ... they, I say, that stayed at Leiden feasted us that were to go at our pastor's house being large, where we refreshed ourselves after our tears, with singing of Psalms, making joyful melody in our hearts, as well as with the voice, there being many of the congregation very expert in music; and indeed it was the sweetest melody that ever mine ears heard." Caleb Johnson, *Of Plymouth Plantation: Along with the Full Text of the Pilgrims' Journals*, 92, quoted in Edward Winslow's *Hypocrisy Unmasked* (London, 1646).

[49] Noyes, *Women of the Mayflower*, 75.

focus on them steadfastly participating in services on the Sabbath, submitting to the preaching of the Word, ensuring that even the most restless of children were exercising the same attentiveness.

The godly women were faithfully led by the godly men among them. Bradford described Elder Brewster's ministry to the colony as a "diligent dispensing of the Word of God:" he taught "twice every Sabbath powerfully and profitably"[50] and had the "singularly good gift of prayer."[51] Governor Carver was described as "a gentleman of singular piety," "rare humility," and when the "poor people were in great sickness and weakness," he did not turn any away, for even as leader no work was considered too lowly for him.[52]

The Pilgrim women were active members of this spiritual community, their testimonies known and heard, their spiritual lives held accountable by leaders whom they obeyed, respected, and relied on for spiritual guidance. The teaching and counsel of their leaders would have spoken profoundly into their suffering.

The Vital Presence of the Pilgrim Women in Plymouth Colony

A compelling observation made by some historians is that the presence of the Pilgrim women contributed to the survival of Plymouth colony. While the men were exploring, building, hunting, and establishing ties with the Indians, the women made a "home" to which the men could return. The will and purpose of the men were fortified by the Pilgrim women's presence in the colony.[53] Against the backdrop of untamed and unpredictable surroundings—the women, in carrying on with the more "ordinary" activities (perhaps so ordinary they were not written about), provided for the men a place of comfort and affection: "The household, the hamlet, the village, the town, the city, the state rise out of her 'homely toils' though her destiny is obscure."[54] One historian observed that the "Puritans' religious emphasis on domestic life helped make women agents of the kind of domestic sociability that contributed to social stability."[55] Thus, the wife in the Christian family unit, virtually absent in past expeditions, was an anchor for the *Mayflower* passengers—the Puritan ethic of the Pilgrim woman not just a refined or civilizing influence but a saintly one, embodying such biblical virtues as Christ-like submission, sacrifice, and devotion that lent itself to the thriving of a struggling colony. In persevering in the face of pain and the mundane, the Pilgrim women played a major role in sustaining the Separatist community's vision.

---

[50] Bradford, *Plymouth Plantation*, ed. Paget, 208.

[51] Bradford, *Plymouth Plantation*, ed. Paget, 208–209.

[52] Johnson, *Mayflower*, 114.

[53] Noyes, *Women of the Mayflower*, 86–87, 117.

[54] Fowler, *Woman on the American Frontier*, 33.

[55] Amanda Porterfield, "Women's Attraction to Puritanism," *Church History* 60 (1991): 208.

A Final Scene

After recounting a distressing incident following the Separatist community's flight to the Netherlands in which the women were "weeping and crying on every side … crying for fear and quaking with cold," Bradford, recalling how "pitiful it was to see the heavy case of these poor women in this distress," breaks mid-narrative and writes, "But that I be not tedious in these things, I will omit the rest, though I might relate many other notable passages and troubles which they endured and underwent in these their wanderings and travels both at land and sea; but I haste to other things."[56] We who are keen on learning about the experiences of the Pilgrim women might instinctively wish that Bradford had not omitted the rest of those precious details. Although we naturally long to see further scenes of the women on record, our longing may perhaps be allayed when weighing Bradford's purpose in chronicling the origins and development of the colony. His manuscript opens with his intentions: to relay events in "plain style, with singular regard unto the simple truth in all things."[57] The Plymouth governor endeavored to illuminate a story of a former generation, one that pictured the Pilgrims' faith, sacrifices, and commitment to God's purposes in the face of adversity. He assembled accounts from the flight from England all the way to the establishment of a colony and often dispensed with particularities (there is also marginal detail about the *Mayflower* vessel and the Pilgrims' famous thanksgiving celebration) in order to convey the "simple truth" of that story.[58] Yet, continuing the same narrative of that flight to the Netherlands, Bradford writes: "I must not omit, however, to mention the fruit of it all. For by these public afflictions, their cause became famous, and led many to inquire into it; and their Christian behaviour left a deep impression on the minds of many. Some few shrank from these first conflicts, and no wonder; but many more came forward with fresh courage and animated the rest."[59] And so, while countless scenes of individual Pilgrim women have not been captured, these women are nonetheless remembered and honoured for their incredible courage, strength, and endurance in the midst of extraordinary circumstances, and most importantly, for the fruit of it all.

---

[56] William Bradford, *Of Plymouth Plantation, 1620–1647*, ed. Samuel Eliot Morison (New York: Alfred A. Knopf, 1952), 14.

[57] Bradford, *Plymouth Plantation*, ed. Morison, 3.

[58] Bunker writes: "But in telling the story of the voyage, the Pilgrim left out almost every fact that most readers, then and now, would consider relevant or essential. The name, design, and dimensions of the ship and the number of crew members: none of these appear in Bradford's history … Bradford never talks about food, drink, armaments, pirates, the last view of land … He says nothing whatever about the route. These gaps were unusual, even by the standards of his age … From what must have been many incidents, during the sixty-six days between the English Channel and the Cape, he selected only very few." See *Mayflower Pilgrims and Their World*, 58–59.

[59] Bradford, *Plymouth Plantation*, ed. Paget, 8.

Statue of a Pilgrim Father in
Central Park, New York
(Public Domain)

CHAPTER FIFTEEN

The Pilgrims and Religious Liberty

RYAN RINDELS

In June 1974, *The New Yorker* featured a comic by Donald Reilly with two Pilgrims on an ocean vessel. One says to the other, "Religious freedom is my immediate goal, but my long-range plan is to go into real estate."[1] Imbedded in the humor is incredulity that religious liberty is a sufficient explanation for a journey to the New World, revealing perhaps more about modern America than the seventeenth-century pilgrims. It is true that the settlement of Plymouth by English Separatists was made possible in part by the expectation of commercial benefit to King James I. This should not obscure, however, the prominence of religious liberty in the civic and ecclesial life of the Pilgrims.[2] Modern America hardly resembles Separatist Plymouth of the 1620's, yet the nation has a higher religiosity relative to other nations with origins in Latin Christendom. A sectarian offshoot of English Puritanism that took root in New England established a precedent which, over time, would lead to expanded understandings of religious liberty. If this result was not intended by the Pilgrims, their very existence as Separatists made an indispensable, even inevitable contribution to the flourishing of Christianity in the United States.

The phrase "religious liberty" rings differently in modern ears than it did to

---

[1] *The New Yorker* (June 3, 1974): 46.

[2] The "Merchant Adventurers," a group of seventy London investors with Puritan sympathies understood their purpose in financing as colony in America as a means "to plant religion." Nathaniel Philbrick, *Mayflower: Voyage, Community, War* (New York, NY: Penguin, 2006), 20

those who landed at Cape Cod in 1620. North Americans of a secular bent, drawing on notable Supreme Court cases—whose focus was on the right to refuse patrons on grounds of religious convictions—commonly interpret such appeals as a cover for bigotry and discrimination. Conversely, a casual religious admirer may anachronistically cite the Pilgrims as purveyors of denominational freedom more akin to that of Baptists such as Isaac Backus (1724–1806) and John Leland (1754–1841). In the conclusion to his recent history, *They Knew They Were Pilgrims*, John G. Turner captures the difficulty in drawing a connection between religious freedom in the seventeenth-century and what emerged in America at the close of the eighteenth when he writes, "the Pilgrims and other inhabitants of Plymouth Colony left behind both a complicated legacy of human bondage and unresolved debates about liberty."[3] If the contours of the debate have shifted, contemporary American Protestants in the free church tradition still share ecclesiological goals with the Pilgrim Fathers, though few would advocate the stringent, even brutal measures to achieve such goals. Among these are a congregational and covenantal understanding of the local church, and a missionary ethos.

Arrival

The *Mayflower* departed from Plymouth on September 6, 1620, and arrived at Massachusetts 67 days later, on November 11. In his *History of Plimoth Plantation*, governor William Bradford poignantly described the colonists act of supplication, performed, incidentally, before their feet touched New England's shore:

> Being thus arrived in a good harbor and brought safe to land, they fell upon their knees & blessed ye God of heaven, who had brough them over ye vast & furious ocean, and delivered them from all ye periles & miseries thereof.[4]

Having survived nine harrowing weeks on the North Atlantic with two live births and only one death was fortuitous by the standards of seventeenth-century sea travel. In the same month, the Pilgrims drafted the renowned Mayflower Compact, a charter that served as a basis for the Plymouth colonists' perilous, if not functional, autonomy. The signers, "loyall subjects of [their] dread soveraigne Lord, King James," claimed to plant a colony "for ye glorie of God, and advancement of ye Christian faith, and honor of our king & countrie."[5] Drawing from Old Testament patterns and the Reformed theological tradition,

---

[3] John G. Turner, *They Knew they Were Pilgrims: Plymouth Colony and the Contest for American Liberty* (New Haven, CT: Yale University Press, 2020), 365.

[4] William Bradford, *Of Plimoth Plantation* (Boston, 1901), 94–95. On Bradford's life, see Bradford Smith, *Bradford of Plymouth* (New York, NY: J.B. Lippincott, 1951).

[5] Bradford, *Of Plimoth Plantation*, 94.

they swore to "covenant and combine [them] selves togeather into a civill body politik, for [their] better ordering & preservation, & furtherance of ye ends foresaid."[6]

A reader today may find it difficult to believe that the aforementioned persons had separated from the King's church and were in their present location in part, due to persecution by the church over which he was head. The deferential language should not obscure several salient points. The settlers articulated a distinctly theological mission: "for ye glory of God, and advancement of ye Christian faith."[7] Furthermore, they envisioned a commonwealth—civill body politik"—that would uphold and promote the same Christian faith. As Separatists, the Plymouth colonists strove zealously to maintain the congregational autonomy of their churches and doctrinal purity according to their reading of the Bible. These tight boundaries would invariably put the Pilgrims in conflict with newer arrivals from England. Initially, Puritans whose toleration of, or practice of rites within the Church of England were understood as a threat to the very existence of Plymouth Plantation. In subsequent years, Baptists and Quakers experienced persecution at the hands of Plymouth's leadership, who only grudgingly granted toleration, often for political expedience. When Plymouth was officially absorbed into Massachusetts Bay Colony in 1691, the consensus stood that Congregational churches should be funded by taxpayers irrespective of their denominational affiliation. Religious liberty by Pilgrim reckoning was paradoxically restrictive.

Which religion? Whose liberty?

"Religion" and "liberty" are two words that resist simple definition, yet their meanings will in large part, impact an assessment of the Pilgrims' views. Though works such as Samuel Johnson's *Dictionary of the English Language* (1755) and Noah Webster's 1828 dictionary provide brief definitions of "religion," lexicographer Thomas Blount's *Law Dictionary and Glossary* (1656), a precursor to the modern dictionary, provides no proper definition of the term. Considering that Blount's *Glossary*, published within the first generation of Plymouth's settlement, assumes, rather than defines "religion," is an illuminating example. For their own entries, Johnson and Webster include "future rewards and punishments" in their respective definitions of religion, thereby including some non-Christian systems of worship. Merriam-Webster's modern dictionary renders religion "the service and worship of God or the supernatural," and "commitment or devotion to religious faith and observance."[8] A theistic, and specifically Christian definition—

---

[6] Bradford, *Plimoth Plantation*, 94. Cf. Jeremy Dupertuis Bangs, *New light on the Old Colony: Plymouth, the Dutch context of toleration, and patterns of Pilgrim commemoration* (Boston: Brill, 2020).

[7] Bradford, *Plimoth Plantation*, 94.

[8] Merriam Webster Dictionary (https://www.merriam-webster.com/dictionary/religion accessed October 6, 2020).

stated or implied—is eclipsed by inclusive terminology that resists connection to any specific tradition.

"Liberty" for its own part, presents challenges, for the Pilgrims had in mind a specific kind of freedom, namely, the permission to worship and govern according to their own convictions.[9] "Liberty of conscience," used synonymously with religious liberty was not religious freedom. Even former Plymouth pastor and early Baptist Roger Williams, whose advocacy of "soul liberty"—e.g. separation of church and state—did not advocate religious freedom in a pluralistic sense.[10] Plymouth's settlers possessed an idea of freedom akin to Medieval theologians who distinguished freedom *from* something as distinct from freedom *for* something. Liberated from the Established Church, Plymouth's Pilgrims retained a vision of ecclesial homogeneity. Harried in their native country, exiled in the Netherlands, the *Mayflower's* original passengers had paid a heavy price for nonconformity. William Bradford, for example, forfeited his inheritance in order to sail with John Robinson and William Brewster to the Netherlands in 1607.[11] It should come as no surprise then, that these Separatists were averse to accommodation, zealous as they were to defend their vision of the church.

The extent to which Plymouth's inhabitants maintained religious principles is evident in their decision not to receive the sacraments without their pastor John Robinson. Robinson, who never journeyed to America, maintained regular correspondence with the church, offering counsel, and weighing-in on major decisions.[12] The Plymouth congregation took neither the Lord's Supper, nor baptised any person, infants included, for over a decade. Only after a qualified, congregationally-chosen pastor was instated did the Pilgrims receive the sacraments. Such remarkable commitment to the Reformed Protestantism—which their enemies regularly maligned—ostensibly explains why the Pilgrims staunchly resisted new arrivals who did not share their principles.

Dissent

Plymouth's history from 1620 to 1691 provides instances of conflict, including several episodes modern readers may find surprising, if at times humorous. In December 1621, several settlers, recently arrived from the *Fortune*, refused to work on Christmas Day, claiming it "wente against their consciences."[13]

---

[9] Turner, *They Knew They Were Pilgrims*, 165.

[10] Even Martin Luther (1483–1546) in his later years, opposed religious freedom, conceding that capital punishment was warranted for heretics. Cf. Michael G. Baylor, *Action and Person: Conscience in Late Scholasticism and the Young Luther* (Leiden: Brill, 1977), 254–262.

[11] Philbrick, *Mayflower*, 13.

[12] Turner, *They Knew They Were Pilgrims*, 100. John Robinson would weigh in on Plymouth's politics, even pronouncing the unlawfulness of Myles Standish's murder of Pecksuot in 1622.

[13] Bradford, *Plimoth Plantation*, 135.

William Bradford initially objected, and only grudgingly conceded to their request. When these Anglicans proceeded to play outdoor games, an English Christmas tradition, the governor intervened.[14] Plymouth's Separatists resisted any celebration that resembled Roman Catholicism and resented residents who would not labor during what they believed was a normal work day. Spartan simplicity entailed no eulogies at burials, strictly civil weddings, and a calendar marked by a single holiday. Such tight boundaries could not avoid clashes with incomers. Investor Thomas Morton's decision to erect a May Pole at an outpost called Merry Mount where English and Indians reveled, led to swift reprisals—an episode scorned by subsequent generations of historians and novelists who judged the event the embodiment of Pilgrim bigotry.[15]

In 1624, John Lyford, an Oxford-educated minister was chosen to be the Plymouth church's pastor. Though Lyford gave testimony of God's regenerating work in his life, a spiritual requisite for church membership in New England congregations, the amicable union was short-lived. Plymouth's request that Lyford "renounce his calling to the office of the ministry, received in England, as heretical and papistical," was too much, and the pastor demurred.[16] When authorities later apprehended letters written by Lyford criticising the Pilgrims, the minister was forced to apologise publicly. Lyford's decision to baptise infants and administer communion to a minority of Anglicans was a source of conflict that not only led to Lyford's expulsion, but prompted the men of Plymouth to inflict corporal punishment on Thomas Oldham, who defended the minister.[17]

Interestingly, Lyford claimed in one letter that the Separatist's chief concern was pandering to church members at the expense of the unconverted. William Bradford replied to this accusation by defending the rigour of the church, noting that the colony enforced church attendance, punishing those who were "idling and neglect[ing] the hearing of the word."[18] Like Massachusetts Bay later, attending public worship was compulsory in Plymouth—a conviction shared with New England's Puritans—on grounds that outward religious conformity provided the best context for personal conversions to occur. Separatists, however, were not Puritans, and the emergence of more radical elements would stretch the boundaries of the Pilgrims' religious toleration.

As noted earlier, Roger Williams' insistence that the state not coerce individuals

---

[14] Bradford, *Of Plimoth Plantation*, 135.

[15] Turner, *They Knew They Were Pilgrims*, 132. Turner mentions Nathaniel Hawthorne's short story, *The May-Pole of Merry Mount* (1832) in which Hawthorne framed Merry Mount and Plymouth as a contrast between "jollity and gloom," and William Carlos Williams' praise for Thomas Morton as "a New World pioneer taking his chances in the wilderness" (Turner, *They Knew They Were Pilgrims*, 120).

[16] Turner, *They Knew They Were Pilgrims*, 112.

[17] Turner, *They Knew They Were Pilgrims*, 114.

[18] Turner, *They Knew They Were Pilgrims*, 115.

Statue of Roger Williams in
Roger Williams Park,
Providence, Rhode Island
(Photo: Michael A.G. Haykin)

into religious compliance was not warmly received by the majority of his contemporaries. Among other objections—oath-taking for example—Williams denied that the magistrate could inflict corporal punishment on those who violated the first table of the Ten Commandments. Though he would serve as visiting pastor for several months, Williams was expelled from Plymouth and would eventually settle in Rhode Island—pejoratively coined "rogues' island"—where he would join the charismatic midwife-turned-visionary Anne Hutchinson (1591–1643).[19] Unlike Plymouth, residents in Providence were not forced to attend worship services. That religious liberty in America's future would resemble that of Rhode Island rather than Plymouth reflected a primacy of the individual over the community. For the Pilgrims, liberty was ecclesial in nature. Their identity as a people covenanted before God superseded the private convictions of individuals to establish alternative forms of worship on grounds of destructive sectarianism.

Several years later, William Vassal, a member of Plymouth's church clashed with William Bradford and future governor Edward Winslow over the extent of religious liberty. During the English Civil Wars, religious toleration was expanded under Oliver Cromwell to a degree that was unacceptable to Plymouth and Massachusetts Bay leadership.[20] Travelers who spent time in England were sympathetic to the possibility that Baptists, Quakers, even Roman Catholics could worship freely according to their consciences. In 1643, Vassal and another family formed their own congregation in Scituate. When Plymouth's church accused the party of unlawful separation, pastor Charles Chauncy insisted that they should not receive the sacraments. Vassal objected by appeal to worship in accordance with one's conscience.[21] A bill passed in 1645 however, quashed religious dissent. Vassal drafted a counterproposal that would "allow and maintain full and free tolerance of religion to all men that would preserve the civil peace, and submit unto government."[22] Bradford and Winslow again won the day, but victory was short-lived and tenuous. Religious minorities would begin to arise from within as much as from without.

Plymouth's brittle toleration would be tested to its fullest extent with the arrival of the Quakers. Originating with the shoemaker and mystic George Fox, the Friends, as they preferred to be called, incited controversy for their heterodox beliefs and unconventional public conduct. Early Quakers attended worship services, only to publicly denounce the minister at the completion of the sermon. Some Quakers, taking suit from the prophet Isaiah, walked naked in the

---

[19] Orthodox Puritans began to call Rhode Island the "sewer of New England."

[20] See Susan Hardman Moore, *Pilgrims: New World Settlers and the Call of Home* (New Haven, CT: Yale University Press, 2007), 55–73.

[21] Turner, *They Knew They Were Pilgrims*, 201–203.

[22] Turner, *They Knew They Were Pilgrims*, 207.

streets. In the civic sphere, the Friends refused to swear oaths, to remove their hats before superiors, or pay taxes to support the local minister. When missionaries Ann Austin and Mary Fisher arrived in 1656, Boston's magistrates banished them to Barbados. Despite fines, imprisonment, expulsion, and even execution, the Friends found sympathetic hearers and established a community at Sandwich.[23] Plymouth residents faced ten-shilling fines for attending their meetings. When Quakers refused to pay taxes to the church, their property was seized. Notwithstanding impoverishment, Quakers could not be rooted out. As with the Baptists, Plymouth's settlers would cease actively persecuting Quakers, though the colony never granted religious toleration, nor abrogate mandatory taxation for the local clergyman's salary.

As the preceding accounts indicate, the colony's understanding of religious liberty was incompatible with dissent that continued to challenge Plymouth. Yet the colony's grip was loosening, even if incrementally. By 1655, New Plymouth had allowed a Baptist, Henry Dunster to settle in Scituate.[24] Four years later, the colony repealed its compulsory church attendance law.[25] Concessions to religious liberty should not, however, overshadow the fact that an original *Mayflower* passenger like William Bradford never lost the theologically-oriented vision for founding the colony. Two years prior to his death in 1657, Bradford expressed deep despair over Plymouth's "degenerate" ways, notably, the colony's growing materialism and sexual immorality. Despite misgivings about the community's trajectory, the spiritual life of Plymouth was not extinguished. Though in its nascent stages, missionary labors that began with John Eliot in Massachusetts Bay would enjoin Plymouth's ministers in the coming decades—evidence that liberty for the Separatists had not lost its religious character, nor was the colony a mere enclave of insular sectarians indifferent to the spiritual condition of their indigenous "heathen" neighbours.

Mission

The *Mayflower*'s voyage and Plymouth's founding was made possible by a company of investors called the "Merchant Adventurers," many of whom had Puritan sympathies. This is evident from a statement that the colonists "plant religion" in America. Nevertheless, missionary activity lagged by

---

[23] Puritans in Massachusetts Bay distanced themselves from Plymouth on grounds of sectarianism, though in fact, the Pilgrims proved more tolerant of Dissenters than their cousins to the north. Unlike Massachusetts Bay, Plymouth never executed Quakers, or any religious dissenters for that matter.

[24] Henry Dunster, the first president of Harvard College, withheld his fourth child from baptism and had to resign his pastorate the next year.

[25] Turner, *They Knew They Were Pilgrims*, 241.

several decades.²⁶ The Pilgrims accepted that the Christian gospel should be preached to all nations and their failure to do so in the early years prompted criticism from John Robinson in Leiden.²⁷ John Lyford's reproach that Plymouth's citizens cared not for the unconverted elicited a rebuttal by William Bradford, thereby revealing that missionary activity of some kind was expected. By mid-century, the eminent Edward Winslow personally raised money for missionary work among New England's native tribes.²⁸ John Eliot, seventeenth-century New England's most famous missionary came from Massachusetts Bay, yet the fruit of Eliot's labours would extend to Plymouth. Some Wampanoag Christians who passed through the colony requested that a minister instruct them in the faith.²⁹ By 1651, the pastor William Leverich of Sandwich took on this responsibility. Leverich's successor, Richard Bourne continued a ministry that trained a network of Wampanoag evangelists and preachers. By 1666, Bourne concluded that a church should be established at Mashpee. In 1670, the congregation was founded and the Wampanoag Christians ordained Bourne as their minister.³⁰ Another of Plymouth's ministers, the controversial John Cotton, who received a stipend from *The Society for the Propagation of the Gospel in New England*, began preaching to Wampanoags who lived in a town southeast of Plymouth, in the fall of 1670. During a period of several decades, many natives accepted Christianity. The tragedy that was King's Philip War (1675–1676) elicited mistrust of the so-called "Praying Indians" (e.g. converted aboriginals), though a reputation of loyalty and bravery in battle shifted public opinion.³¹

Plymouth's participation in missionary activity among the Wampanoags

---

²⁶ Turner, *They Knew they Were Pilgrims*, 58–59. If the Mayflower Compact is a religiously thin document, with no reference made to doctrine or church polity, a secular reading of the *Compact* is, however, a fundamental mistake A simple explanation for the brevity of the *Compact* is the haste with which the Pilgrims composed the draft. In years after the American Revolution, figures such as John Quincy Adams and Daniel Webster found in the Mayflower Compact an embryonic example of the new Republic's constitution. In fact, the Compact bore little resemblance to a constitution or bill of rights. There is no reference to terms of office, voting rights, civil liberties.

²⁷ Upon hearing of Miles Standish's murder of Peckusot, Robinson protested, "oh how happy a thing it had been, if you converted some before you had killed any" (D. Hamilton Hurd, *History of Plymouth County, Massachusetts: With Biographical Sketches of Many of Its Pioneers and Prominent Men* [Philadelphia: J. Lewis, 1884], 88).

²⁸ "Papers related to the proceedings of the Corporation for the Propagation of the Gospel in New England, 1649–1656," Bodleian, MS. Rawl. D. 934, fol. 1v, as cited in Moore, *Pilgrims*, 253, n. 36.

²⁹ The Wampanoag nation was established by the Pokanoket sachem Massassoit after a military raid led by Myles Standish at Wessagusset, See David J. Silverman, "Indians, Missionaries, and Religious Translation: Creating Wampanoag Christianity in Seventeenth-Century Martha's Vineyard," *William and Mary Quarterly* 3ʳᵈ ser., 62, no. 2 (April 2005): 141–174.

³⁰ Turner, *They Knew They Were Pilgrims*, 253.

³¹ Captain Michael Pierce's "Cape Indians" showed remarkable heroism despite being overwhelmed by a significantly larger contingent of fighters. See Edward Field, *State of Rhode Island and Providence Plantations at the End of the Century: A History* (Boston: Mason Publishing, 1902), 1:411.

suggests that religious liberty possessed value, not merely to preserve the rights of an existing covenanted congregation, but to propagate the Christian gospel and establish indigenous churches. Freedom to establish an autonomous local church carried the obligation to win converts from paganism. The labour of preaching to a foreign people over several decades reflects the Pilgrims' teleological understanding of religious liberty, one that carried a weighty obligation to proselytize non-Christians.

Covenant

From its beginnings as a Separatist congregation in Leiden, covenants proved instrumental for the Pilgrims in religious and civic spheres alike. That persons were expelled from Plymouth for ecclesiological and theological reasons testifies to the importance of a communal identity deeply tied to the solemn oaths common in the Old Testament. A letter written by John Robinson to elder William Brewster in 1617 referred to the original congregation's "most strict and sacred bond."[32] The Pilgrims broke with the Church of England on conviction that the established church lacked a New Testament model of ethical rigour. Their vision of life in the New World was a society guided principally by the Bible and subject to the decisions of the members who comprised this body. Understandably, this meant giving due attention to the personal conversion of those in its midst, and withholding membership from persons who could not provide testimony of regeneration.[33] The rigorous standards enforced by church leaders created controversy, particularly over the question of whose children should receive baptism. Like the centuries-long parish model, the Pilgrims preferred a single church per town. That a Plymouth citizen could attend worship at a new congregation, much less join membership there, was considered an odious schismatic act. The covenant bond was solemn and binding, and those who departed without communal consent could be judged harshly by the community they left.[34]

Despite severance from the English Church, the Pilgrims neither foresaw, nor welcomed offshoots, even if dissenters employed similar arguments, appealing to conscience and the right to interpret the Bible as they believed God required. High standards for church membership would inexorably lead to the establishment of new denominations, but would likewise guard against

---

[32] Ashbel Steele, *Chief of the Pilgrims: The Life and Time of William Brewster* (Philadelphia: J.P. Lipincott, 1857), 194.

[33] As the late historian Perry Miller observed, "The fundamental problem of life of English Puritans was not social: it was salvation of the soul, out of which would flow a purification of the church and a regeneration of the state" (Perry Miller, *The New England Mind: From Colony to Province* [Boston, MA: Beacon Press, 1953], 2:54).

[34] One of New England's critics, William Rathband, alleged that if a member wished to leave against the church's wishes, he or she went away, "tacitly accused, slandered, yea, virtually cast out and cursed," as cited in Moore, *Pilgrims*, 96.

the kind of nominalism that conflated one's faith with their national identity. The Pilgrims of course, staunchly opposed the formation of new churches and firmly believed that giving people liberty to worship God as they saw fit would lead to atheism. Corresponding by letter during the 1680's, John Cotton Jr., wrote to Thomas Hinckley decrying that liberty would not only undermine social order, but lead to religious indifference and chaos.[35] While it could be argued that an upended social order and periodic chaos has accompanied the kind of religious liberty these men loathed, irreligion has yet to win the day.

Declaration and Independence

Several notable Pilgrim myths emerged in the nineteenth century. Among these included the notion popularized by John Quincy Adams, James Madison and Daniel Webster that among Plymouth's leaders, the Mayflower Compact was a proto Declaration of Independence, and that the Separatists were the United States of America in embryonic form.[36] The Pilgrim Fathers would likely have judged the Declaration's claim that men possess "the rights to life, liberty and the pursuit of happiness" as incomplete, if not uncomfortably hedonistic, more akin to Epicurus than the apostle Paul.[37] These devout colonists would have staunchly opposed Thomas Jefferson's famous "wall of separation" between church and state as contrary to the plantation's very existence—an elect, covenanted community akin to ancient Israel—not a pluralistic society where private citizens worship according to their consciences. Considering Plymouth's early ecclesial hegemony, it should come as no surprise that Jefferson's proposed "wall" was written in an 1802 letter to reassure Connecticut Baptists that America's future would be unlike its Puritan past, at least in its insistence on denominational conformity. Liberty for the Pilgrims, the freedom to establish a pristine visible church to serve as an example to the world, was in their minds, inconceivable in a pluralistic society.

Conclusion

In the year 1833, Massachusetts became the last state in the union to officially remove a tax levied to support established congregational churches for over two centuries.[38] The cleavage of church and state was complete, even if William Brad-

---

[35] Turner, *They Knew They Were Pilgrims*, 346.

[36] Daniel J. Boorstin called the Mayflower Compact "the primeval document of self-government" and cites John Quincy Adams' well-known claim that the compact was "perhaps the only instance, in human history, of that positive, original social compact, which speculative philosophers have imagined as the only legitimate source of government" (Daniel J. Boorstin, *Hidden History: Exploring our Secret Past* [New York: Harper and Row, 1987], 68–69).

[37] This well-known phrase comes from the United States Declaration of Independence.

[38] Pamela Durso and Keith E. Durso, *The Story of Baptists in the United States* (Brentwood, TN: Baptist History and Heritage Society, 2006), 68.

ford's dream of a community of saints in New England had died much earlier. Among the New England literati, Nathaniel Hawthorne had in mind the traditions of his seventeenth-century ancestors when, speaking through the person of Clifford in *The House of the Seven Gables* (1851) wrote,

> It is my firm belief and hope, that these terms of roof and hearth-stone, which have so long been held to embody something sacred, are soon to pass out of men's daily use, and be forgotten. Just imagine, for a moment, how much of human evil will crumble away, with this one change! What we call real estate—the solid ground to build a house on—is the broad foundation on which nearly all the guilt of this world rests.[39]

Hawthorne's prophecy of a humanity liberated from the fetters of their Pilgrim forefathers has not come to pass in exactly the manner Clifford predicted. It is true, America has grown more secular. For many, the "terms of roof and hearth-stone" have passed "out of daily use." On the other hand, the nation has grown more religious. Despite the secularization of the modern West, a majority of Americans believe religion, notably Christianity, is important to them. Recent surveys cite monthly church attendance hovering around 37%. By contrast, in Britain, the Plymouth settlers' country of origin, only 10% attend services monthly.[40] America's religious trajectory has puzzled historians and sociologists for decades.[41] Max Weber's thesis that as a society becomes more industrial and urban it grows more secular has proven true throughout the West, with the exception of the United States.[42]

At face value, the theological, ecclesial and civic boundaries the Pilgrims fought to maintain were a failed attempt at Christendom *redivivus*. From another perspective, America's religiosity, particularly its autonomous, congregationally-led churches whose members number in the tens of millions today, fulfills the Pilgrim Fathers' original vision. As newer generations of "Separatists," e.g. Baptists, Quakers, broke away from Plymouth, colony-sanctioned persecution deepened the commitment of afflicted minorities, leading many to embrace the lessons instilled from their forefathers concerning obedience to Scripture, the primacy of conscience, and a covenanted community. Plymouth's leadership

---

[39] Nathaniel Hawthorne, *The House of the Seven Gables* (Pleasantville, NY: The Readers Digest Association, 1985), 229.

[40] Thomas Kidd, *A Religious History of the American People* (Grand Rapids, MI: Zondervan, 2019).

[41] For further discussion, see Charles Taylor, *A Secular Age* (Cambridge, MA: Harvard University Press, 2007), 423–472.

[42] Kevin M. Shultz and Paul Harvey, "Everywhere and Nowhere: Recent Trends in American Religious History and Historiography," *Journal of the American Academy of Religion* 78, no.1 (March 2010): 129–162. Cf. William Herberg, *Protestant, Catholic, Jew: An Essay in American Religious Sociology* (Chicago, IL: University of Chicago Press, 1955). South Korea has also been an exception to this rule.

should have been less surprised by defections than they were.

Presently, European nations who have maintained a union of state and church, a desire shared by the Pilgrim Fathers, have witnessed a diminishing number of adherents who attend worship regularly and serve in a local congregation. In a paradoxical way, the Pilgrims succeeded through failure. Their convictions, which precluded the acceptance of independent congregations within the community, further instilled a streak of nonconformity in matters of faith. If the furtherance of the gospel was the Pilgrims' chief goal, they certainly laid the foundations for a nation where this would be possible, even if it did not come in ways they intended. The dissenting offshoots that emerged from Plymouth kept the strict communal commitments that characterized its humble beginnings. America's religious future would be marked by a seemingly endless array of emerging sects, providing a novel alternative to older forms.

Intellectual trends in modernity and postmodernity have proven inimical to traditional expressions of Christianity in America. Indifference to the faith, however, on account of church and state being conflated has not. For such reasons, the story of the Pilgrims and religious liberty exudes an ironic element that has characterized the nation from its beginning, memorably captured by Reinhold Niebuhr, in his *Irony of American History* (1952), who wrote:

> Irony ... prompts some laughter and a nod of comprehension beyond the laughter; for irony involves comic absurdities which cease to be altogether absurd when fully understood.[43]

If Pilgrim history provides reasons for laughter, America's ongoing battles over religious liberty prove that four hundred years is not sufficient to achieve full understanding. In this respect, wisdom does not preclude, though it certainly tempers our laughter.

---

[43] Reinhold Niebuhr, *The Irony of American History* (1952 Reprint, Chicago, IL: University of Chicago Press, 2008), 2.

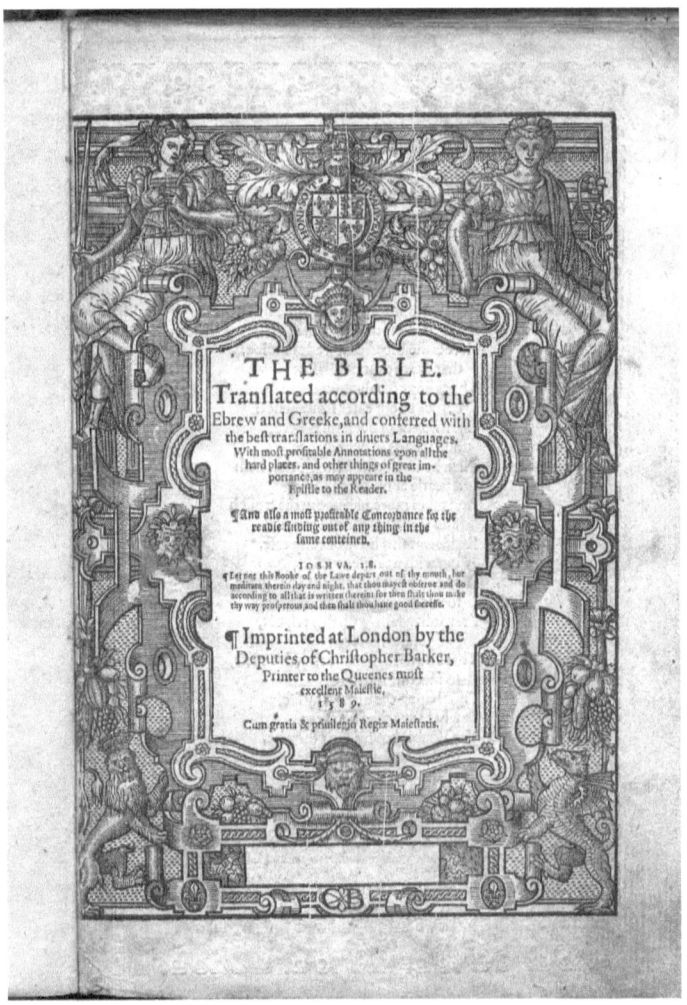

Geneva Bible Title Page, 1589
(Wikipedia Commons)

CHAPTER SIXTEEN

The Spirituality of the Pilgrim Fathers

NATE PICKOWICZ

I have the blessing of ministering in the Pilgrims' backyard. While the state of New Hampshire was not founded until 1629, our whole region still retains the ancient markers of their influence. I've had the opportunity to drive down Standish Avenue in Plymouth. I've visited Plymouth Rock. I've stepped foot on the *Mayflower*. More than this, I've read the writings of John Robinson, William Bradford, and Edward Winslow. I've prayed over passages of Scripture from the Geneva Bible. I even married a Pilgrim descendent! But most of all, as a Christian, I share the same Christian faith of the Plymouth settlers. In short, their story is immensely important to me. Why? Because of their serious devotion and spirituality.

I often cringe when I read books and articles that treat the Pilgrims as purely social or political figures. They were deeply devout and spiritual people who sought, first and foremost, the freedom to worship Jesus Christ according to their consciences. Every decision they made and every discipline they practiced was borne out of their deep-seated Christian belief; out of their profound spirituality. And while we should see them as individuals who came together in the bonds of Jesus Christ, there were commonly-held beliefs that guided and directed everything they would attempt in their new American life. As we conclude this exploration into the Pilgrims, I want to briefly glance at four key areas of their religious devotion—a devotion that is not common to many today, but is desperately needed.

Devotion to God
Far greater than their devotion to family, community, or society, the Pilgrims were primarily devoted to God. They believed in the God of Scripture; the triune God maintained in Christian orthodoxy—Father, Son, and Spirit. And they saw the powerful ministry of God in every realm of life.

The providence of God
The Pilgrims acknowledged God as their heavenly Father, guiding and directing their lives. They knew that whether they were in England, the Netherlands, or America, they needed to put their faith squarely in God, and trust in his providential hand to protect them. Edward Winslow noted that "[God] had been our only Shield and Supporter."[1] In his account of their perilous journey, William Bradford wrote:

> Being thus constrained to leave their native soil and country, their lands and livings, and all their friends and familiar acquaintance ... those things did not dismay them, though they did sometimes trouble them; for their desires were set on the ways of God and to enjoy his ordinances; *but they rested on his providence*, and knew whom they had believed.[2]

In the years to follow, their faith in God in the midst of great trials became legendary throughout Old and New England. Captain Edward Johnson, a resident of Massachusetts Bay Colony, recounted the Pilgrims' courageous endeavor, noting specifically that they were "guided by the provident hand of the most high."[3] At every step, the Pilgrims knew that God was working out his sovereign plan in their lives, and would glorify himself at every point. They were firmly convinced of "[God's] glory as a principal, and all other outward good things but as accessories."[4]

The glory of Christ
The Pilgrims' understanding of the workings of God came through their saving knowledge of Jesus Christ. Throughout all their writings—journals, histories, and treatises—they professed their profound love for Christ. To him they confessed their sins; in him they placed all of their faith and hope. All of them

---

[1] Edward Winslow, *Good News from New England*, ed. Kelly Wisecup (Amherst, MA: University of Massachusetts Press, 2014), 100.

[2] William Bradford, *Of Plymouth Plantation*, ed. Samuel Eliot Morrison (New York: Knopf, 1952), 11. Italics added.

[3] Edward Johnson, *Johnson's Wonder-Working Providence, 1628-1651*, ed. J. Franklin Jameson (New York: Charles Scribner's Sons, 1910), 42.

[4] Winslow, *Good News from New England*, 115.

understood that "among men there is given none other name under heaven, whereby we must be saved."[5]

More than simply believing the message of salvation for themselves, the Pilgrims firmly believed that it was their responsibility and delight to share that gospel message with others. William Bradford attested to their "great hope and inward zeal ... for propagating and advancing the gospel of the kingdom of Christ in those remote parts of the world."[6] In fact, Edward Winslow articulated their sincere hope to bring the gospel to the natives, "converting them to the true knowledge and worship of the living God, and so consequently the salvation of their souls by the merits of Jesus Christ."[7] In short, the Pilgrims were a gospel-centered people.

The ministry of the Spirit
While they held to their firm convictions about Jesus Christ, the Pilgrims also understood that no one becomes converted or experiences true transformation apart from the powerful ministry of the Holy Spirit. They believed the promise of Jesus to the disciples, that the Spirit "dwelleth with you, and shall be in you."[8] Furthermore, they were keenly aware that nothing or no one else could sustain them, "but the Spirit of God and His grace."[9] They were a Spirit-led people.

However, what would separate them from other religious sects who relied on inward promptings, subjective reasoning, and personal experiences? The Pilgrims knew that, left to their own devices, they would invariably follow their sinful hearts into ruin. Instead, they submitted themselves wholeheartedly to the word of God—the Holy Scriptures.

Devotion to the Scriptures
As a movement, Puritanism (as well as the Separatism of the Pilgrims) was heavily influenced by several Christian pastors and theologians. They had great love and respect for men like John Calvin, William Perkins, and William Ames. However, there was no greater formative and regulative influence than the Bible.

The biblical text
The Pilgrims did not read or study King James's Authorized Version of the Bible. Rather, their Bible of choice was an English translation produced during John Calvin's ministry known as "The Geneva Bible." While they understood

---

[5] Acts 4:12 (Geneva Bible, 1599).

[6] Bradford, *Plymouth Plantation*, 25.

[7] Winslow, *Good News from New England*, 55.

[8] John 14:17 (Geneva Bible, 1599).

[9] Bradford, *Plymouth Plantation*, 63.

that the translation itself, along with the footnotes, were of human invention, the biblical text was inspired of God—infallible, authoritative, and sufficient for them. Speaking to the absolute centrality of the Bible, Edward Winslow wrote,

> Our practice being, for aught we know, wholly grounded on the written word, without any addition or human invention known to us, taking our pattern from the primitive churches, as they were regulated by the blessed Apostles in their own days, who were taught and instructed by the Lord Jesus Christ, and had the unerring and all-knowing spirit of God to bring to their remembrance the things they had heard.[10]

Far and away, the Bible retained the greatest influence over Pilgrim life and belief, and they were careful to evaluate any and every doctrine or practice against the revealed word of God. In fact, so staunch was this belief, the Pilgrims ultimately rejected and separated from the Church of England because they believed its practices to be wholly unbiblical. Contrariwise, Edward Winslow explains,

> The primitive churches [in the New Testament] are the only pattern which the churches of Christ in New England have in their eye, not following Luther, Calvin, Knox, Ainsworth, Robinson, Ames, or any other, further than they follow Christ and his Apostles.[11]

The regular practice of Bible-reading
One of the hallmarks of the Protestant Reformation, as well as the Puritan movement, was the individual's right of access to the word of God. Many of the first settlers brought small libraries with them to Plymouth. Both William Bradford and William Brewster owned four hundred volumes each, and even Miles Standish had his own collection of military science, history, and religion. Several Pilgrims possessed works of theology and biblical commentaries, but the most valuable book they owned was the Holy Bible. In fact, virtually all of them owned a Bible, with some families owning more than one.[12]

More than merely owning many Bibles (a common reality today), the Pilgrims consistently made the practice of reading and studying the Scriptures. Perhaps more than any other people since the early church, the early New Englanders were "a people of the book." Cotton Mather articulated the common sentiment of all faithful believers in Puritan New England, "Let not

---

[10] Edward Winslow, "A Brief Narration," in Alexander Young, *Chronicles of the Pilgrim Fathers* (Boston, MA: Little, Brown & Co., 1841), 401.

[11] Young, *Chronicles*, 387.

[12] Robert M. Bartlett, *The Faith of the Pilgrims: An American Heritage* (New York, NY: United Church Press, 1978), 45–47.

a day ordinarily pass you, wherein you will not read some portion of it, with a due meditation and supplication over it."[13] Furthermore, they labored greatly to square every aspect of their lives with the truth of Scripture.

Devotion to Spiritual Disciplines
Early on in his history, *Of Plymouth Plantation*, William Bradford noted the Pilgrims' earnest devotion to the Lord. He declared that they had "labored to have the right worship of God and discipline of Christ established in the church, according to the simplicity of the gospel, without the mixture of men's inventions."[14] They rejected the ostentatious displays of formalised religion, pursuing instead a simple focus on spiritual disciplines that were rooted in scripture.

Prayer
Overwhelmingly, the Pilgrims were a people devoted to prayer. As they navigated their way through difficult circumstances, they "[poured] out prayers to the Lord with great fervency."[15] At the height of their struggle, Edward Winslow noted that every person in Plymouth "privately [entered] into examination with his own estate between God and his conscience, and so to humiliation before him: but also more solemnly to humble our selves together before the Lord by fasting and prayer."[16] However, they rejected the rigid, formulaic prayers of the Church of England in favor of more spontaneous, personal prayers. Taking his cues from the early church father, Tertullian, John Robinson noted, "We pray … without any to prompt us, because we pray from the heart."[17] In all of their prayers, they longed to speak to their Creator, head uncovered, with all candor and earnestness.

Personal holiness
The Pilgrims did not view Bible study and prayer as ends unto themselves. Rather, they sought to apply their disciplines to every aspect of their daily life, striving to be more like Jesus Christ. In their efforts, they desired to live their lives in obedience to Leviticus 20:26: "ye shall be holy unto me: for I the Lord am holy."[18] Therefore, they reformed their speech and behaviour, engaged in

---

[13] Cited in Leland Ryken, *Worldly Saints: The Puritans as They Really Were* (Grand Rapids, MI: Zondervan, 1986), 139.

[14] Bradford, *Plymouth Plantation*, 6.

[15] Bradford, *Plymouth Plantation*, 47.

[16] Winslow, *Good News from New England*, 100.

[17] Cited in Bartlett, *Faith of the Pilgrims*, 268–269.

[18] Geneva Bible, 1599.

the frequent confession of sins, restrained their sinful appetites, sought goodness and kindness toward others, and carried themselves with seriousness and diligence. One such example of a model Pilgrim was William Brewster, who was memorialized by Governor Bradford as being

> wise and discreet and well spoken, having a grave and deliberate utterance, of a very cheerful spirit, very sociable and pleasant amongst his friends, of an humble and modest mind, of a peaceable disposition, undervaluing himself and his own abilities and sometimes overvaluing others.[19]

Worship of the Assembly
One of the key reasons for their flight from Europe was the free exercise of religion. The Pilgrims had grown to believe that the Church of England had become apostate and had fallen away from the way of the churches in the New Testament. In establishing their Christian practice in New England, Edward Winslow maintained that "the Primitive Churches were and are their and our mutuall patternes and examples."[20]

The Pilgrim church assembly was simple. They did not employ much liturgy, only worship practices they found in the Bible: preaching, singing, prayers, and the ordinances of baptism and the Lord's Supper. While in England and the Netherlands, they were blessed by the biblical preaching of Pastor John Robinson, but when half the congregation removed to New England, Robinson stayed behind. They would not have a regular minister for nine years. However, Elder William Brewster did what he could to fill the gap of teaching and leadership. While he served in all ways pastoral, he did not administer the ordinances, as he was not an ordained minister. While they would have acknowledged that all of life could be lived in worship to the Lord, the Pilgrims especially treasured worship in the context of the assembly.

Devotion to a Well-ordered Society

While the Pilgrims maintained a personal devotion to godliness, they readily acknowledged that they were not living isolated lives apart from those around them. They knew that if they were to flourish, they would have to maintain healthy communities, which could only be done through a well-ordered society.

The sanctity of marriage
The primary building block of healthy society was marriage. The Pilgrims believed in the beauty and sanctity of marriage. John Robinson taught that "God

---

[19] Bradford, *Plymouth Plantation*, 327.

[20] Cited in George D. Langdon, Jr., *Pilgrim Colony: A History of New Plymouth, 1620–1691* (New Haven, CT: Yale University Press, 1966), 112.

hath ordained marriage … for the benefit of man's natural and spiritual life."[21] It was more than a tool for prosperity or procreation; marriage was an expression of divine love manifested in the bond between a husband and a wife. Building on the teaching of Ephesians 5:25, Robinson expressed that a husband's love for his wife must be "like Christ's to his church: holy for quality, and great for quantity."[22] Likewise, the wife should submit herself to her husband in all godliness. However, as John Winthrop noted, her submission is "her honor and freedom … Such is the liberty of the church under the authority of Christ."[23] Marriage in Plymouth was celebrated, and the Pilgrims themselves were not stingy with their love, companionship, even their sanctified sexuality. They believed that marriage was the vehicle of many blessings.

The blessing of family
According to J.I. Packer, "The Puritans crusaded for a high view of the family, proclaiming it both the basic unit of society and a little church in itself."[24] They put a premium on marriage, as well as the blessing of children; they worked hard at the well-ordered unity of the family structure. Unlike the cold, seemingly-loveless view of children in the Middle Ages, the Pilgrims treasured their young ones, regarding them as "the inheritance of the Lord."[25] In fact, one of the key reasons for the Pilgrims' emigration from the Netherlands was the well-being of their families, namely the children. Bradford records, "of all sorrows most heavy to be borne, was that many of their children … were drawn away by evil examples into extravagant and dangerous courses, getting the reins off their necks and departing from their parents."[26] They went to the farthest extremes out of love for their children, even risking their lives to cross an ocean, in hopes of giving them a better future.

Community and government
One of the great concerns the Pilgrims had prior to sailing to America was how they might govern themselves. In rejecting the power structure of the State Church, they desired to live and worship with freedom of conscience, yet in submission to the authority of God (Romans 13:1–8). In his farewell address, Pastor John Robinson offered a prescription for them:

---

[21] Cited in Ryken, *Worldly Saints*, 49.

[22] Cited in Ryken, *Worldly Saints*, 76.

[23] Cited in Ryken, *Worldly Saints*, 77.

[24] J.I. Packer, *A Quest for Godliness: The Puritan Vision of the Christian Life* (Wheaton, IL: Crossway, 1990), 270.

[25] Psalm 127:3 (Geneva Bible, 1599).

[26] Bradford, *Plymouth Plantation*, 5.

Whereas you are become a body politic, using amongst yourselves civil government ... let your wisdom and godliness appear, not only in choosing such persons as do entirely love and will promote the common good, but also in yielding unto them all due honour and obedience in their lawful administrations, not beholding in them the ordinariness of their persons, but God's ordinance for your good ... And this duty you both may the more willingly and ought more conscionably to perform, because you are at least for the present to have only them for your ordinary governors, which yourselves shall make choice of for that work.[27]

Upon their arrival in America, aboard the *Mayflower*, they drafted the Mayflower Compact, which reflected Robinson's sentiments to "Covenant and Combine ourselves together into a Civil Body Politic" for the purpose of preserving and furthering their goal of community flourishing.[28] They maintained, "We are knit together as a body in a most strict and sacred bond and covenant of the Lord ... by virtue whereof we do hold ourselves straitly tied to all care of each other's goods and of the whole by every one and so mutually."[29]

They selected their own leaders—a radical notion in those days. Further, they covenanted together as freemen to work for the common good and uphold the laws of God expressed in Scripture. Within a few years, however, they found that their communal work efforts were not keeping up with their growth, and the Colony began to starve. With Governor Bradford's instituting of private ownership, each family labored for their own wellbeing, setting aside provisions for the poor among them. This executive decision away from the socialistic "Common Course and Condition" saved the Colony. Furthermore, they got to experience the blessing of working hard and helping others. John Robinson commented, "[God] hath ... chosen to make some rich, and some poor, that one might stand in need of another, and help another, that so he might try the mercy and goodness of them that are able, in supplying the wants of the rest."[30] In this way, the Pilgrims laboured faithfully toward prosperity and peace in the midst of a well-ordered society.

Conclusion

The world has changed since the Pilgrims arrived in Plymouth Colony. Much has happened in the span of four hundred years. We have seen the rise and fall of Puritanism in New England, two Great Awakenings, two World Wars, the

---

[27] Bradford, *Plymouth Plantation*, 370.

[28] Recorded in Bradford, *Plymouth Plantation*, 75–76.

[29] John Robinson and William Brewster, Letter to Sir Edwin Sandys, cited in Bartlett, *Faith of the Pilgrims*, 25.

[30] Cited in Ryken, *Worldly Saints*, 70.

birth of the modern Missions movement, and the expansion of a large number of Evangelical denominations. But we have also seen culture's freefall into depravity, the likes which have scarcely been seen since the last days of the Roman Empire. Far from being sympathetic to Christian values, America has become largely hostile to God. And what is even worse, professing Christianity has spent the last half-century flirting with worldliness. We need a spiritual and doctrinal revival! We need a biblical awakening! And while we can never wind the clock backwards—nor should we want to—we need a return to the earnestness, godliness, faithfulness, and devotion of those first American Pilgrims.

Let us seek the Lord to revive in us a devotion to God—a theological revival that embraces God as provident and sovereign Lord; Jesus Christ as our only Redeemer and Saviour; and the Spirit of God as the indwelling sanctifier and comforter.

Let us ask the Lord to revive in us a devotion to the Scriptures—an intellectual and spiritual illumination by which we build our lives and practices according to the word of God, accepting it as "God-breathed" (2 Timothy 3:16) revelation—inspired, inerrant, authoritative, and sufficient for all of life and godliness.

Let us entreat the Lord to revive in us a devotion to spiritual disciplines—that we would love righteousness and chase godliness; that we would confess our sins to God and spurn them; that we could engage in regular Bible-reading, prayer, and public worship.

May we plead with the Lord that he might grant to us a well-ordered society—that he would preserve the sanctity of marriage, a love for family and children, and a treasuring of Christian community; may our Christian churches reject all forms of worldliness and preach the gospel of Jesus Christ as the only Saviour from sins through repentance and faith; and that our nation would submit to God for life, vitality, and prosperity!

Of course, we know that genuine spirituality does not come by way of human means, but by way of the Father's providence, and Son's salvation, and the Spirit's ministry. However, let our anthem be this: "[God] whose name be ever glorified in us, and by us, now and evermore. *Amen.*"[31]

---

[31] Winslow, *Good News from New England*, 116.

English Blue plaque commemorating
Island House as visited by
the Pilgrim Fathers on the Barbican, Plymouth
before sailing for the New World
(Public Domain)

Afterword

MICHAEL A.G. HAYKIN

For a considerable period of time, the landing of the Pilgrim Fathers and their families in the New World has been central to the narrative of the history of colonial America. It has been seen as the start of what ultimately became the United States of America. This past year, this narrative has been challenged by the *New York Times* in its initiation of what it called "The 1619 Project." This project has the goal of reframing American history around slavery and the contributions of African Americans to U.S. history, since 1619 was the year that for the first time a group of Africans were sold into slavery at the English colony of Jamestown. This project raises vital questions such as "Was America founded as a slavocracy, and are current racial inequities the natural outgrowth of that? Or was America conceived in liberty, a nation haltingly redeeming itself through its founding principles?"[1] This celebratory book of the 400th anniversary of the landing of the Pilgrims has not sought to answer this question per se, but the essays in it do indicate that however one tells the story of the United States—and I, for one, would not wish to deny the central role that African Americans have played in this story—the landing of the Pilgrims is still of central significance as a key turning-point in the history of the Christian Faith and more generally, Western culture.

---

[1] See, for example, Adam Serwer, "The Fight Over the 1619 Project Is Not About the Facts" (https://www.theatlantic.com/ideas/archive/2019/12/historians-clash-1619-project/604093/; accessed August 24, 2020).

Bibliography

Ahlstrom, Sydney E. *A Religious History of the American People*. 2nd edition New Haven: Yale University Press, 2004.
Ainsworth, Henry. *An Animadversion to Mr. Clyftons Advertisement*. Amsterdam: n.p., 1613.
———. *An Apologie or Defence of Such True Christians as Are Commonly (but Uniustly) Called Brownists*. Amsterdam: n.p., 1604; Ann Arbor, MI: University Microfilms, STC 238, n.d.
Allan, Sue. *William Brewster: The Making of a Pilgrim*. Burgess Hill, West Sussex: Domtom Publishing, 2016.
Anderson, Douglas. *William Bradford's Books: Of Plymouth Plantation and the Printed Word*. Baltimore, MD: Johns Hopkins University Press, 2003.
Ashley, Maurice. *England in the Seventeenth Century Pelican History of England 6*. Baltimore, MD: Penguin Books, 1975.
A True Confession. The Reformed Reader website. http://www.reformedreader.org/ccc/atf.htm.
Baillie, Robert. *A Dissuasive from the Errours Of the Time*. London, 1645.
Bailyn, Bernard. *The Barbarous Years: The Peopling of British North America: The Conflict of Civilizations, 1600–1675*. New York: Alfred A. Knopf, 2012.
Bartlett, Robert M. *The Faith of the Pilgrims: An American Heritage*. New York: United Church Press, 1978.
Baylor, Michael G. *Action and Person: Conscience in Late Scholasticism and the Young Luther*. Leiden, the Netherlands: Brill, 1977.
Benge, Dustin and Nate Pickowicz, *The American Puritans*. Grand Rapids, MI: Reformation Heritage Books, 2020.

Boorstin, Daniel J. *Hidden History: Exploring our Secret Past*. New York: Harper and Row, 1987.

Bozeman, Theodore Dwight. *To Live Ancient Lives: The Primitivist Dimension in Puritanism*. Chapel Hill, NC: University of North Carolina Press, 1988.

Bradford, William. "A Dialogue or the sume of a Conference between som younge men borne in New England and sundry Ancient men that came out of holland and old England Anno dom 1648." *Publications of the Colonial Society of Massachusetts*, 22. Boston: The Colonial Society of Massachusetts, 1920.

———. "A Dialogue, or 3d Conference betweene some Young-men borne in New-England, and some Ancient-men, which came out of Holland and Old England, concerning the Church, and the Gouerment thereof." *Proceedings of the Massachusetts Historical Society* 2, 1870.

———. "Governor Bradford's First Dialogue." *Plymouth Church Records, 1620–1859*, 22. Boston: Publication of the Colonial Society of Massachusetts, 1920.

———. *Bradford's History of "Plimoth Plantation."* Book 2, "Anno 1621," 127 Project Gutenberg e-book. http://www.gutenberg.org/files/24950/24950-h/24950-h.htm#a1621.

———. *Bradford's History of "Plimoth Plantation."* Book 2, "The Remainder of Anno 1620," 111. http://www.gutenberg.org/files/24950/24950-h/24950-h.htm#a1620.

———. *Of Plymouth Plantation*. Edited by Samuel Eliot Morrison. New York: Alfred A. Knopf, 1952.

Bremer, F.J. *The Puritan Experiment: New England Society from Bradford to Edwards*. Hanover, NH; London: University Press of New England, 1995.

Brewster, Dorothy. *William Brewster of the Mayflower: Portrait of a Pilgrim*. New York: New York University Press, 1970.

Bridge, William. *A Sermon Preached unto the Volunters of the City of Norwich and also to the Volunters of Great Yarmouth in Norfolk*. London: Ben Allen, 1642.

———. *Babylons Downfall*. London: John Rothwell, 1641.

———. *Seasonable Truths in Evil-Times*. London: Nath. Crouch, 1668.

———. *Scripture Light, the Most Sure Light*. London: Peter Cole, 1656.

———. *The Wounded Conscience Cured, the Weak One strengthened, and the doubting satisfied*. London: Benjamin Allen, 1642.

———. *The Works of the Rev. William Bridge, M.A*. London: Thomas Tegg, 1845.

Browne, John. *History of Congregationalism and Memorials of the Churches in Norfolk and Suffolk*. London: Jarrold and Sons, 1877.

Brown, John. *The Pilgrim Fathers of New England*. London: The Religious Tract Society, 1897.

Bunker, Nick. *Making Haste from Babylon*. London: The Bodley Head, 2010.

Burgess, Walter H. *John Robinson, Pastor of the Pilgrim Fathers, a Study of His Life and Times*. London: Williams and Norgate, 1920.

———. *John Smith, the Se-Baptist*. London: James Clarke & Co., 1911.

Burrage, Champlin. *The Early English Dissenters in the Light of Recent Research (1550–1641)*. New York: Russell & Russell, 1912.

Bush, Sargent, ed. *The Correspondence of John Cotton*. Chapel Hill: NC: The University of North Carolina Press, 2001.

Butler, Jon. "Two 1642 Letters from Virginia Puritans." *Proceedings of the Massachusetts Historical Society* 84 (1972).

Caffrey, Kate. *The Mayflower*. New York: Stein and Day, 1974.

Calvin, John. *Institutes of the Christian Religion*. Edited by John T. McNeill. Translated by Ford Leis Battles. Louisville, KY: Westminster John Knox, 1960.

Carlson, Eric Josef. "Book Reviews: Richard Greenham: Portrait of an Elizabethan Pastor. John H. Primus." *The Sixteenth Century Journal* 30, no.1 (Spring, 1999): 239–40.

Carlson, Leland, and Albert Peel. *The Writings of Robert Harrison & Robert Browne*. London: Routledge, 1853.

Clyfton, Richard. *An Advertisement Concerning a Booke Published by C. Lawne*. Amsterdam, 1610.

Conforti, Joseph. *Saints and Strangers: New England in British North America*. Baltimore: Johns Hopkins University Press, 2006.

Coolidge, Calvin. "Speech on the 300th Anniversary of the Mayflower Compact." *The New York Herald*. New York, NY, Nov. 23 1920. https://www.loc.gov/item/sn83045774/1920-11-23/ed-1/.

Cooper, Ian. *The Pilgrim Fathers*. Leominster, Herefordshire: Day One Publications, 2015.

Cooper, James. *Tenacious of their Liberties: The Congregationalists in Colonial Massachusetts*. Oxford: Oxford University Press, 1999.

Cotton, John. *A sermon preached by the Reverend Mr. John Cotton deliver'd at Salem, 1636*. Boston, 1713.

———. *The Way of Congregational Churches Cleared from the Historical Aspersions of Mr. Robert Baylie*. London, 1648.

Cushman, Robert. *Sin and the Danger of Self-Love Described, in a Sermon Preached at Plymouth, in New England, 1621*. Boston: Charles Ewer, 1846.

Deetz, James and Patricia Scott Deetz. *Times of their Lives: Life, Love, and Death in Plymouth Colony*. New York: Freeman and Company, 2000.

Dexter, Henry Martyn. *The Congregationalism of the Last Three Hundred Years as Seen in Its Literature*. New York: Harper, 1880.

Dickens, A.G. *Lollards and Protestants in the Diocese of York*. Oxford: Oxford University Press, 1982.

Dillon, Francis. *A Place for Habitation*. London: Hutchinson, 1973.

Doe, Ted. "Nonconformity in Norwich." *Norwich Heart*. http://www.heritagecity.org/research-centre/churches-and-creeds/noncomformity-in-norwich.htm.

Durso, Pamela and Keith E. Durso. *The Story of Baptists in the United States*. Brentwood, TN: Baptist History and Heritage Society, 2006.

Edwards, Thomas. *Antapologia: Or, A Full Answer to the Apologeticall Narration of Mr Goodwin, Mr Nye, Mr Sympson, Mr Burroughs, Members of the Assembly of Divines*. London: John Bellamie, 1644.

Emerson, Everett. *Puritanism in America: 1620–1750*. Boston, MA: Twayne Publishers, 1977.

Evans, James. *Emigrants: Why the English Sailed to the New World*. London: Weidenfeld & Nicolson, 2017.

Ferne, Henry. *The Resolving of Conscience, upon this Question, Whether upon such a Supposition or Case, as is now usually made (The King will not discharge his trust, but is bent or seduced to subvert Religion, Laws, and Liberties) Subjects may take arms and Resist? and Whether that Case be now?* Cambridge: Edward Freeman and Thomas Dunster, 1642.

Foner, Eric, and John A. Garraty. *The Reader's Encyclopedia to American History*. Boston: Houghton-Mifflin, 1991.

Fowler, William W. *Woman on the American Frontier. A Valuable and Authentic History of the Heroism, Adventures, Privations, Captivities, Trials, and Noble Lives and Deaths of the "Pioneer Mothers of the Republic."* Hartford, CT: S.S. Scranton & Company, 1879.

George, Timothy. *John Robinson and the English Separatist Tradition*. Macon, GA: Mercer University Press, 2005.

Goodall, Sandra. "Beyond Bradford's Journal: The Scrooby Puritans in Context." PhD dissertation, Arizona State University, 2015.

Goodwin, Thomas, Philip Nye, Sidrach Simpson, Jeremiah Burroughs, and William Bridge. *An Apologeticall Narration, Humbly Submitted to the Honourable Houses of Parliament*. London: Robert Dawlman, 1643.

Googins, Mary Soule. "Women of the 'Mayflower' and Plymouth Colony." *Medford Historical Society Papers* 25 (1921). http://www.perseus.tufts.edu/hopper/text?doc=Perseus%3Atext%3A2005.05.0026%3Achapter%3D2.

Greaves, Richard L. "William Bridge." In *Oxford Dictionary of National Biography*, ed. H.C.G. Matthew and Brian Harrison. Oxford: Oxford University Press, 2004.

Gullotta, Daniel. "The Great Awakening and the American Revolution." *Journal of the American Revolution* (2016). https://allthingsliberty.com/2016/08/great-awakening-american-revolution/.

Hall, Leora. "Understanding Puritan Womanhood in Feminist America." Unpublished Paper. https://www.lagrange.edu/resources/pdf/citations/2011/10_Hall_History.pdf.
Haller, William. *The Elect Nation: The Meaning and Relevance of Foxe's Book of Martyrs*. New York: Harper, 1963.
Harris, Rendel, Stephen K. Jones, and Daniel Plooij. *The Pilgrim Press: A Bibliographical & Historical Memorial of the Books Printed at Leyden by the Pilgrim Fathers*. Cambridge: W. Heffer and Sons, 1922.
Hawthorne, Nathaniel. *The House of the Seven Gables*. Pleasantville, NY: The Readers Digest Association, 1985.
Haykin, Michael A.G. "A Boanerges and a Barnabas." *Tabletalk*, 36, no.3 (March 2012): 32–33.
Heaton, Vernon. *The Mayflower*. Exeter, Devon: Webb & Bower, 1980.
Heimert, Alan, and Andrew Delbanco, eds. *The Puritans in America: A Narrative Anthology*. Cambridge, MA: Harvard University Press, 1985.
Helwys, Thomas, and Richard Groves. *A Short Declaration of the Mystery of Iniquity (1611/1612)*. Macon, GA: Mercer University Press, 1998.
Herberg, William. *Protestant, Catholic, Jew: An Essay in American Religious Sociology*. Chicago, IL: University of Chicago Press, 1955.
Hodge, Charles. *Systematic Theology*. Reprint, Peabody, MA: Hendrickson, 2008.
Howe, John. *The Principles of the Oracles of God, Lecture X in The Whole Works of the Rev. John Howe, M.A.* Edited by John Hunt. London: F. Westley, 1822.
Hosmer, James Kendall, ed. *Winthrop's Journal "History of New England" 1630–1649*. New York: Barnes and Noble, 1908.
Howard, Alan. "Art and History in Bradford's Of Plymouth Plantation." *William and Mary Quarterly* 28 (1971):.
Hubbard, William. *A General History of New England, from the Discovery to MDCLXXX*. Boston: Charles C. Little and James Brown, 1878.
Johnson, Caleb H. *The Mayflower and Her Passengers*. n.p.: Xlibris, 2006.
_____. *William Bradford of Plymouth Plantation, Along with the full text of the Pilgrims' journals for their first year at Plymouth*. n.p.: Xlibris, 2006.
Johnson, Edward. *Johnson's Wonder-Working Providence, 1628–1651*. Edited by J. Franklin Jameson. New York: Charles Scribner's Sons, 1910.
Johnson, Francis. *A Brief Treatise Conteyning Some Grounds and Reasons, Against Two Errours of the Anabaptists*. Amsterdam, 1609.
_____. *A Christian Plea Conteyning Three Treatises*. Amsterdam, 1617.
_____. *A Treatise of the Ministery of the Church of England. Wherein Is Handled this Question, Whether It Be to Be Separated From, or Joyned Unto*. London, 1959.

_____. *Certayne Reasons and Arguments Proving it is not Lawfull to Heare or Have any Spirituall Communion with the Present Ministers of the Church of England*. Amsterdam, 1608.

Johnson, G. *A Discourse of Some Troubles in the Banished English Church at Amsterdam*. Amsterdam, 1603.

Johnston, O.R. "Richard Greenham and the Trials of a Christian." In *Puritan Papers. Volume 1 1956–1959*, edited by J.I. Packer,. Phillipsburg, NJ: P&R Publishing, 2000.

Kidd, Thomas. *A Religious History of the American People*. Grand Rapids, MI: Zondervan, 2019.

Kirk-Smith, Harold. *William Brewster: The Father of New England*. Boston: Richard Kay, 1992.

Kraus, C. Norman. "Anabaptist Influence on English Separatism as Seen in Robert Browne." *Mennonite Quarterly Review* 34 (January 1960): 5–19.

Land, Richard Dale. "Doctrinal Controversies of English Particular Baptists (1644–1691) as Illustrated by the Career and Writings of Thomas Collier." DPhil thesis, Regent's Park College, Oxford University, 1979.

Langdon, George D., Jr. *Pilgrim Colony: A History of New Plymouth. 1620–1691*. New Haven, CT: Yale University Press, 1966.

Laud, William. *A Speech delivered in the Starr-Chamber ... at the Censure, of John Bastwick, Henry Burton, & William Prinn; Concerning pretended Innovations in the Church*. London, 1637.

Lawne, Christopher, et al. *The Prophane Schism of the Brownists or Separatists, With the Impietie, Dissensions, Lewd and Abominable Vices of that Impure Sect*. London, 1612.

Letham, Robert. *The Westminster Assembly: Reading its Theology in Historical Context*. Philipsburg, NJ: P&R Publishing, 2009.

Levy, Babette. "Early Puritanism in the Southern and Island Colonies." *American Antiquarian Society Proceedings* 70 (1960).

Lincoln, Abraham. "Proclamation of Thanksgiving" (October 3, 1863). *Abraham Lincoln Online*. http://www.abrahamlincolnonline.org/lincoln/speeches/thanks.htm.

Lincoln, Abraham, and Gore Vidal. *Selected Speeches and Writings*. New York: Library of America, 2009.

Luther, Martin. *To the Christian Nobility of the German Nation*. Translated by Charles M. Jacobs. Revised by James Atkinson. In *Three Treatises from the American Edition of Luther's Works*. Philadelphia: Fortress, 1970.

Marble, Annie Russell. *The Women Who Came in the Mayflower*. Boston: The Pilgrim Press, 1920.

MacCulloch, Diarmaid. *Thomas Cranmer: A Life*. New Haven, CT: Yale University Press, 1998.

Mason, Thomas W., and B. Nightingale. *New Light on the Pilgrim Story*. London: Congregational Union of England & Wales, 1920.

Mather, Increase. *The Life and Death of that Reverend Man Richard Mather*. Cambridge, 1670.

Miller, Perry. *The New England Mind: The Seventeenth Century*. Cambridge, MA: Harvard University Press, 1939.

_____. *The New England Mind: From Colony to Province*. Volume 2. Boston: Beacon Press, 1953.

Moore, Susan Hardman. *Pilgrims: New World Settlers and the Call of Home*. New Haven, CT: Yale University Press, 2007.

Morgan, Edmund S. *Visible Saints: The History of a Puritan Idea*. Ithaca, NY: Cornell University Press, 1963.

Morison, Samuel Eliot, ed. *The Pilgrims' Progress: Of Plymouth Plantation, 1620-1647*. New York: Alfred A. Knopf, 1952.

Niebuhr, Reinhold. *The Irony of American History*. Reprint, Chicago, IL: University of Chicago Press, 2008.

Noyes, Ethel J.R.C. *The Women of the Mayflower and Women of Plymouth Colony*. Plymouth, Mass: Memorial Press, 1921.

Nuttall, Geoffrey F. *Visible Saints: The Congregational Way 1640-1660*. Repr. Weston Rhyn, Oswestry, Shropshire: Quinta Press, 2001.

Olsen, V. Norskov. *John Foxe and the Elizabethan Church*. London, 1973.

Olson, Roger E. *Arminian Theology*. Downers Grove, IL: IVP Academic, 2006.

Otis, James. *Mary of Plymouth: A Story of the Pilgrim Settlement*. New York: American Book Company, 1910.

Packer, J.I. *A Quest for Godliness: The Puritan Vision of the Christian Life*. Wheaton: Crossway, 1990.

Parini, Jay. "Of Plymouth Plantation," *Promised Land: Thirteen Books That Changed America*. New York: Anchor Books, 2008.

Parker, Kenneth L. and Eric J. Carlson. *'Practical Divinity': The Works and Life of Revd Richard Greenham*. Aldershot, Hampshire: Ashgate, 1998.

Peterson, Mark. *The City-State of Boston: The Rise and Fall of an Atlantic Power, 1630-1865*. Princeton, NJ: Princeton University Press, 2019.

Philbrick, Nathaniel. *Mayflower*. New York: Penguin Books, 2006.

_____. *Mayflower A Voyage to War*. London: Harper Collins, 2006.

Porter, H.C. *Reformation and Reaction in Tudor Cambridge*. Cambridge: At the University Press, 1958.

Porterfield, Amanda. "Women's Attraction to Puritanism." *Church History*, 60, no. 2, 1991, pp. 196–209., doi:10.2307/3167525.

Read, David. "Silent Partners: Historical Representation in William Bradford's 'Of Plymouth Plantation.'" *Early American Literature* 33, no. 3 (1998), 291-314.

Reason, Joyce. *Robert Browne (1550?-1633)*. London: Independent Press, 1961.
Reid, James. *Memoirs of the Lives and Writings of those Eminent Divines, who convened in the Famous Assembly at Westminster, in the Seventeenth Century*. Paisley, Renfrewshire: Stephen and Andrew Young, 1811.
Reay, Barry. *The Quakers and the English Revolution*. New York: St. Martin's Press, 1985.
Robinson, John. *A Justification of Separation from the Church of England*. Amsterdam, 1610.
_____ *The Works of John Robinson. Volumes 1-3*. Edited by Robert Ashton. London: John Snow, 1851.
Rumburg, H. Rondel. *William Bridge: The Puritan of the Congregational Way*. n.p.: Xulon Press, 2003.
Ryken, Leland. *Worldly Saints: The Puritans As They Really Were*. Grand Rapids: Zondervan, 1986.
Sargent, Mark L. "The Best Parts of Histories: The Letters in William Bradford's Of Plymouth Plantation." *Lives out of Letters: Essays on American Literary Biography and Documentation in Honor of Robert N. Hudspeth*. Edited by Robert D. Habich, . Cranbury, NJ: Fairleigh Dickinson University Press, 2004.
Sargent, Mark. "William Bradford's 'Dialogue' with History." *New England Quarterly* 65, no. 3 (1992),.
Scheffer, J. De Hoop. *History of the Free Churchmen Called the Brownists, Pilgrim Fathers and Baptists in the Dutch Republic, 1581-1701*. Edited by William Elliot Griffis. Translated by J. De Hoop Scheffer. Ithaca, NY: Andrus & Church, 1922.
Shakespeare, J.H. *Baptist and Congregational Pioneers*. London: Kingsgate Press, 1907.
Sherwood, Mary B. *Pilgrim: A Biography of William Brewster*. Falls Church, VA: Great Oak Press of Virginia, 1982.
Shultz, Kevin M., and Paul Harvey. "Everywhere and Nowhere: Recent Trends in American Religious History and Historiography." *Journal of the American Academy of Religion* 78 no. 1 (2010).
Silverman, David J. "Indians, Missionaries, and Religious Translation: Creating Wampanoag Christianity in Seventeenth-Century Martha's Vineyard." *William and Mary Quarterly*, 3rd ser., 62, no. 2 (2005).
Smith, Bradford. *Bradford of Plymouth*. New York: J. B. Lippincott, 1951.
Smith, Dwight C. "Robert Browne (c 1550-1633) as Churchman and Theologian". unpublished PhD, University of Edinburgh, 1936.
Starkey, Marion. *The Congregational Way: A Narrative of the Role the Pilgrims, the Puritans, and Their Heirs Played in Shaping American History*. Garden City, NJ: Doubleday, 1966.

Stearns, Raymond P. "Assessing the New England Mind." *Church History*, 10, no. 3, 1941, pp. 246–262., doi:10.2307/3160253.

Steele, Ashbel. *Chief of the Pilgrims, or, The Life and Time of William Brewster*. Philadelphia: J.B. Lippincott, 1857.

Taylor, Charles *A Secular Age*. Cambridge, MA: Harvard University Press, 2007.

Tomkins, Stephen. *The Journey to the Mayflower: God's Outlaws and the Invention of Freedom*. London: Hodder & Stoughton, 2020.

Toon, Peter. *The Pilgrims' Faith*. Reading, Berkshire: Bradley and Son, 1970.

Trump, Donald. "Presidential Proclamation on Thanksgiving Day, 2019" (November 27, 2019). WhiteHouse.gov. https://www.whitehouse.gov/presidential-actions/presidential-proclamation-thanksgiving-day-2019/.

Turner, John. "Dorothy Bradford Did Not Commit Suicide." *Anxious Bench*. Patheos. December 5, 2019. www.patheos.com/blogs/anxiousbench/2019/12/dorothy-bradford-did-not-commit-suicide/.

Turner, John G. *They Knew they Were Pilgrims: Plymouth Colony and the Contest for American Liberty*. New Haven, CT: Yale University Press, 2020.

Vile, John. "Mayflower Compact." *The First Amendment Encyclopedia*. https://www.mtsu.edu/first-amendment/article/869/mayflower-compact.

Waldrup, Carole Chandler. *Colonial Women: 23 Europeans Who Helped Build a Nation*. Jefferson, NC: McFarland, 1999.

Walton, Robert C. *The Gathered Community*. London: Carey Press, 1946.

Washington, George. "Thanksgiving Proclamation." October 3, 1789. National Archives. https://founders.archives.gov/documents/Washington/05-04-02-0091.

Watts, Michael R. *The Dissenters. Vol. 1: From the Reformation to the French Revolution*. Oxford: Clarendon Press, 1978.

Webster, Daniel. "Plymouth Oration, December 22, 1820." Dartmouth University Website. https://www.dartmouth.edu/~dwebster/speeches/plymouth-oration.html.

Webster, Francis J., and Thomas Bremer, eds. *Puritans and Puritanism in Europe and America: A Comprehensive Encyclopedia*. Santa Barbara, CA; Denver, CO; Oxford:ABC-CLIO, 2006.

Webster, Tom. Godly *Clergy in Early Stuart England: The Caroline Puritan Movement, c. 1620–1643*. Cambridge: Cambridge University Press, 1997.

Weis, Frederick Lewis. *The Colonial Clergy and the Colonial Churches of New England*. Baltimore, MD: Society of the Descendants of Colonial Clergy, 1977.

Westminster Assembly. *The Reasons Presented by the Dissenting Brethren Against Certain Propositions concerning Presbyteriall Government*. London: Humphrey Harward, 1648.

White, Barrington Raymond. *The English Separatists Tradition*. London: Oxford University Press, 1971.

Whitehead, George. *The Law and Light Within*. [London, c. 1656].

Whittock, Martyn J. *Mayflower Lives: Pilgrims in a New World and the Early American Experience*. New York: Pegasus Books, 2019.

Willen, Diane. "Godly Women in Early Modern England: Puritanism and Gender." *The Journal of Ecclesiastical History* 43, no. 4, (1992), 575–578.

Willison, George F. *Saints and Strangers*. New York: Reynal & Hitchcock, 1945.

Winship, Michael P. *Godly Republicanism: Puritans, Pilgrims, and a City on a Hill*. Cambridge, MA: Harvard University Press, 2012.

_____. *Hot Protestants: A History of Puritanism in England and America*. New Haven, CT: Yale University Press, 2018.

Winslow, Edward, and John Bradford. *Mourt's Relation: A Journal of the Pilgrims at Plymouth, 1622, Part VI*, The Plymouth Colony Archive Project. http://www.histarch.illinois.edu/plymouth/mourt6.html.

Winslow, Edward. *Good News from New England*. Edited by Kelly Wisecup. Amherst, MA: University of Massachusetts Press, 2014.

_____. *Hypocrisy Unmasked*. London, 1646.

Worthley, Harold Field. "Doctrinal Divisions in the Church of Christ at Plymouth, 1744–1801." In *They Knew They Were Pilgrims: Essays in Plymouth History*, ed. L.D. Geller. New York: Poseidon Books, 1971.

Yarbrough, Slayden. "The Influence of Plymouth Colony Separatism on Salem: An Interpretation of John Cotton's Letter of 1630 to Samuel Skelton." *Church History* 51, no. 3 (1982), .

Young, Alexander. *Chronicles of the Pilgrim Fathers*. London: Dent & Sons 1920.

_____. *Chronicles of the Pilgrim fathers of the colony of Plymouth, from 1602-1625*. London: E. P. Dutton,1923.

Ziff, Larzer. "The Salem Puritans in the 'Free Aire of a New World.'" *Huntington Quarterly Library* 20 (August 1957), .

www.ingramcontent.com/pod-product-compliance
Lightning Source LLC
Chambersburg PA
CBHW021423070526
44577CB00001B/34